BILTON BANKS

The Pit and Its People

by Barry Stewart

First published in the United Kingdom, 2012,
by Stenlake Publishing Ltd.
54–58 Mill Square, Catrine,
Ayrshire, KA5 6RD.

Telephone: 01290 551122
www.stenlake.co.uk

ISBN 9781840335910

Acknowledgements

Thanks are due to the following for the use of pictures in this book: Mary Anderson, Audrey Bell, Peter Bowart, David Brewis, Dennis P. Dalby, Gordon Egdell, Alan Gilholm, Elizabeth Haddow, Roger Harrison, Victor Henderson, Doreen and Adrian Ions, Roger Jermy, Ronnie Knox, John F. Mallon, Vera Mallon, Billy and Sandra McKnight, Ken Middlemist, Tom Pattinson, Sadie Rennison, Esther Shell, Margery Slater, Joyce Snaith, Raymond Straker, Ian Varty, Ken and Stella Willcox, and Dave Young.

Thanks are also due to the many people from Alnwick, Amble, Green Rigg, Hampeth, Hipsburn, Lesbury, Newton on the Moor, Shilbottle and Brackley who shared their memories of life in and around Bilton Banks; and to the archivists at Northumberland Record's Office, the North East Mining Institute, Northumberland and Alnwick Castle Archives.

Introduction

Generations of families have depended on coal for their livelihood, especially in the North East. But many young men of my era managed to avoid life as a pitman and I count myself amongst that fortunate group.

My single visit down a mine was as a fourteen year old schoolboy on a trip with my classmates. At the same age, in 1933, my father had already left school and was working at the bottom of the shaft at Shilbottle Grange Pit, as the 'on- setter's' assistant. His role was to control the incoming full coal tubs entering the cage, while simultaneously attaching the empty, returning tubs, to the coupling chain and the endless rope hauler, to create two sets of seventeen tubs for transmission back towards the coal face.

It is very humbling to know that my different lifestyle and my career opportunities were made possible by my father's labours underground, in extremely harsh working conditions.

During his lifetime I hardly enquired about his work experiences, but like him I have returned to Shilbottle and particularly to the 'Callishes',[1] where no doubt my footprints have indented soil, clay and coal dust previously walked by my ancestors.

I have an indistinct recollection of the 'Old Pit' yard at Bilton but clearly recall once seeing 'Buddy' Douglas, his wheelchair among the potato 'shaws' and him standing with the aid of crutches, working in his garden at the 'Manager's House'. If it hadn't been for these memories, I think I could be forgiven for dismissing the hillside at Bilton as being just another field.

Bilton Banks is not just another field. It is where families lived in stone and brick-built houses, sometimes three generations of men there being miners.

So it is with respect and affection that I dedicate this book to those who laboured at Longdyke Colliery, brought their wives to live there, forged a proud community and raised their families at Bilton Banks.

The first part of the book deals with mining and Longdyke Colliery. Later sections cover life in Bilton Banks village, and the final pages incorporate pictures and stories of individuals who worked or lived at the 'Old Pit'.

Barry Stewart

---

[1] 'Callishes' – the local pronunciation of Cawledge – related to the burn, passing through land north of Longdyke and named on early maps as 'Calludge'.

Coal – some facts

Put simply, coal – the commodity 'won' by my father's labours – and his numerous forebears and colleagues underground, is a combustible black or brownish-black sedimentary rock.

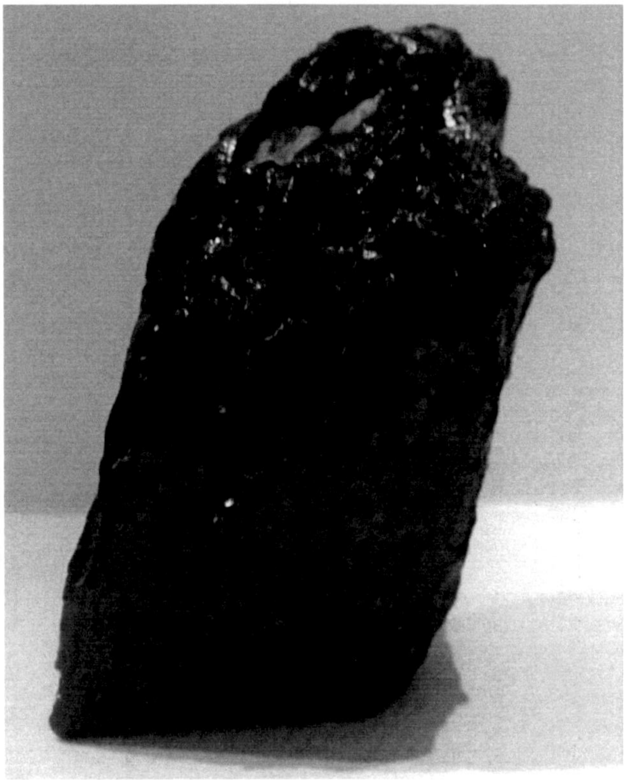
[2]

Coal normally occurs in rock strata in layers or veins.

Coal is composed primarily of carbon and variable, smaller quantities of hydrogen, sulphur, oxygen, nitrogen and other minor trace elements.

Coal owes its origin to plant matter, which during the Carboniferous period between 295 and 259 million years ago, accumulated at the bottom of water and mud. This prehistoric plant matter was compressed over millennia, most commonly in an acidic culture, which helped keep it free from oxidisation and biodegradation. In this unadulterated form, the compressed coal retains its essential organic qualities, which over the centuries have proved valuable as a source of energy.

Until recent times, coal has been the world's largest converter of energy.

There are different grades of coal. The highest rank, except graphite, is anthracite.

Anthracite coal is harder and glossier than lignite, sub-bituminous and bituminous coal, and has therefore been used primarily for domestic and commercial heating.

[2] A piece of Shilbottle coal.

Evidence of Ancient Use of Coal

It is known that coal has been mined for centuries. Evidence exists of surface and outcrop coal being used in Bronze Age funeral pyres in Britain between 5,000 and 4,000 years ago.[3] Historians can point specifically to coal being used as fuel in Greece 300 years before the birth of Christ *especially by those who worked with metals*.[4] By the end of the second century of the Common Era, it is known that the Romans were busily extracting coal across most major coalfields in England and Wales.[5] A thousand years later, in the 13th century, coal was in such demand it was being shipped from Newcastle to London for use by smiths and lime burners employed in the building of Westminster Abbey.[6] During the Industrial Revolution there was large-scale use of coal when steam engines took over from water wheels across the developing world. During the 18th century Britain produced over 80% of the world's coal.

Coal Mining in Northumberland

Bell Pits

Early mine labourers extracted coal from surface outcrops. Once they had exhausted the surface mineral, they progressively sank a shaft to reach the coal which was then excavated by primitive picks and shovels and transported to the surface by buckets and winches.

Bell pits got their name because, in cross-section, the excavated sub-surface mine resembled a bell.

Typically, no supports were used and mining continued outwards in the depths of the cavity, from the foot of the pit, until it became too dangerous to work or the walls of the pit collapsed. At this stage another mine was started, usually close by.

Bell pits had limited life span. They lacked a drainage system and were liable to flooding.

It is known that bell pits were common in Northumberland. In the region around Ford, a few miles south of the Scottish border, bell pits were still operating into the 20th century.[7]

Excluding bell and outcropping pits, by 1869, there were 139 collieries listed as operating in the Northumberland Coalfield ranging from Berwick-upon-Tweed in the north, to the River Tyne in the south, west across Northumberland to its border with Cumbria, and east under the North Sea.[8]

---

[3] Britannica, 2004, *Coal Mining: ancient use of outcropping coal.*

[4] Mattusch, Carol (2008): 'Metal Working and Tools', in: Oleson, John Peter (Ed): *The Oxford Handbook of Engineering and Technology in the Classical World*, OUP, Oxford.

[5] Smith, A.H.V. (1997) 'Provenance of Coals from Roman Sites in England and Wales'. *Britannica* Vol. 28, pp. 297–324.

[6] Cantrill, T.C. (1914). *Coal Mining*, Cambridge, England CUP, pp. 3–10.

[7] Forebears of the James Robert Punton, who later lived at Bilton Banks and then Shilbottle, worked at Ford Common Colliery on Ford Moss, where there remains much evidence of bell pit mining.

[8] Collieries of the United Kingdom at Work in 1869, http://freepages.genealogy.roots.ancestory.com

Coal Mining in Shilbottle

There are three seams of coal in the Shilbottle area. These are Townsend, Cannel and Shilbottle.[9] They are part of the Middle Limestone Series. The upper measures are missing because of erosion. The coal-winning area is effectively an island on the eastern side of the Northumberland Coalfield, it being physically separated from the rest of the coalfield by the Great Whin Sill Dyke to the west and north, and to the south by the Hauxley Fault.[10]

The Shilbottle seam begins to outcrop to the west of Longframlington and dips eastwards. As the seam approaches Newton on the Moor it hits a fault which throws it up 270 feet where it next outcrops in the Whittle area. It then dips eastwards. It is believed that monks, based at Hulne Abbey, near Alnwick Castle, were mining coal at Deanmoor from the 12th century.[11]

John Green, a Shilbottle man (shown below as a boy) deposited with Northumberland Records Office, a handwritten story of Longdyke and Bilton Banks.[12] His account was written when he was a mature adult.

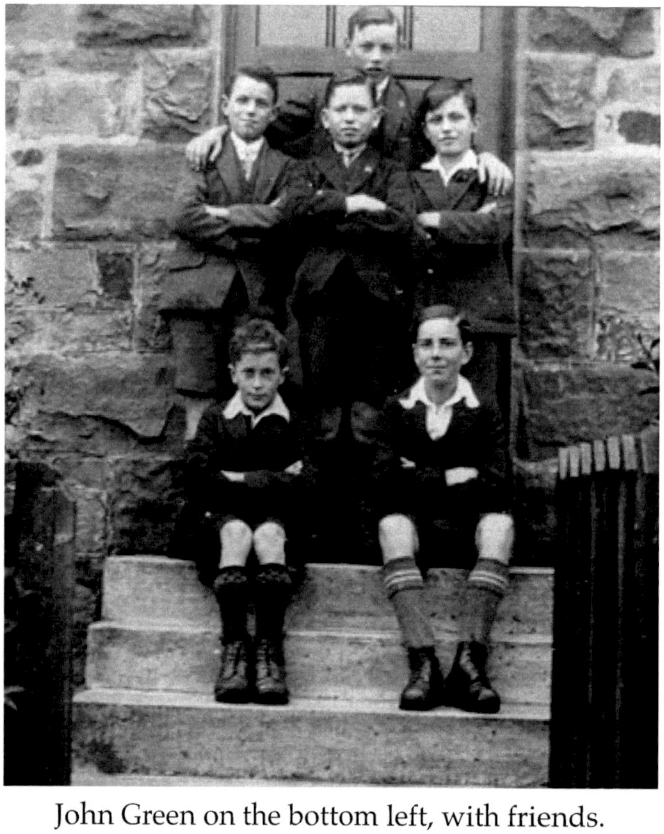

John Green on the bottom left, with friends.

[9] Tuck, James T., *The Collieries of Northumberland Vol. 1*, Newcastle: Trade Union Printing Services, 1993 p. 89.

[10] According to Hodgson, John Crawford, F.S.A., *History of Northumberland Vol. 5* (Newcastle: Andrew Reid, 1899) p. 335, the Great Whin Sill comes into conflict with the Six Yard Limestone sub-strata which outcrops at Buston Granary. Here Hodgson relies heavily on George Tate (the 19th century geologist)'s geological expertise which Hodgson quotes extensively throughout his huge literary work.

[11] Research carried out by Mrs. Joyce Snaith for a school/church project and for presentation to Felton Local History Society, relying heavily on Hodgson, *ibid* Vol. 5.

[12] Green, John, *Mining in Shilbottle* (NRO 2205/1/2) held at the Northumberland Archives.

Mr. Green refers to fields to the west of Hitchcroft, near the A1 road, where mounds of earth reveal ancient coal workings.[13] He speculates that boggy ground in these places represent filled in coal shafts which had been between 10 and 20 feet deep and were worked until poor ventilation beat the labourers. Green also refers to coal seams being found in three or four places, very near surface level, when builders were excavating the ground in readiness for the building of the Farne View housing estate at Shilbottle in the 1950s. Survey documents held by the Newcastle Society of Antiquaries show that coal was being mined in the manor of Shilbottle from a very early period. A survey carried out for the Percy Estates in 1567 by William Gray of Alnwick states that: *there ys within these fields of Shilbottell one coole myne which is much profitable for the tenants and th'inhabitants of the towne thereabouts.*[14] A later survey, carried out in 1585 states that within the manor of Shilbotel there is *a good and riche myne of coles verye profitable to the country thereabouts.*[15] The 'winning' of coal in this area, Shilbottle and Whittle, was the subject of several commercial undertakings, the right to rent the mine workings passing from 'William Gray of Alnewicke,' in 1585 to 'William Bednell and other burgesses of Alnewicke' for £4 12s 0d annually. Seventeen years later the coal mining rights were held under lease to Griffin Butler and William Harte at the rent of £15 annually.

In 1685, Whittle (west of Shilbottle) was sold by Thomas and Gilbert Swinhoe to Timothy Davison and Matthew Jefferson of Newcastle, who purchased the tenements, farm holding and the *coal mines there* in trust, for the Mayor and Burgesses of Newcastle, for use by the Master and brethren of the newly founded Holy Jesus Hospital in Newcastle.[16]

During the 18th century the coal mines around Deanmoor, Whittle and 'Shilbotel' were held under successive leases retained by the family of Archbold of Cawledge Park, Alnwick. Warburton, writing around 1715, describes 'Whitley' (Whittle) as *containing valuable seams of coal and lime – the latter having been worked for local use.*[17] In 1734 it was stated that there *are several coal pits that are present in use, and produce abundance of very good coals that serve most of the neighbouring villages.*[18] Coal from the mines was being taken by horse and cart in sacks for sale in Alnwick as a source of heating and light. Prior to 1762 the collieries were worked by Alnwick Corporation. After this date ownership transferred to the Duke of Northumberland, who in 1766 purchased land, known as Shilbottle Lodge, from Henry, Hugh and Thomas Taylor. In a colliery plan bearing the date 14th April 1764, in possession of the Newcastle Society of Antiquaries,[19] a Windmill Pit is shown in a field west of Deanmoor, which is one mile west of Shilbottle on the road towards Rugley.

The shaft for the Windmill Pit, managed by Mr. Archbold, is thought to have been sunk close to Tuffy's Well, near the drainage bridge, close to the turn off to Snipe House on the Rugley road. It is thought that this pit was opened on 22nd June 1763.[20]

---

[13] Gordon Straughan of Colliery Farm, Shilbottle had to haul a young heifer out of bell pit workings near Hitchroft, in 2010, where it had strayed and got stuck.

[14] Hodgson, *ibid* p. 425.

[15] Hodgson, *ibid* p. 426.

[16] Hodgson, *ibid* p. 456.

[17] Hodgson, *ibid* p. 456

[18] Mark's Survey Inedited Contributions to the History of Northumberland, Hodgson p.426

[19] Brown, William, *Colliery Plans,* (1764) Newcastle Society of Antiquaries. A similar plan, drawn by William Brown, and dated 25th April 1765, is held in the Collections of the Duke of Northumberland ref DP/D1/I/100. This plan indicates 63 bell pits in the process of being sunk, presently working or abandoned, running south from the Windmill Pit towards Whittle.

[20] Jermy, Roger, *Northern Northumberland's Minor Railways, Volume two – Colliery & Associated Lines,* (Usk, Mon., Oakwood Press, 2011) p. 11.

Tuffy's Well

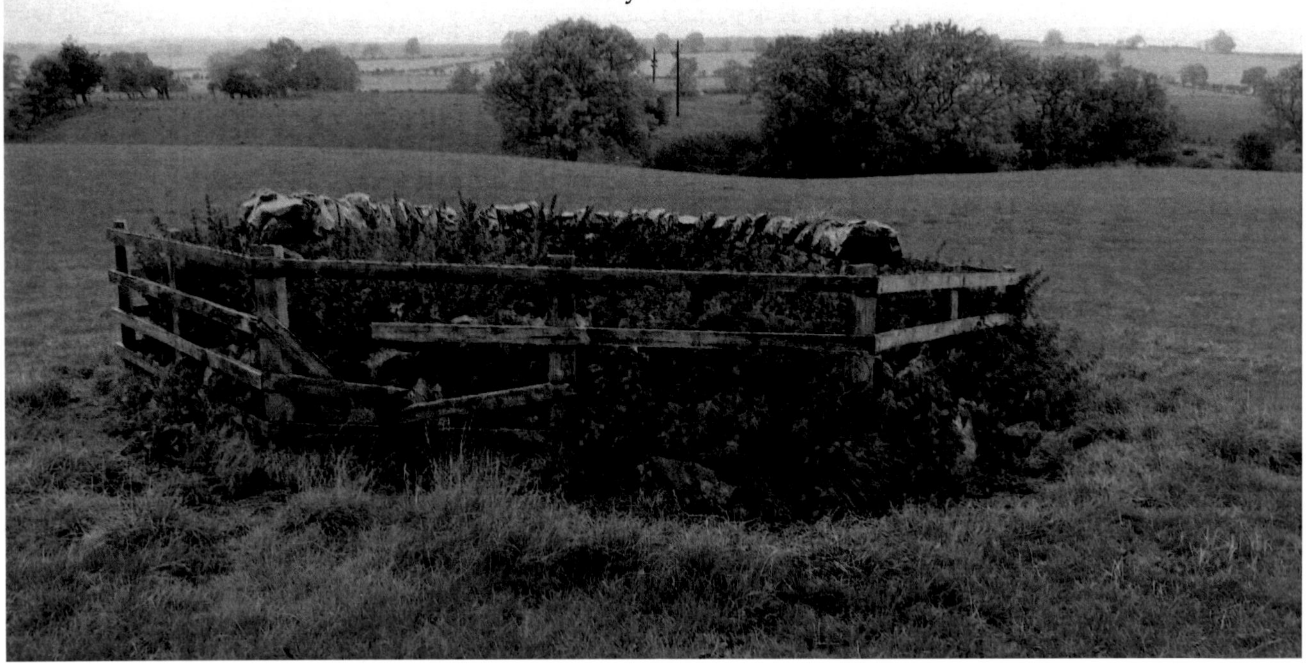

Close examination of the structure of the well shows brickwork which once formed the inner lining. To the north of the well is a 1950s pumping station which releases water into a nearby stream. It is thought that this is the site of the former Windmill Pit, the windmill being used to pump water from the mine to prevent flooding.[21] William Brown's surveying record shows that coal was being 'won' at the Windmill Pit at a depth of 13 fathoms (78 feet).[22] Mr. Brown's plans show tracings of numerous small air shafts, on *the rise-side of a road* leading to Deanmoor, which suggest that coal seams were being extensively worked over longer, underground distances.

In the 18th and 19th centuries it was common for a single shaft to be divided with a 'brattice', which was a wooden partition, to effectively create two shafts. Warmer air from the bottom of the shaft would rise up one shaft, creating a vacuum to draw fresh air down the other side of the shaft and thus provide essential ventilation. Coal, in ancient pits with a 'brattice', was hauled to the surface in baskets which did not interfere with the shaft's division.

Deeper mines were later sunk in and around Shilbottle. Six shafts are recorded near Blue Lodge Farm. The first was sunk in 1780 and five closely followed. These were in an arc running from the north east perimeter of the farm. They were roughly 150 to 200 yards apart. On 1st August 1787 the Duke of Northumberland granted permission for coal to be led away from Shilbottle with horses, wains, carts and carriages. The principal colliery then was in possession of Robert Readhead and permission for leading off the coal was given to John Byerly George Forster and John Wailes. Three of the pits were named – *Hatchet, Hawley* and *Smokey*[23] and these operated for about 20 years, working the Townsend seam, using then two shafts for ventilation. The deepest went to 36 fathoms (216 feet) with a principal seam of 32 inches.

---

[21] W.S. Armstrong and Sons (Mineral Agents for the Duke of Northumberland) and North of England Mining Institute documents show survey work being carried on the quoted date at Shilbottle.

[22] A fathom was originally based on the distance between the fingertips of a man's outstretched arms of between 5 feet 6 inches and 6 feet, generally accepted as 6 feet.

[23] John Green's account Northumberland Archives ref. NRO 2205/1/2.

Evidence of workings can be found along the Shilbottle to Hitchcroft road, especially the fields west of the Green Lonnen when they have been ploughed and coal spoils and black dust are brought to the surface.

On 31st May 1802 coal workings known as Shilbottle Colliery were offered by lease from Thomas Taylor of Newburn and taken up by John Taylor. Following this, in 1807, the Blue Lodge shaft at Colliery Farm[24] (which, along with Engine, New East or Furnace Pit, provided the alternative name for the pit) was sunk. The shaft walls were lined with bricks. The method of working this pit included *headings 60ft apart, 6ft wide and boards 15ft wide, leaving pillars 9ft 9ins wide as supports.*[25] A second level of working is shown in the ancient plans to reveal mining under the village.

On 21st February 1807 John Buddle,[26] the renowned colliery viewer and engineer, brought in by the owners of Shilbottle Colliery, advocated a cast iron railway from the colliery to a depot at Alnwick; the carriages were to be of 10cwt tubs, horse driven with the expectation that six carriages at a time could be hauled.[27]

The 'spoil heap' for the Blue Lodge has been grassed over but is still visible in the fields opposite the private house which is now used as a cattery. A degree of imagination is required at this location, but a discerning observer will note how the grassed-over surface drops away in the foreground and then rises again over a more elevated aspect of the former spoil heap. A small amount of digging will provide evidence of the minerals which were mined with the coal and now form the anonymous looking heap. The records show that the pit shaft at Blue Lodge was 10 feet in diameter and twice as big as previous pits in the area. The shaft was capped by the National Coal Board after 1947.

In 1830 The Keeper's Pit, which was near Town Foot, on the unclassified Shilbottle to Alnwick Road (shown as Shilbottle Colliery, towards the north, on the map on page 10), was sunk to allow working in a southerly direction and up to the low side of the old workings from the Blue Lodge pit, near Colliery Farm. The workings from the Blue Lodge pit were used to assist with ventilation,[28] and a stationary steam engine drove a ventilator to allow deeper workings to be exploited away from the shaft bottom.[29] Men were lowered on a chain with four leather straps attached, where they inserted one foot. They hung on to the chain as they were lowered and used their free foot to avoid bodily contact with the shaft's wall. Coal was brought from the face on sledges which were drawn by boys and men. There were no tubs and no wheels, so the work was hard and laborious. The Keeper's Pit had a big house next to it which in the late 1930s was occupied by one of the Duke of Northumberland's gamekeepers, who also did work as a joiner and stone mason. The occupation of the resident of this house may have been the reason for the name 'Keeper's' being used for this pit.[30]

---

[24] The Newcastle Society of Antiquaries hold plans dated 16th November 1814 for this pit.

[25] This, board-and-pillar, (board alternatively spelled bord) method of mining is known as partial extraction. Road or work-ways are driven in a regular lattice-work manner leaving pillars between the boards to support the roof. Tuck, *ibid* p. 14.

[26] John Buddle junior's memorial plaque reads: 'In his profession of a mining engineer and viewer of collieries he occupied the highest rank, and was extensively employed and consulted not only in this kingdom but in other countries. He had the merit of being the originator of various improvements in coal mining.' When he died in 1843, aged 70 his funeral procession was over a mile long. It took three hours to proceed from his home in Wallsend to his burial ground in St James' Churchyard in Benwell.

[27] Collections of the Duke of Northumberland, Ref. DP/D2/I/125. A detailed account of the haulage system and carriageway is to be found in Jermy, *ibid* pp. 11–17.

[28] John Green's account refers to him viewing documents which show the sinking to have been on 14th October 1845 which is confirmed in the records of Durham Mining Museum.

[29] An underground map held by the Collections of the Duke of Northumberland shows that the coalfield was being worked from a quarter of a mile east of Hampeth, towards the Beacon, across to Colliery Farm, north of the Keepers to the foot of Bilton Banks.

[30] In the 1950s this house was occupied by Mr. Hood and his family (including his children Tina and Willie) until it was demolished.

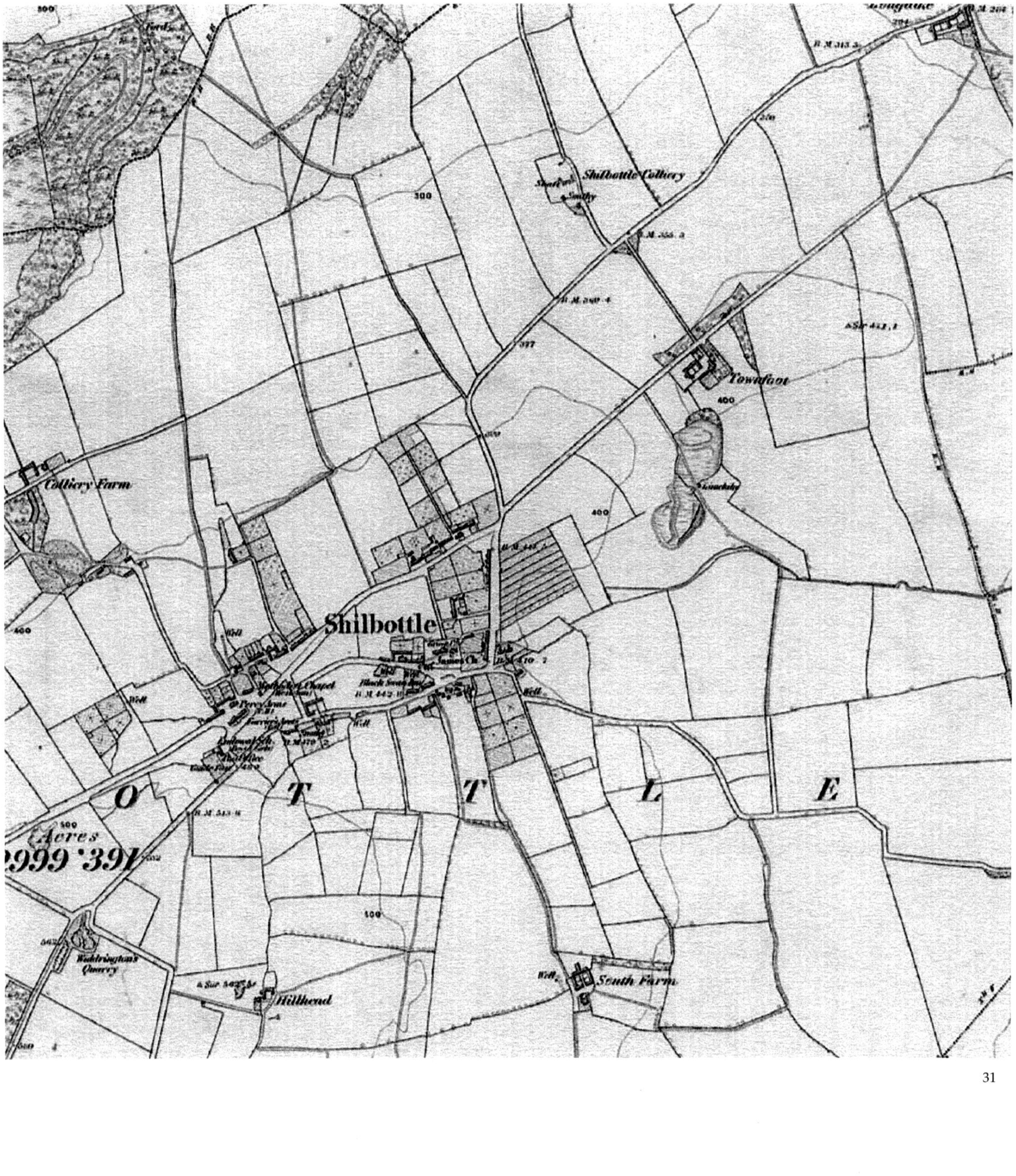

[31]

[31] Ordnance Survey 1st Edition; reproduced with permission of Northumberland Archives.

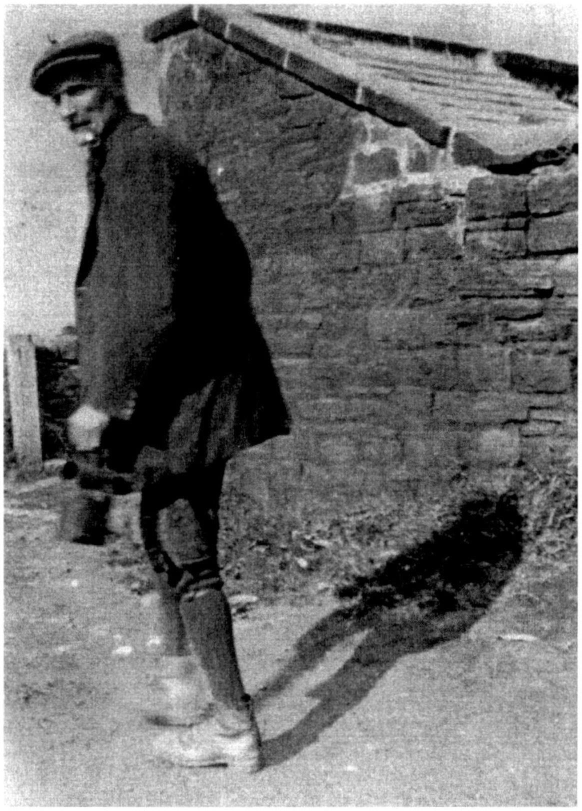

32

In the then centre of Shilbottle village a further mine (The Town Pit) with a 10 feet diameter shaft, was sunk in 1844 to a depth of 45 fathoms.[33] The pit was situated between Rose Cottage, on South Side and the stone-built terraced bungalow opposite the Aged Miners' Cottages, on the North Side, which was, previously known as Cannon Cottage. Cannon Cottage was so named because following the end of hostilities with Germany in 1918, the *Council sought to acquire a German trophy for Shilbottle and it was agreed that a captured German gun, if possible one captured by the 'Northumberlands' would serve as a memento of the Great War*.[34] In the Second World War the cannon was removed, along with other valuable metal, to be smelted down for the manufacture of munitions.

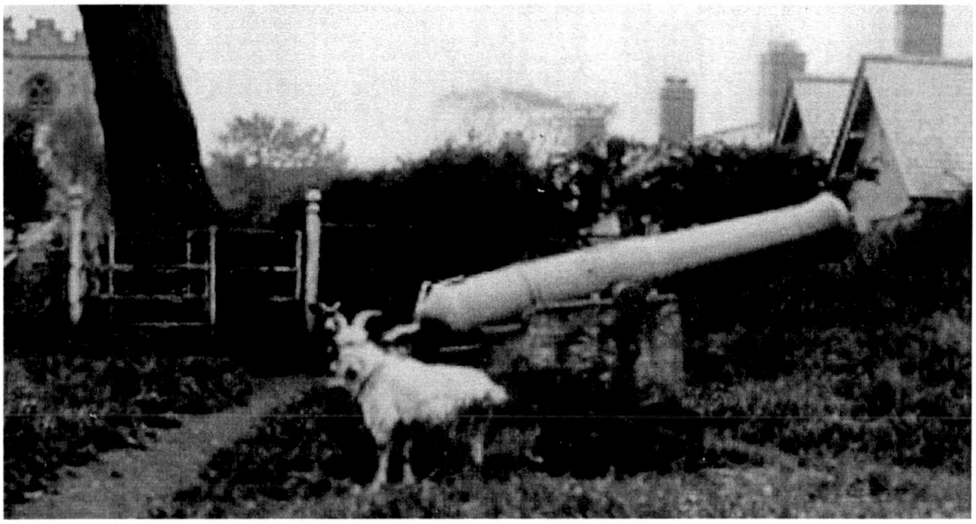

[32] Published with kind permission of the Editors of *Memories of Shilbottle – Millennium Edition,* 2000.

[33] Surveyors before Nationalisation plumbed shafts regularly to check for flooding, so depths can be relied upon with some degree of accuracy.

[34] *Memories of Shilbottle* p. 23.

Before Cannon Cottage became an occupied dwelling, it had been used as the colliery offices for The Town Pit. In 1845 East Pit (also known as Engine Pit or New Engine Pit) was sunk. Prior to this, consideration was being given to a mine at Longdyke.

In 1755 Hugh, Earl of Northumberland issued a lease to William Cooper of Bilton Banks to develop a colliery at Bilton Banks.[35] Mr. Cooper's application was to ascertain whether it was viable to extract coal near Longdyke. In 1796 the Duke of Northumberland issued an amended lease to Sir Grey Cooper of the Township of Bilton and Bilton Banks in which he assigned – *full and free licence, liberty, power and authority to enter upon any part of lands and grounds to drive drift, levels and water courses ... for the purposes of sinking or working or carrying on any other colliery or mine belonging to him ... for the purposes of winning, working, obtaining or getting or recovering coals ... for a period of 21 years.*

Within the lease document the duke's attorney, William Isaacson, included clauses requiring Sir Grey Cooper to – *leave good and sufficient walls and pillars and stone to support the roof ... to keep open and preserve the staple pits, shaft or shafts, drifts or levels, or water courses as should be proper for the winning of coal ... so that the miners be not over-burdened with water or drowned.*[36]

An 1805 map of Greenrigg (drawn by John Taylor)[37] shows 19 bell pits in a dog-leg formation between Greenrigg House, Spy Law and Bilton Village. The depths of these pits range from 3 to 48 fathoms. The legend on the plans states: *It evidently appears that the coal has been wrought up to the Dyke (the sandstone Dyke) at the north or rise side, by virtue of a level driven from the north, which intersects the seam. But as the coal is thrown down such a depth by the Dyke and as machinery for drawing water was not in use when the colliery was wrought near two hundred years since, it follows that to the south, all is whole coal.*

At two pits (south of the Dyke and sunk to 12 and 16 fathoms) a small part of the seam was wrought eighteen years ago by Sir Grey Cooper for the purposes of burning lime, he having permission from His Grace the Duke of Northumberland, to win coals for that use, but not for sale. The lime kilns at that time being discontinued there since. The seam is 32 inches in height and of good quality.

Two specific bell pits, described collectively as Old Pit, are shown on plans of Bilton Banks Estate, dated March 1813.[38] The estate was then in possession of Edward Henderson Esq. These Old Pits were in High Dove Cote Field at Longdyke.

Interestingly, a hand-drawn map[39] prepared by Robert Tate in April 1817 for Earl Percy, the then Duke of Northumberland's son, shows a field off the bridleway between Greenrigg and Bilton Banks which is named Collier's Close. Beyond, to the south, the present Cawledge Burn is spelled Calludge – which perhaps accounts for today's local pronunciation.

In 1817 Thomas and Hugh Taylor held the lease for Shilbottle Colliery, then situated at Colliery Farm. They were still lessees for Shilbottle Colliery in 1860.

---

[35] Collections of Duke of Northumberland Ref SY: M II 12H.
[36] *Ibid* Ref SY: MII 12X.
[37] *Ibid* Ref AC/O/VI: 8.
[38] *Ibid* Ref WA/1/7/36.
[39] *Ibid* Ref AC/O: VI 13.

In historical documents, solicitors, attorneys, agents and mining examiners all seem to refer to the collieries in the Township of Shilbottle, wherever they are or have been located, simply as 'Shilbottle Colliery'. This 'short-hand' way of naming the collieries adds an element of difficulty for anyone seeking to unravel particular events or dates. Thankfully, the Durham Mining Museum is more specific and shows the various pits at Shilbottle, giving them their operational names (Engine, Smoke Staple, Town, East or New Pit and Longdyke). Unfortunately, there is still some confusing cross-referencing with regard to the dates of sinking. Fault cannot be attributed to those maintaining the records however, because dates of sinking were often noted through word of mouth. This was because many of those responsible for manual work at the pits could not read or write. Sometimes, even when the exact date had been recorded, the date referred to could have been the date of starting to sink the mine, the date of completion or the date when coal was first struck. Certainty can rarely be claimed. Accepting this uncertainty, and acknowledging the limitations under which the records are derived, the Durham Mining Museum states that work on sinking the shaft at Longdyke Colliery started on 22nd August 1844, which would be under the Taylor family's ownership. In a later record the date is left blank. The museum's records then show that East Pit's shaft was sunk on 14th October 1845. Elsewhere, in another record it is shown as having been sunk on 22nd August 1844 (apparently the same date as Longdyke). Roger Jermy helps clarify the situation because he refers to an article appearing in the *Alnwick Journal* on 15th March 1860. The article is not directly related to Longdyke Colliery. It is more concerned with describing the excellent 'coal road' or tramway running away from the colliery. The author is walking away from Longdyke on the tramway and in the context of developing a description the writer states – *Nearby ... (there are) houses for the men ... provided rent-free, with coals ... the largest house (being) the residence of the manager.*

The inference, according to Mr. Jermy, is that the author is describing Colliery Farm / Blue Lodge, because the article goes on to mention the writer walking along the waggonway to where – *the old pit was worked, and where, for many years almost all the coal, used in Alnwick, was brought to bank.* The reference, here in 1860, to 'old pit' must be to the pit at Colliery Farm and the waggonway referred to is that which ran from Colliery Farm pit to the depot formerly at Wagonway Road. However, the author in 1860, is referring to walking from Longdyke – which was then in operation and also had a waggonway for the transport of coal to a depot at Alnwick. Around this time the ownership of the colliery at Longdyke had passed from the Taylor brothers to Mr. Henry Augustus Paynter, an Alnwick solicitor and his colleague solicitor, Mr. Nathaniel Dunn of Bedlington. It is known that on 25th March, 1870 the Duke of Northumberland issued a 31 year lease on Shilbottle Colliery which included 26 workmen's cottages and the manager's house at Longdyke. This lease conferred mining rights within the township of Bilton for *workings opened as well as not opened.* In 1867 the colliery at Shilbottle covered an area underground of 2,221 acres. By then 3.5 million tons of coal had been raised. It was estimated that another 5 million tons of coal remained to be 'won'. This was despite the coal face being half a mile from the foot of the 150 feet deep shaft. During the next decade the colliery at Longdyke was making at least one shilling and one penny per ton profit and had plant at or in the pit worth close on £5,000. It was considered sufficiently viable as a colliery to merit public ownership.

---

[40] Durham Miners Museum www.dmm2.org.uk

[41] Jermy, *ibid* p. 16.

[42] The manager (of Colliery Farm pit) is named Wilson, the owners' agent at Shilbottle was initially Hugh Wilson and then William Wilson.

[43] Northumberland Estates Archive ref: A 3800.5. There is also a lease document for Bilton Banks Farm. This is from 1855 and mentions particularly the quarry in the name of West Quarry Fields. Northumberland Estates Contract Agreement: Archive ref A2456.

[44] Jermy, *ibid* p. 17.

In the 1880s a 'Limited' share release was issued under the Companies Act, 1862 and 1880. This offered opportunities for selected individuals to purchase £1 shares up to £30,000 in the establishment of The Shilbottle Coal Company. This was to be under the directorship of R.S. Garwood Esq, H.A. Paynter Esq, and J.T. Garwood Esq, who together retained a £20,000 share holding.

The resident manager (and secretary) of the proposed company was to be Mr. Nichol Cheeseman, Bilton Banks, Northumberland.

For Private Circulation only.

The Shilbottle Coal Company, LIMITED.

To be Incorporated under the Companies' Act, 1862 and 1880, whereby the liability of Shareholders is absolutely limited to the amount of their Shares.

CAPITAL, £50,000,

In 50,000 Shares of £1 each. 20,000 Shares are taken by the Vendors.

PAYMENTS AS FOLLOW:—

Five Shillings on Application, Five Shillings on Allotment, and the remainder as required, in Calls not exceeding Two Shillings and Sixpence each, and at Intervals of not less than Three Months.

In the event of no Allotment being made, amounts paid on application for Shares will be returned in full.

The Vendors guarantee a Dividend at the rate of Six per cent. per annum for Five Years, from date of allotment of Shares, on the paid-up Capital.

Provisional Directors.

R. S. GARWOOD, Esq. | H. A. PAYNTER, Esq.

J. T. GARWOOD, Esq.

Bankers.

Messrs. WOODS & CO., Alnwick.

Solicitors.

Messrs. FORSTER & PAYNTER, Alnwick. [45]

[45] Northumberland Estates Archive ref AC: K/1/30.

Following this flotation, The Shilbottle Coal Company was formed. Longdyke was undoubtedly a productive and profitable pit. It operated until 19th August 1925 when the Grange Pit started production.

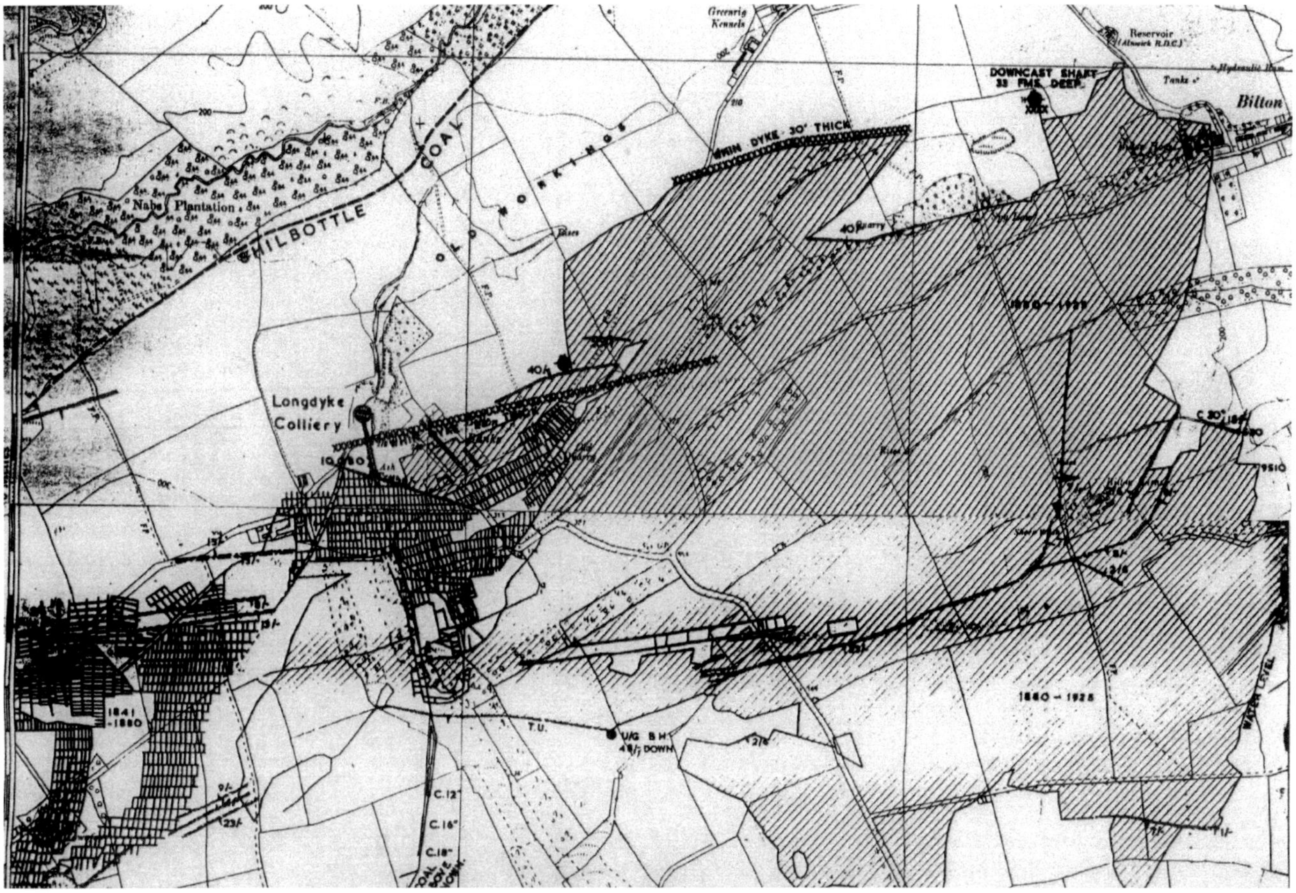

The above map of underground workings at Longdyke show 'board and pillar' working (the squared darker area) up to the southern perimeter of the 30 feet thick sandstone Whin Dyke. To the west, also darker and squared, are the workings from The Keepers and Blue Lodge Pits. The diagonal lines in the larger part of the map show later, more sophisticated, long-wall, underground workings. The Downcast Shaft, which went to 33 fathoms, is located north west of Bilton at the very edge of the coalfield. The central area of the coalfield was worked between 1880 and 1925. The area, near the Longdyke shaft was worked prior to 1880.

Before concentrating the rest of this work on Longdyke and the community at Bilton Banks, it may be helpful to make some observations about changes in the demographic disposition and employment patterns of residents in the Shilbottle area, during the period when coal was being mined in the locality.

Miners and Labourers in Shilbottle and Longdyke/Bilton Banks

19th century Shilbottle was described as comprising five poor law townships of Shilbottle, Shilbottle Woodhouse, Hazon and Hartlaw with Newton-on-the-Moor. The village of Shilbottle comprised 70 cottages. In 1891 it had a population of 454.

The census data for Shilbottle, Bilton Banks and Longdyke over a century are revealing.[46]

[46] It is acknowledged that the first National Census in standard, albeit brief format was not conducted until 1841. These figures come from parish data collected by Hodgson p. 454.

Early, local census returns show the population of Shilbottle to be as follows:

Year	Number	Year	Number
1801	472	1851	601
1811	465	1861	570
1821	548	1871	528
1831	557	1881	428
1841	549	1891	454

Prior to the sinking of the deep mines in and around Shilbottle, church baptism, marriage and burial returns show that most men and boys worked on the farms as agricultural labourers. However, in the latter part of the 19th century the situation began to change, but the change was gradual. For example the census taken on 7th June 1841[47] shows that of the 549 people in the village of Shilbottle, 214 were male. There were 91 houses in the village by then and the records show that 48 men gave their occupation as 'miner'. The surnames of these miners include family names which are still to be commonly found in contemporary census and voters' lists for the village. These include: Anderson, Bell, Elliott, Forster, Gray, Gibbon, Hutchinson, Jeffrey, Riddell, Shepherd, Thompson, Watson and Weightman

Bilton Banks, a short distance north east across the fields from Shilbottle and in the parish of Lesbury, had in 1841 only two families resident there; one a single widowed lady, the other a family headed by James White, 44 years of age, who described his occupation as labourer. He had migrated into the area from Chatton to find work and lived with his wife who was ten years his junior, two sons, who were too young to be employed, and three small daughters. Interestingly, suggesting that mining in this area was beginning to occur, nearby there is one dwelling named in the 1841 census, as New Pitt. This was occupied then by Joseph Hall, a widower, who gave his occupation as colliery banksman.

Longdyke Farm, west of the subsequent site of the Longdyke pit, continued to rely heavily on human labour and in 1841 the farm steward there employed four men who lived in dwellings at the farm. Their families provided three further labourers.

The census for 30th March 1851 for Shilbottle is damaged, but readable sections of it show the attraction of mining, there at that time being a visible influx of miners to Shilbottle from outlying hamlets and villages including Embleton, Bamburgh and Charlton. The familiar names of Bell, Riddell and Huntley appear in the census.

The population of Longdyke Farm was pretty much as it had been a decade earlier, but the census provides evidence of migration from one area to another to find work, one family had moved into the area from Ancroft, near Berwick. The census taken on 7th April 1861 shows that one man, Thomas Hall, 51 years, formerly from Lucker near Belford, was resident at Longdyke Farm. He gave his occupation as coal miner, and he may have been related to Joseph Hall, the occupier of New Pitt.

---

[47] All the census data from Northumberland Archives, relevant to Bilton and Longdyke has been transcribed and is shown at Appendix 1.

The only other family shown on the census record is named Cruddas – consisting of a man aged 82 years, who with his son and daughter-in-law are shown as agricultural labourers. The census for 2nd April 1871, for Longdyke shows that the two families there were Robson and Green, Mrs. Robson being a widow employed as an agricultural labourer, and Francis Green being a shepherd originally from Framlington. Mr. Green's two sons, aged 28 and 15 were employed as agricultural labourers.

The Ordnance Survey map (Second Edition) for the Bilton area shows a rifle range located south east of Bilton Colliery. It is approximately 200 yards from the road and was most probably accessed along the footpath running towards the Dene from the byres and farm labourer's cottage, on the south side of the road, which had been in use prior to the building of the Bilton Banks houses. Rifle shooting was clearly a popular sport as the following images of residents shows.

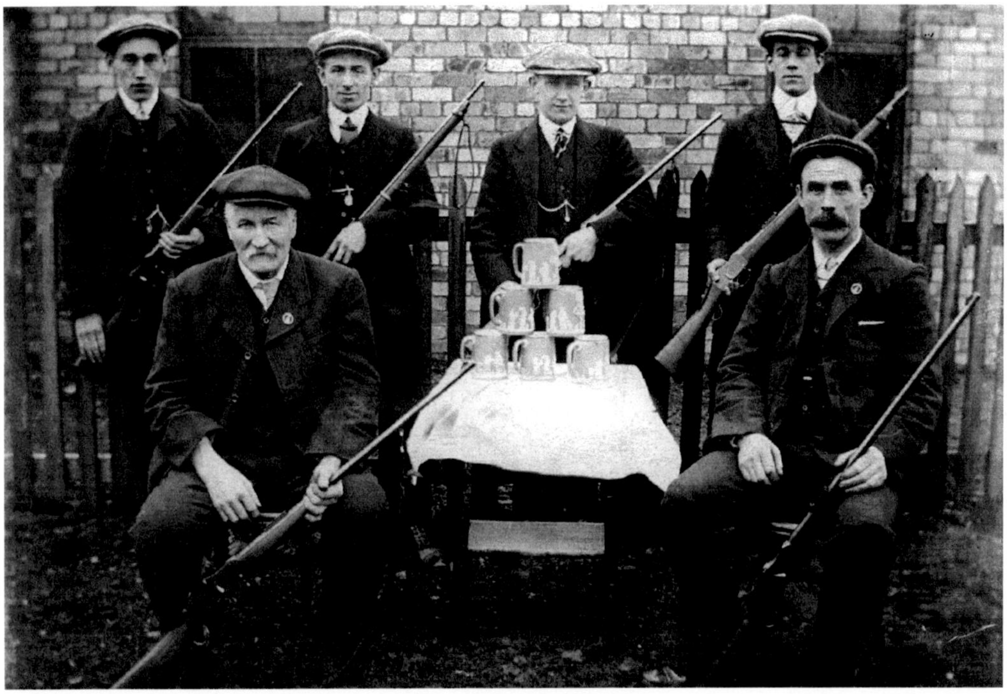

These images are of Mr. W.T. Green with his sons and friends with their trophies.

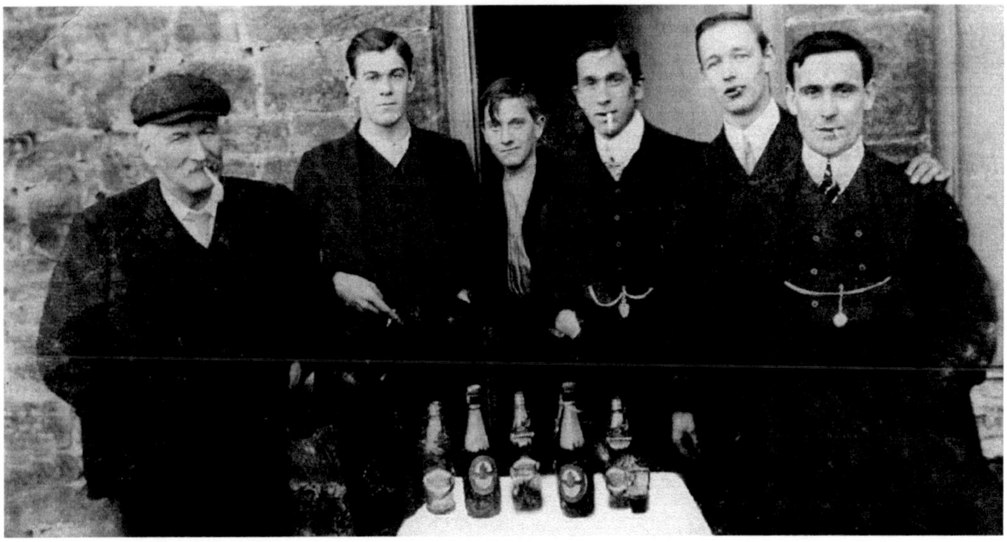

Members of the same group: Mr. W.T. Green, Robert John Green, G. Storey and others (probably – John Green third from left) in their best clothing, celebrating after another days shooting.

Mr. W.T. Green at his cottage door at Bilton Banks.

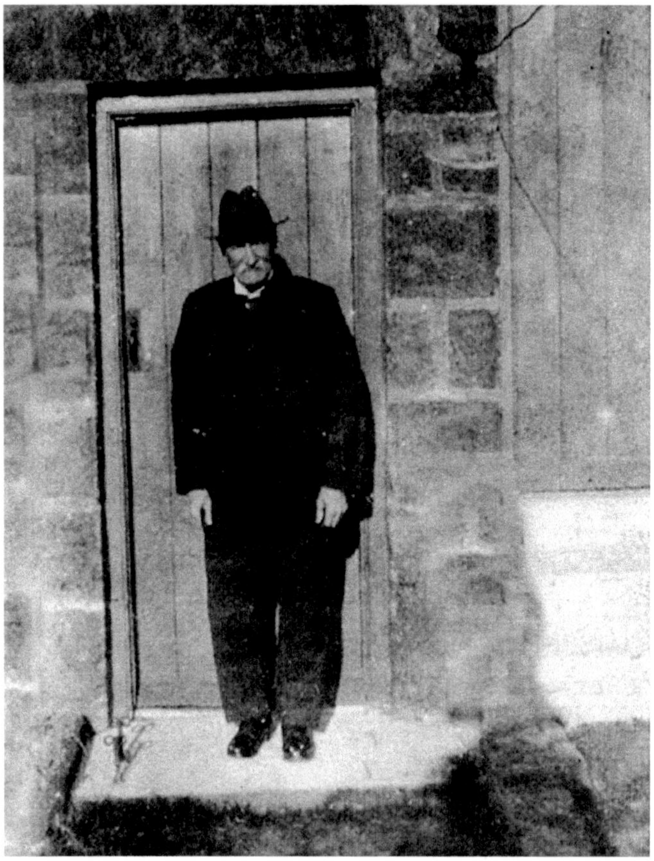
[48]

By the 3rd April 1881, when that decade's census was recorded, the situation at Bilton Banks had changed significantly. By this time, 29 dwellings are listed, with a total of 144 occupants.

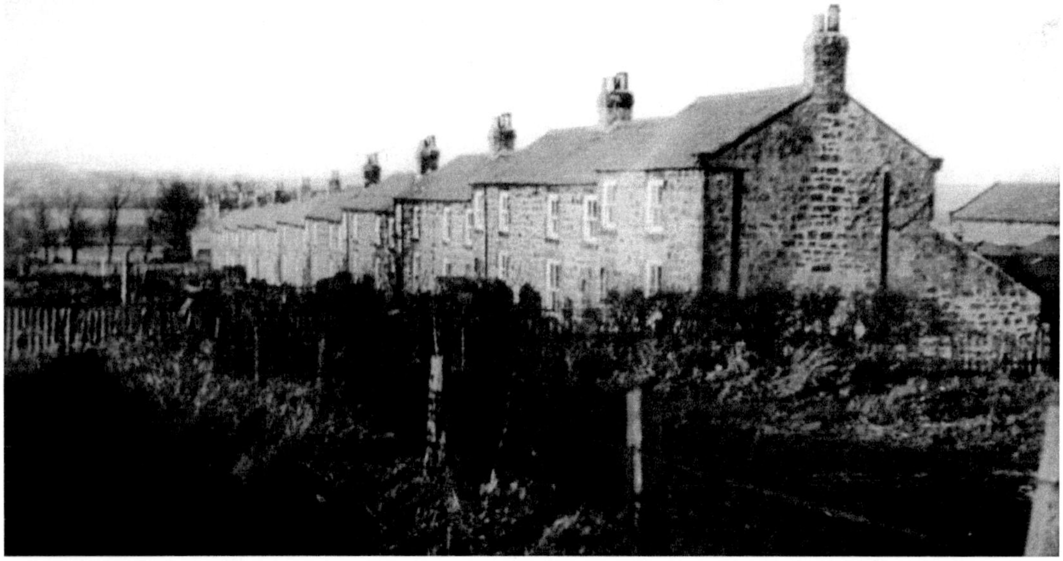

Bilton Banks' houses taken from the east (at a later time) just showing a house from the Short Row, behind the Long Row which is facing onto the road. The manager's house is barely visible at the very bottom of the picture.

[48] The above three images reproduced with permission of Mr. Billy McKnight.

Thirty of the men shown on the census for this period were employed as miners. Six residents in the village however, had more specialised occupations at the colliery including:

Mining engineer
Colliery joiner
Boiler maker
Engine fitter
Winding engineer
Colliery clerk.

Whilst most of the occupants of the two rows of houses, which had been built for some of the workforce, had been born at Shilbottle, some had moved into the area from farming and fishing areas nearby, including Embleton, Bamburgh, Newton-by-the-Sea, Chatton and Earsdon.

The mining engineer, who was effectively the manager, was Mr. William Alexander Ritson. Aged 29 years, he had come into the area from Merthyr in Glamorganshire.

Family names shown in the 1881 census for Bilton Banks, include names which continue in the 21st century to be heard in and around Shilbottle. These include:

Buglass	Hutchinson
Bowey	Punton
Cairns	Thompson
Egdell	Tweedy
Green	Waddle
Hall	Wilson
Henderson	Young

The 1891 census took place on 5th April and shows just 28 dwellings, five of which were occupied by families involved in farming, including Robert Frater the farmer at Longdyke and Thompson Bradford who gave his title as farm steward. The remaining dwellings, except for the home of Robert Thompson, the miller, were occupied exclusively by families whose head worked at the colliery either as a miner, coke burner, blacksmith, engine wright or horse keeper. The manager or mining engineer then was Mr. John Roscamp, who had been born at Wingate in County Durham.

The Village of Bilton Banks in 1891 had a population of 164 out of which 38 men and boys worked at the mine, the majority as underground labourers hewing coal.

The familiar names of Egdell, Hutchinson, Punton, Thompson, Tweedy, Waddle and Young remain prominent. The incomers were from as far away as Cockermouth, Carlisle and Kirkoswald.

The data obtained from the decipherable elements of the 1901 census, taken on 31st March 1901, reveal a similar situation. Thirty two families were resident at Bilton Banks and 37 men and boys were employed at the mine. The census record describes the residents' occupations in greater detail. These include:

Colliery manager	Putter
Deputy manager	Rope Splicer
Colliery engineer	Carter
Colliery deputy	Engineman
Colliery blacksmith	Hewer
Pump engineer	Filler
Coal miner	Drawer

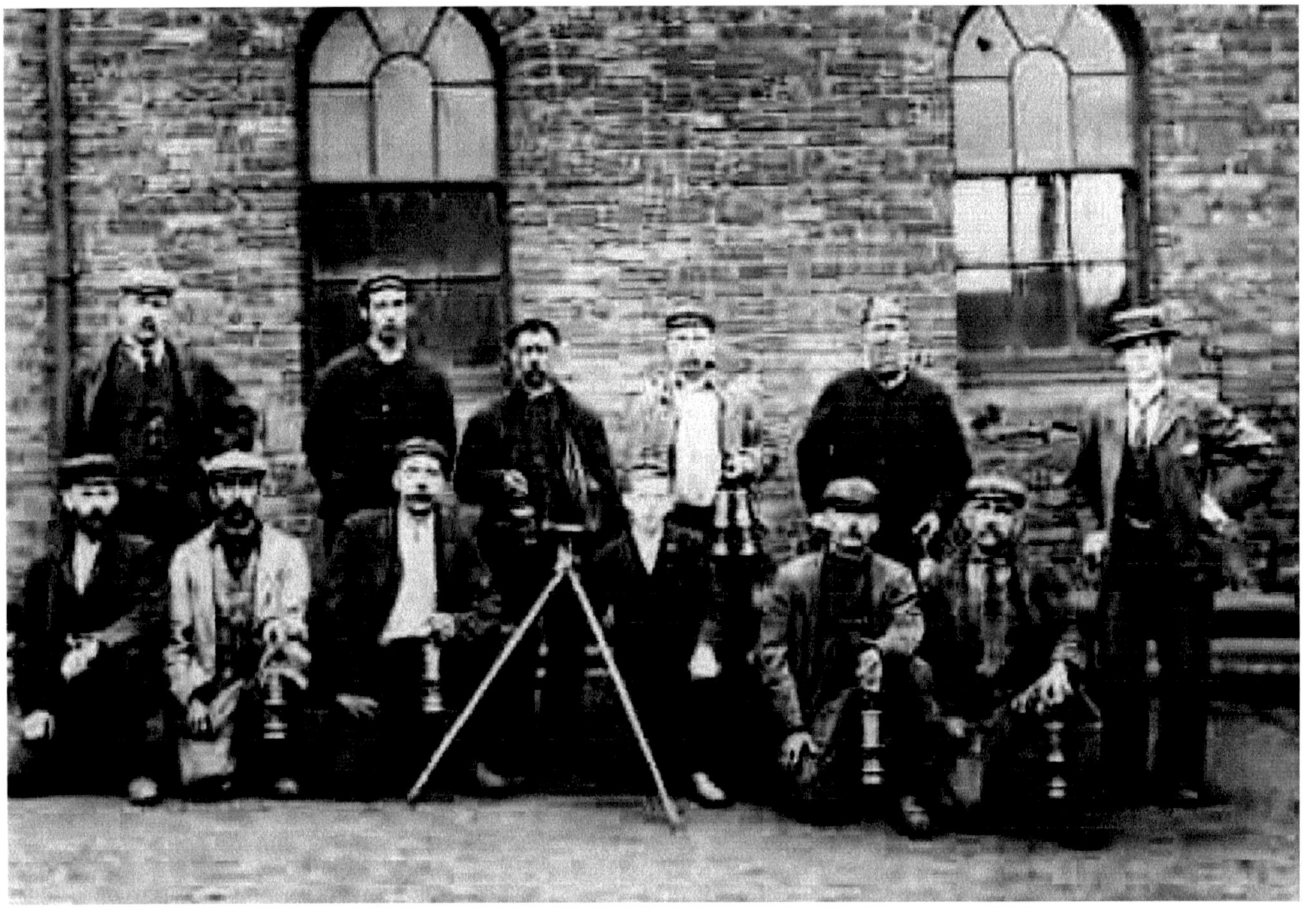

Officials at Shilbottle Colliery, 1890[49]

The manager in 1901 was still Mr. Roscamp. His deputy manager was John Hilton from Shilbottle. The pit deputy was Thomas Temple, who hailed from Dipton. The colliery engineer was William Jeffreys and the blacksmiths were Samuel Egdell and Robert Air. Many of the people from the previous census were still at Bilton Banks.

Opposite: The Ordnance Survey Map (Second Edition)[50] clearly shows the relationship between the colliery, the manager's house to the east of the pit yard and the two rows of miner workers' dwellings.

[49] Reproduced with permission of Northumberland Archives ref: NRO 1426/3. The windows are similar to those installed in the Grange Pit which was not sunk until 1925. Nevertheless, the location is believed to be Longdyke.
[50] Re-produced here with permission of Northumberland Archives.

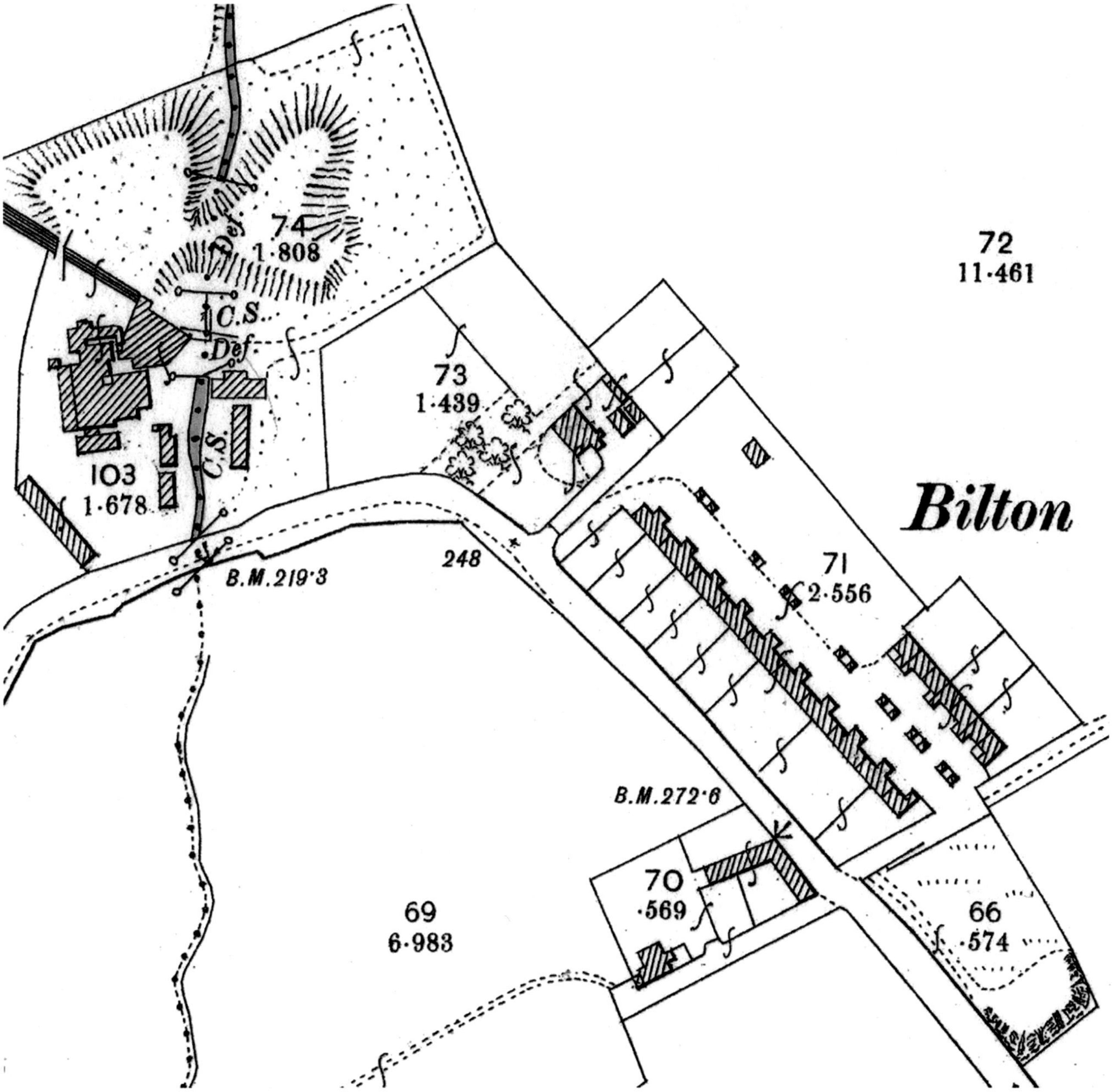

74
1·808
C.S.
Def.
73
1·439
72
11·461
Bilton
103
1·678
C.S.
B.M.219·3
248
71
2·556
B.M.272·6
70
·569
69
6·983
66
·574

Mr. John Green helpfully drew a rough plan of the colliery yard which, with some modifications, is reproduced below.[51]

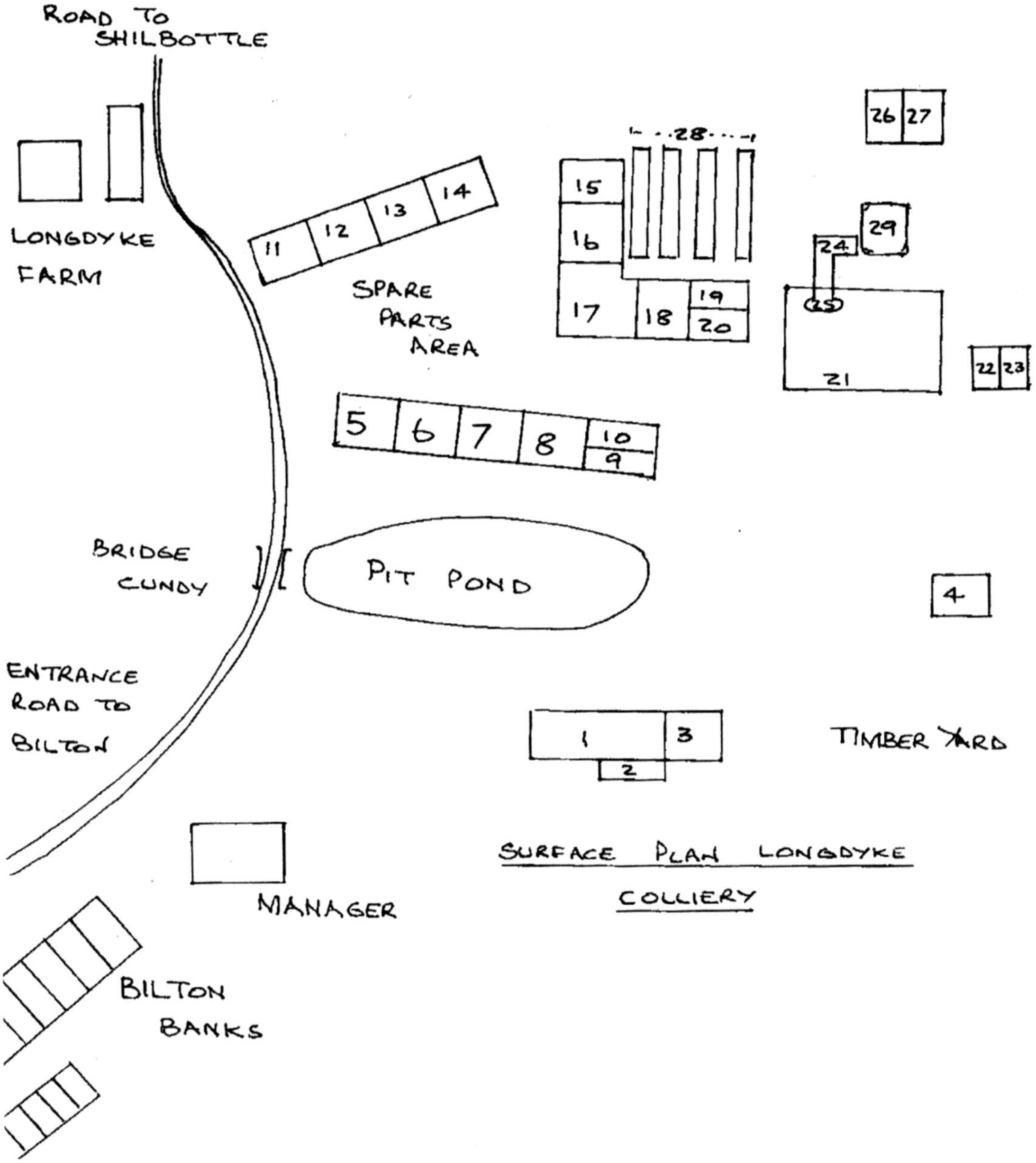

Plan of Longdyke – Old Pit

1	Electric	11	Stables	21	Screens
2	Token lamps	12	Electric shop	22–23	Banksman's cabin
3	Engine/electric	13	Joiners	24	Fan & tunnel
4	Powder cabin	14	Blacksmith	25	Shaft
5	General office	15	Store	26	Boiler-pump
6	Manager	16	Timber store	27	Fireman's cabin
7	Overman's office	17	Main hauler	28	Boilers (4)
8	Oil store	18	Winding engine	29	Fire hose chimney
9	Weigh cabin	19	Screen engine		
10	Weigh cabin	20	Tramway engine		

[51] Original deposited at Northumberland Archives ref: NR 2205/2 – and copied with permission.

It will be noted that in the plan, the colliery is described as Longdyke – Old Pit, but only because by the time the plan was being drawn, there was a new pit at Woodhouse Farm, in Shilbottle, known as the Grange Pit. Bilton Banks had been decommissioned.

Longdyke's Workings

It can be seen from the above plans and drawings that compared with other pits, Longdyke had a degree of sophistication. The shaft was sunk by the Taylor brothers *circa* 1844/45, who were the owners and had industries at Earsdon and Newburn as well as Shilbottle.

Harry Air, who started at Longdyke as a 14 year old, rose to be overman at Shilbottle Grange Pit.

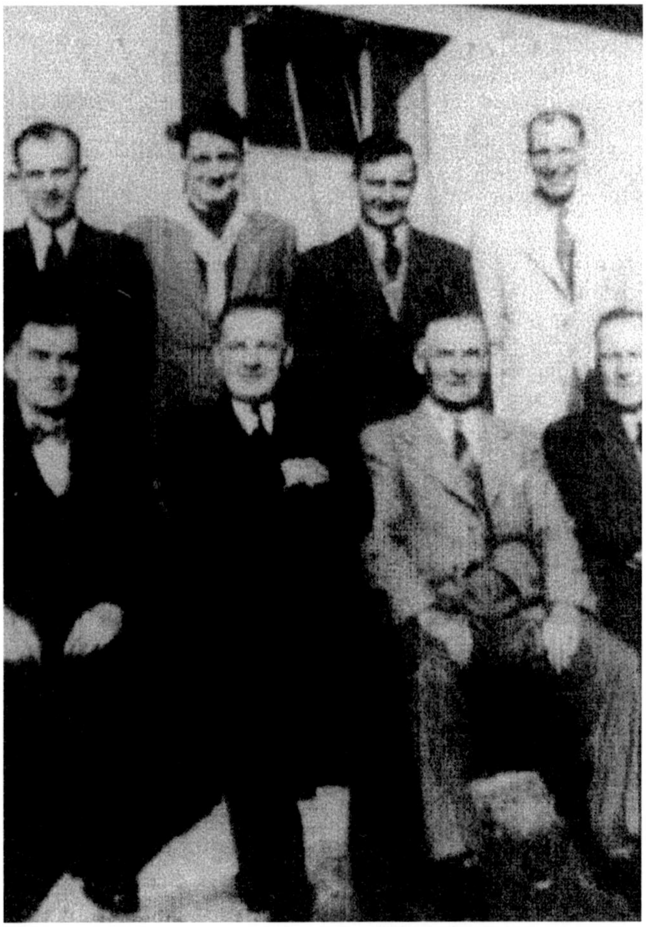
[52]

Mr. Harry Air in his sixties seen seated on the left with colleagues.

Mr. Air wrote a brief outline of working methods at Longdyke. In this he notes that the Taylor brothers built three houses in the parish for use by old people and established a benevolent trust known as 'Taylor's Charity'.[53]

At the beginning of the 20th century the new owners and directors of Longdyke Colliery were Mr. Hugh Augustus Paynter and Mr. Nathaniel Dunn.

---

[52] Reproduced with permission from *Memories of Shilbottle – Millennium Edition*, p. 81.
[53] Air, Harry, a paper entitled *Memories of Longdyke Colliery Working*, (1988) *'Hand Getting' methods 1913 and developments.*

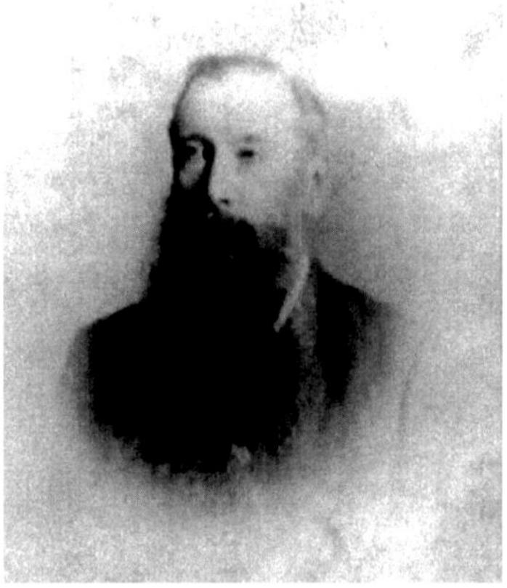

Mr. H.A. Paynter

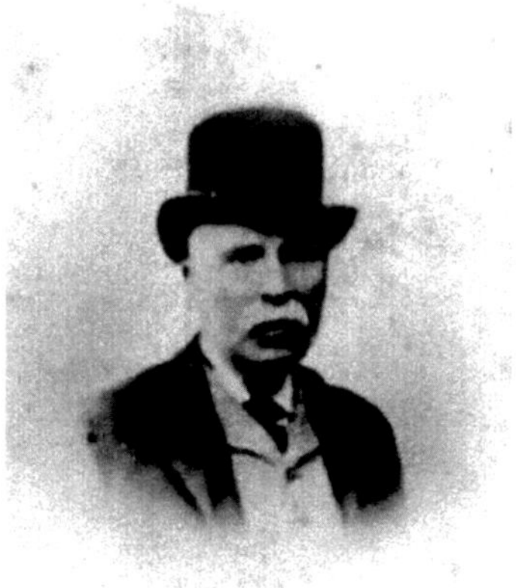
[54]

Mr. N. Dunn

The colliery officials are shown below with the manager Mr. J.A. Dixon in the centre.

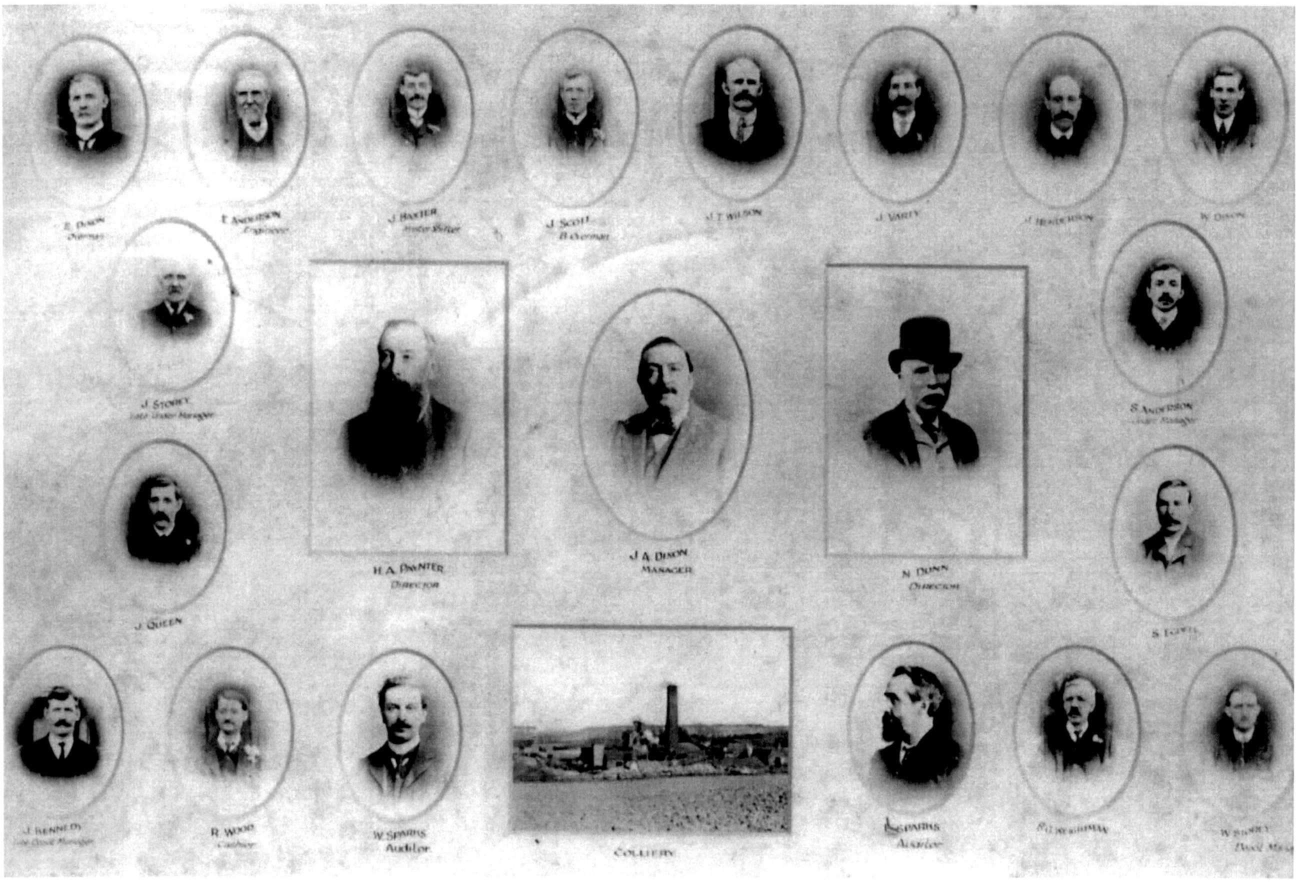

Shilbottle Colliery Officials 1912

The officials are clockwise from top left – E. Dixon (overman), T. Anderson (engineer), J. Baxter (master shifter), J. Scott (Backshift overman), J. T. Wilson, J. Varty, J. Henderson, W. Dixon, S. Anderson (under manager), S. Egdell, W. Storey, (depot manager), B.G. Weightman, L. Sparks (auditor), W. Sparks (auditor), R. Wood (cashier), J. Kennedy (late depot manager), J. Queen, J. Storey (late under-manager).

---

[54] From a photograph provided by Ronnie Knox.

[55] Provided by Mr. Ronnie Knox.

John Green, in his account of life at Longdyke and Bilton Banks, comments that a close knit community existed. He goes on to imply that within the workforce there was a 'pecking order' with some minimal level of favouritism exercised by the management. This is not to say that those who succeeded in securing senior positions did not merit their elevation.

It is known that Coverdale Smith Anderson progressed in his time from labourer to manager and without talent he would not have done that. Within the mining community he became well connected and respected. During his time, some of his relatives also held official positions at Longdyke. His half brother, Edward Kinghorn Anderson, later became under manager at Shilbottle and then manager at Scremerston.

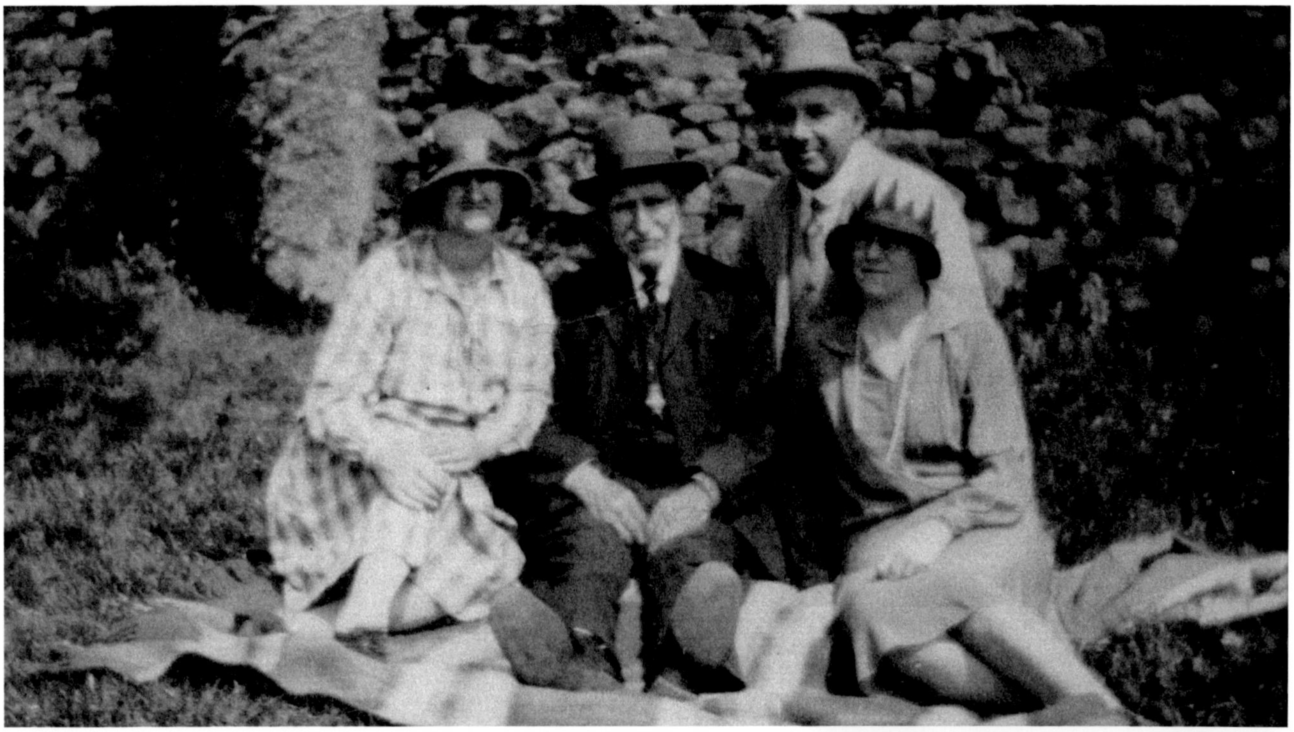

Above: Coverdale Smith Anderson is shown with his father Edward Anderson. His sister Mary Ann Varty and his wife Ursula are on the left and right of the photograph.

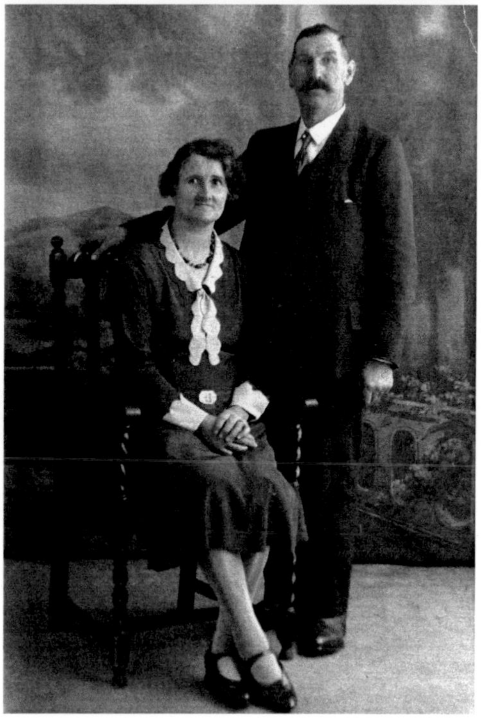

Right: John Varty, Coverdale Smith Anderson's brother-in-law, with his wife Mary Ann (John Varty is third from the right on the composite 1912 image of the officials shown on the previous page).

As the colliery became more profitable, in 1913 the owners negotiated a new lease from the Duke of Northumberland. This gave them permission to extract coal and fireclay and to deepen the existing pit and add one or two new pits at Sturton Grange, Shilbottle.[56]

[56] The above two photographs from the collection of Mr. Leslie Ian Varty, Northants, nephew of Coverdale Anderson.

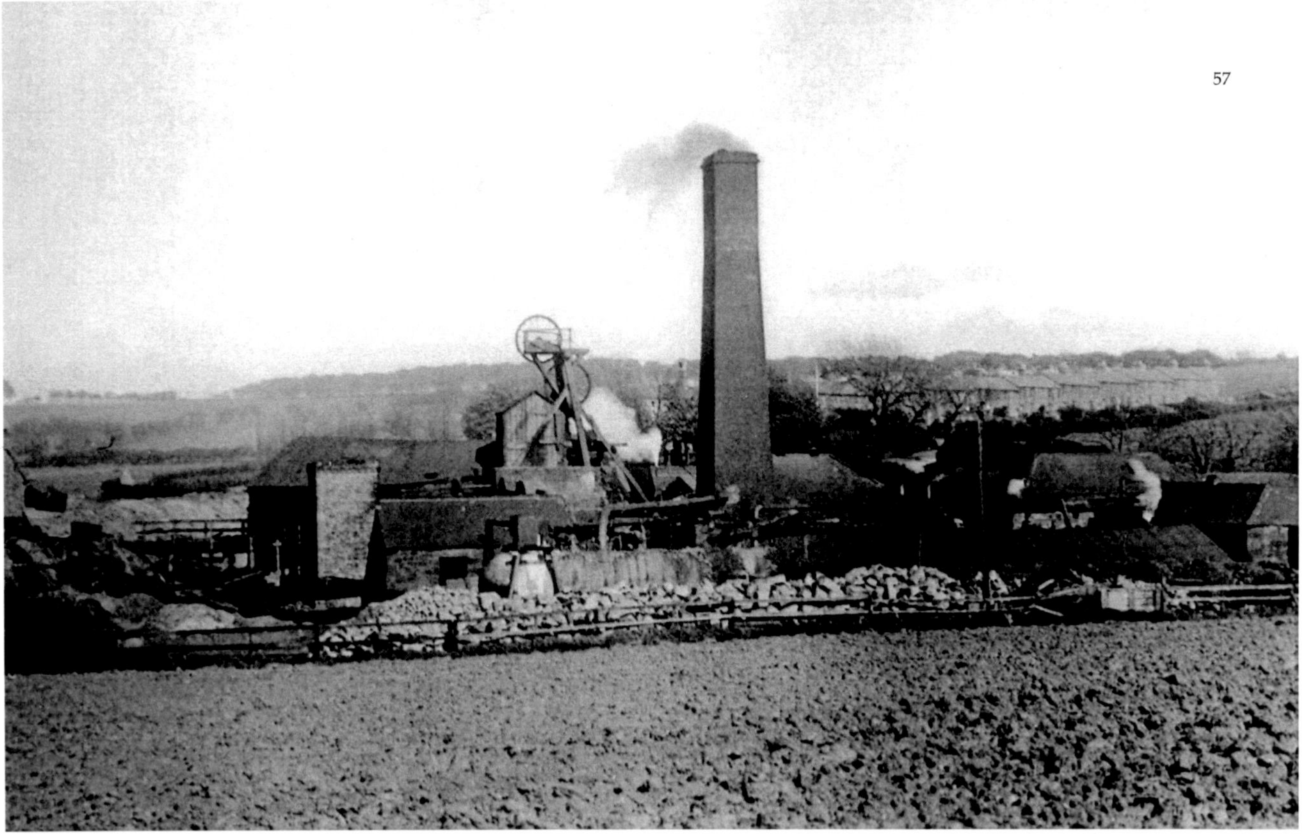

[57]

Longdyke Colliery with its winding house, chimney and outbuildings clearly visible with Bilton Banks in the background.

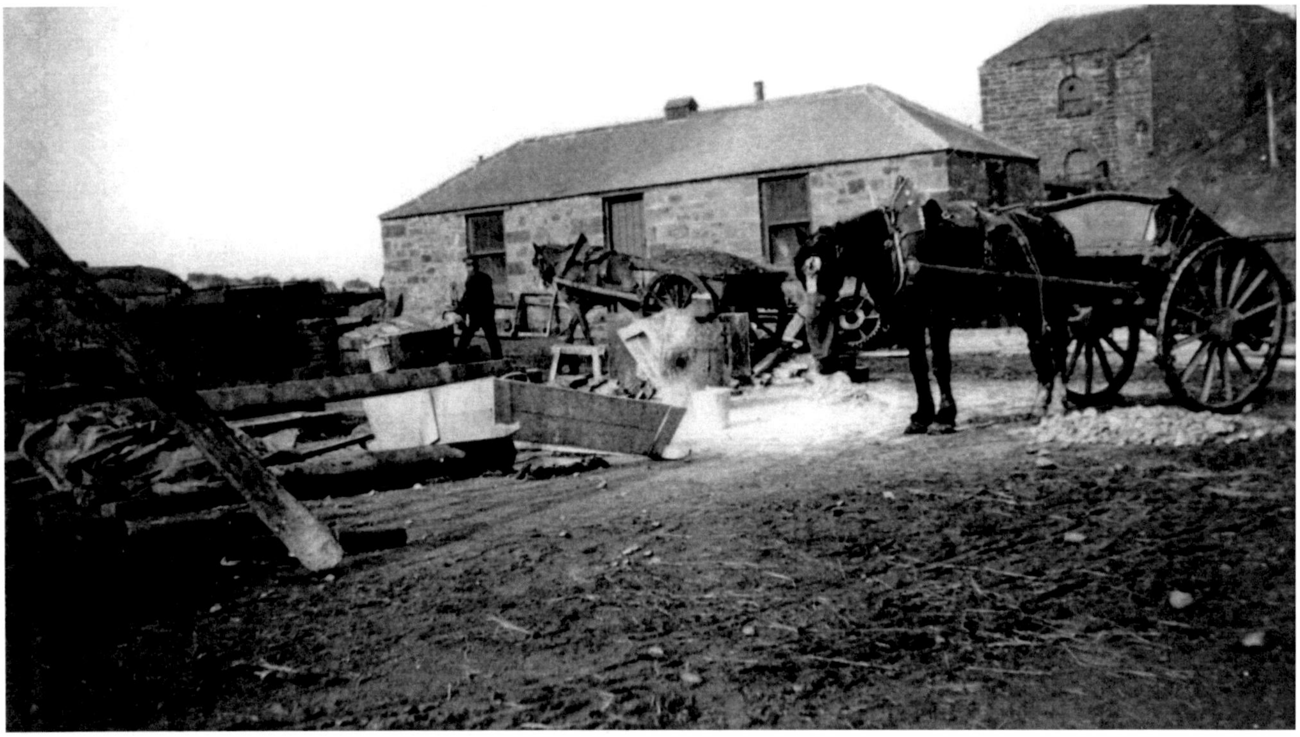

Colliery yard 1904

[57] Image from the author's collection.

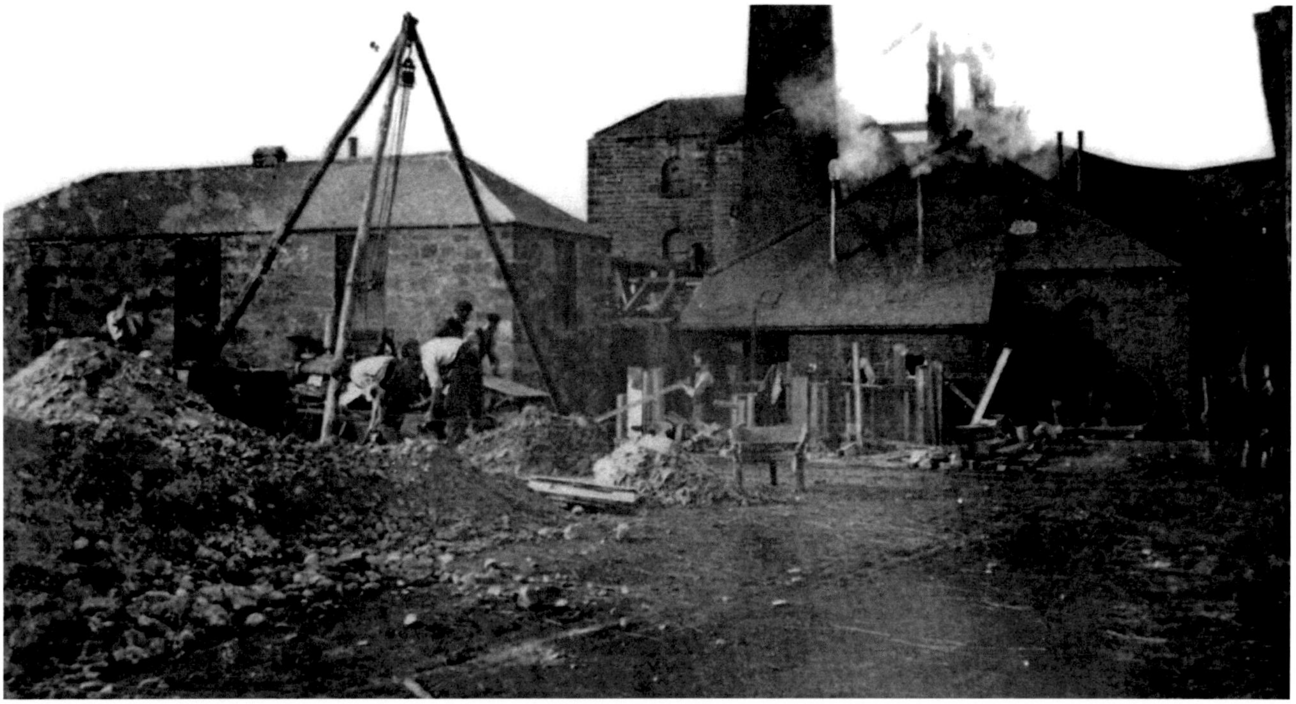

The 'founds' for the then new haulage engine being laid in 1904.

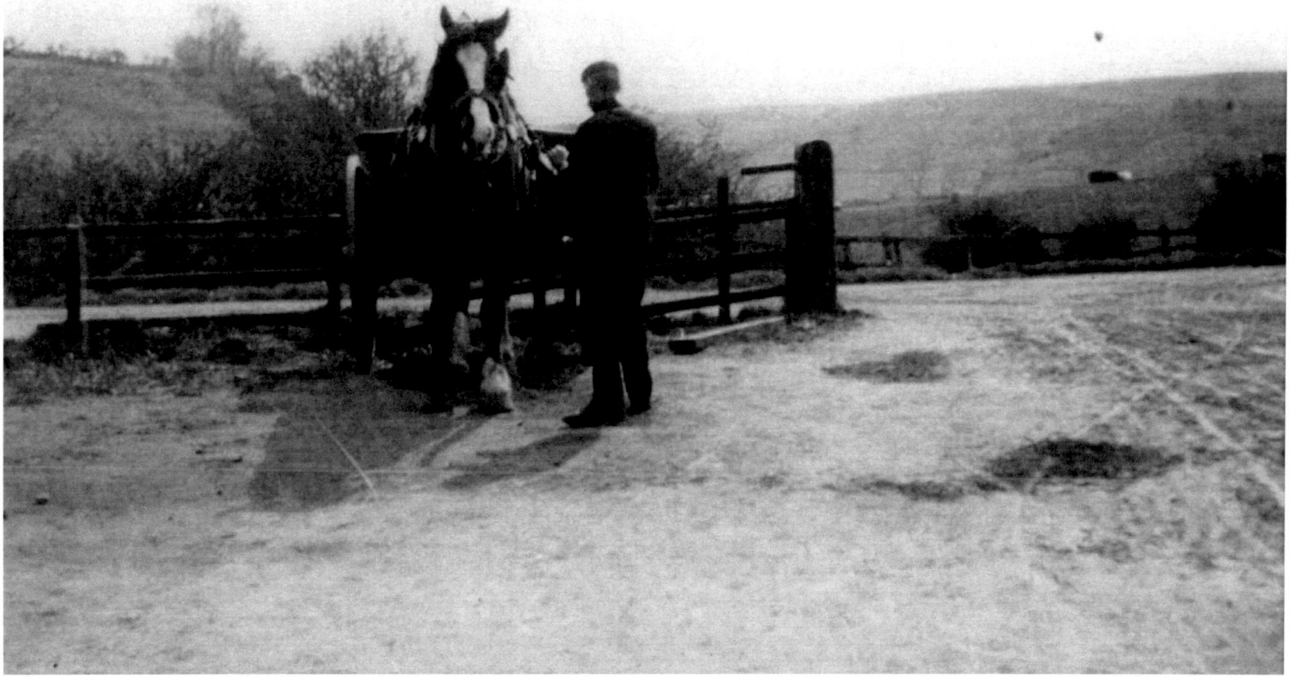

Cartier, W. Wood, at the entrance to the colliery, 1904.

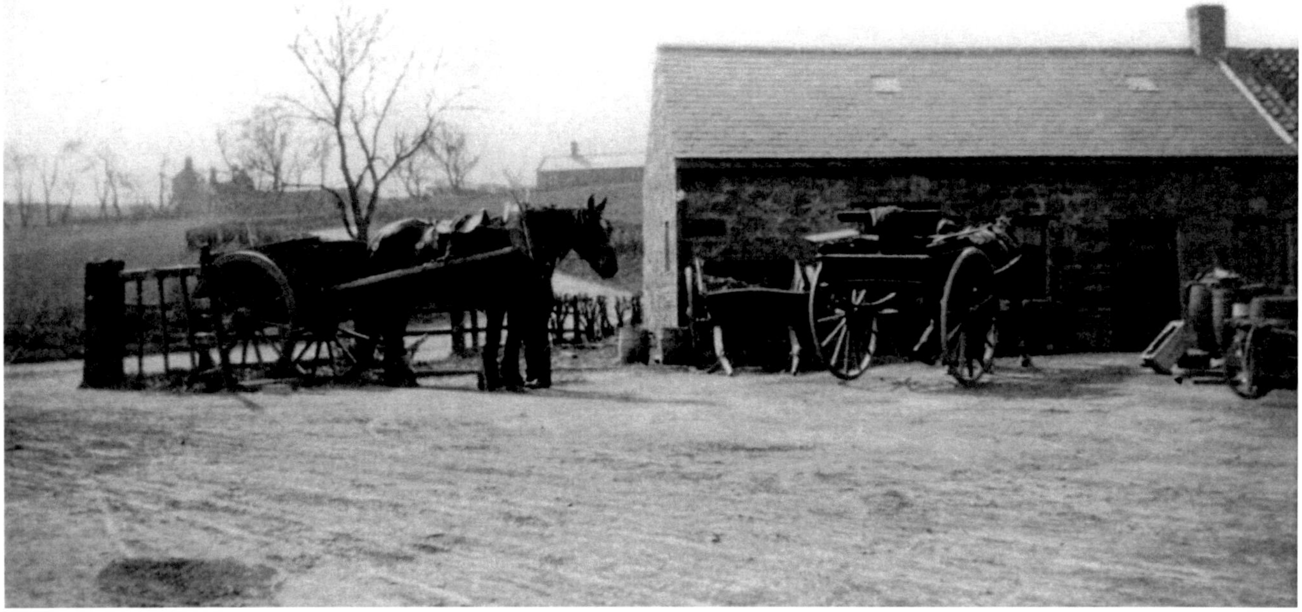

Second entrance with outbuilding in the foreground and dwellings behind.

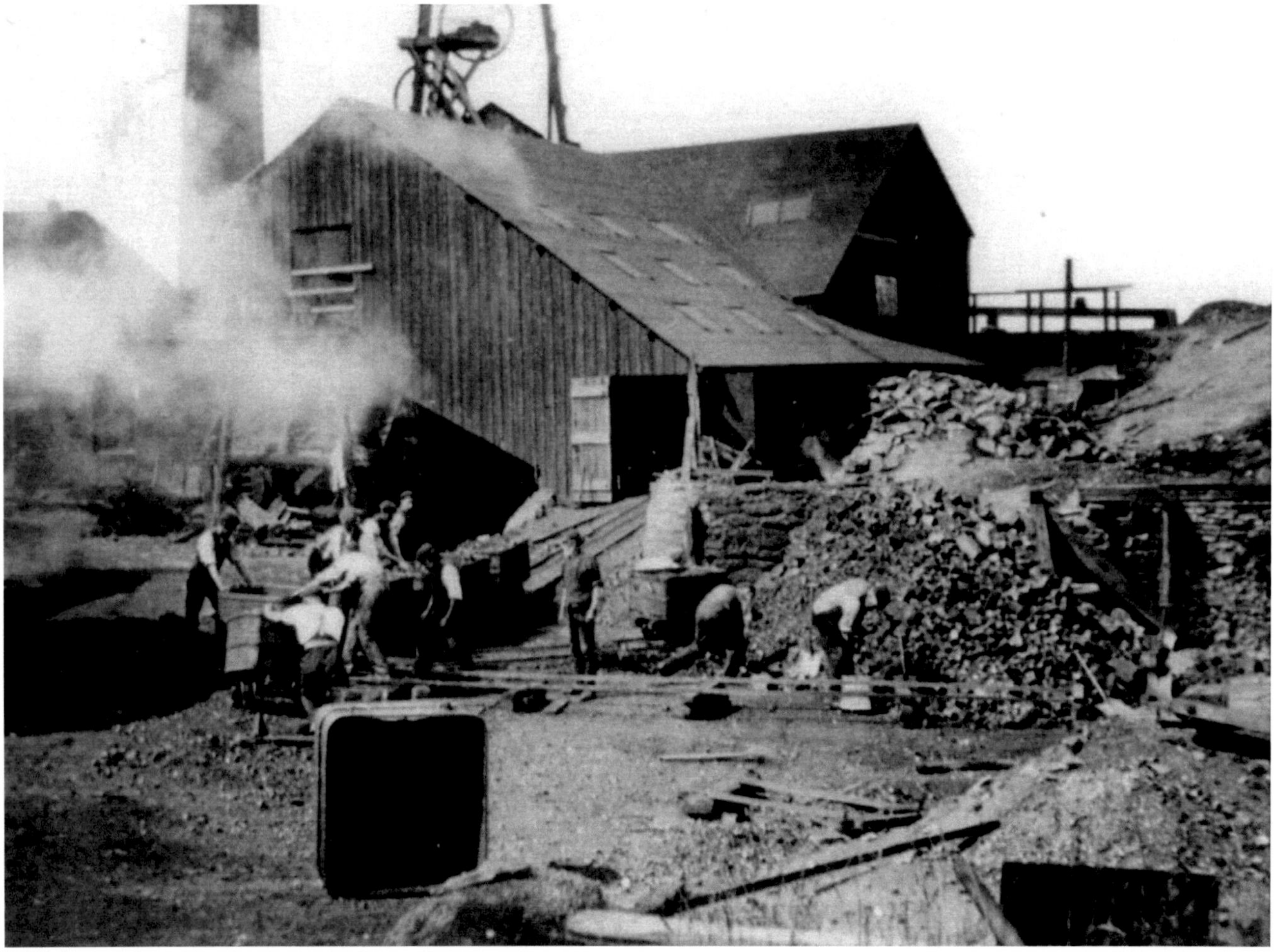

The screens with surface workers man-handling tubs.

[58]

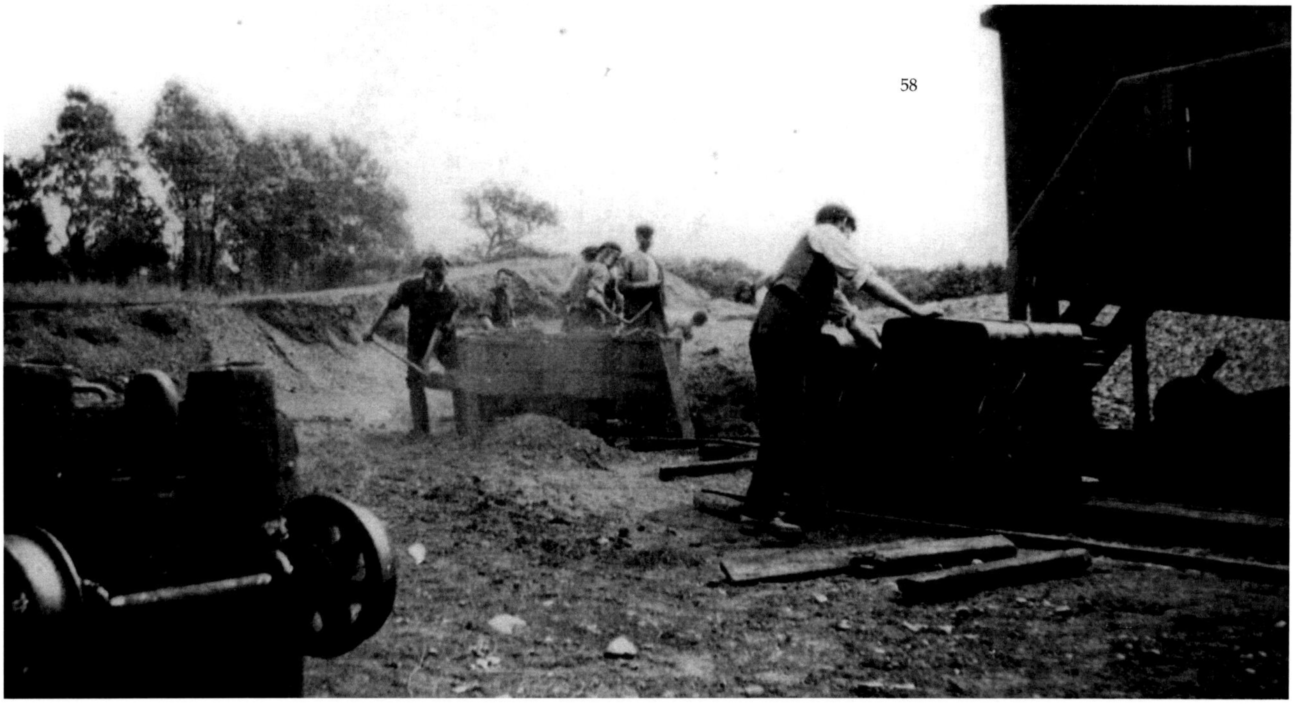

Men filling 'smalls'.

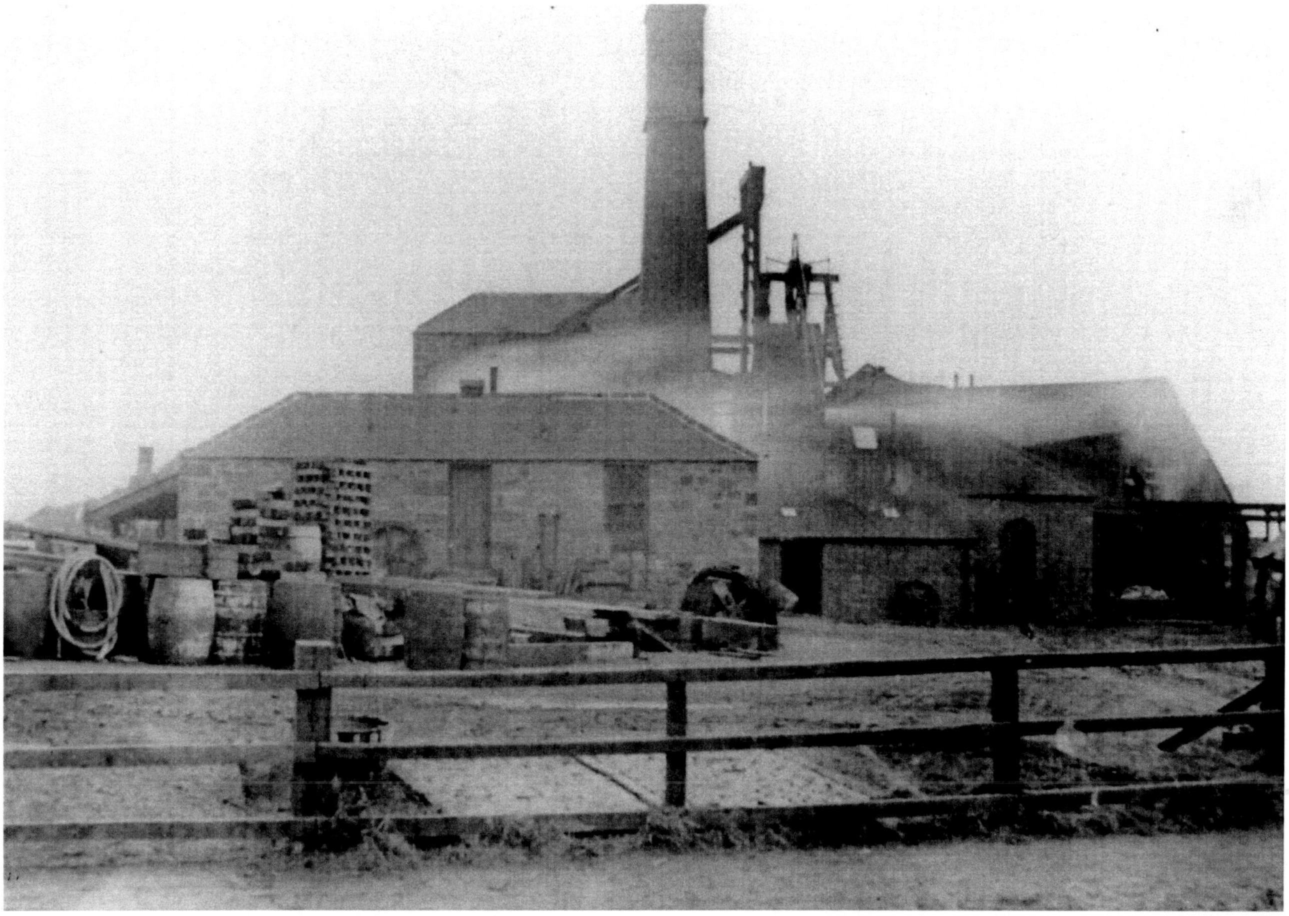

The colliery showing close up views of the outbuildings.

---

[58] The first six photographs above donated by David Brewis – from a collection made by N. Dunn in 1904.

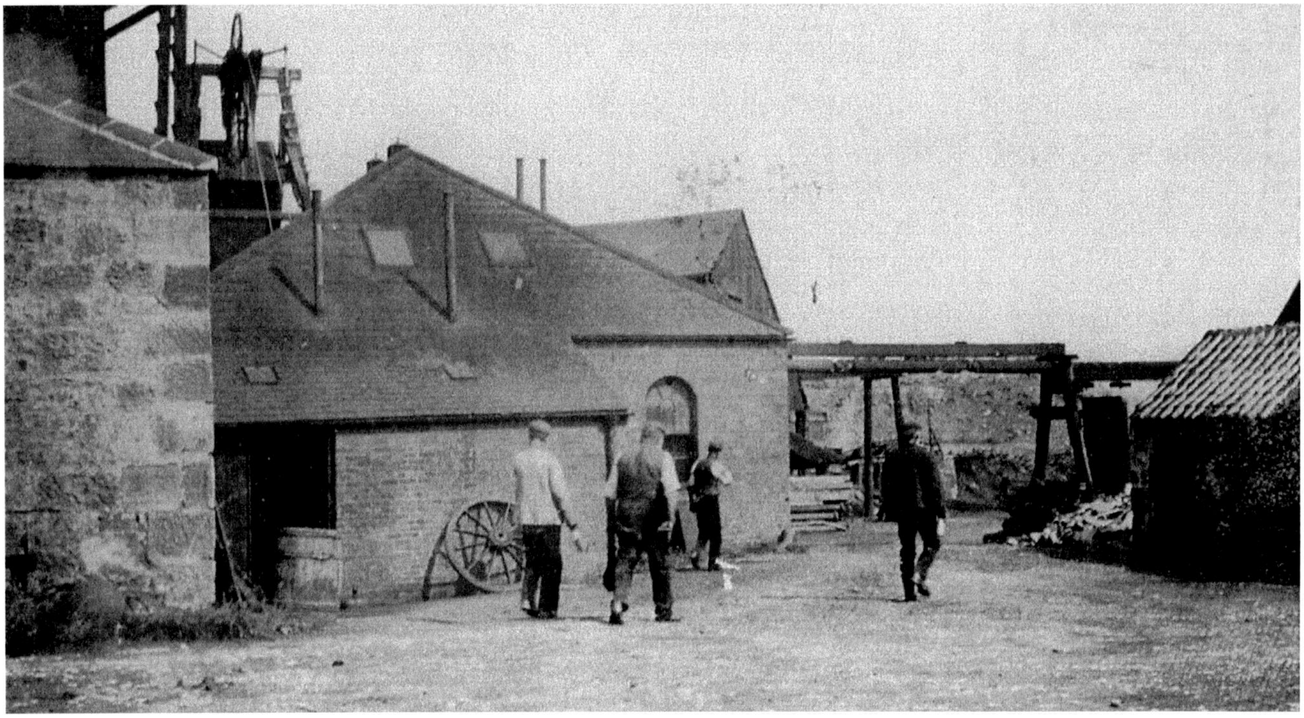

Colliery surface workers retreating from one task and approaching another.

In 1916 the Co-operative Wholesale Society negotiated the purchase of Longdyke Colliery for the sum of £50. It was shortly after this transfer of ownership that Mr. Coverdale Anderson took over as manager.

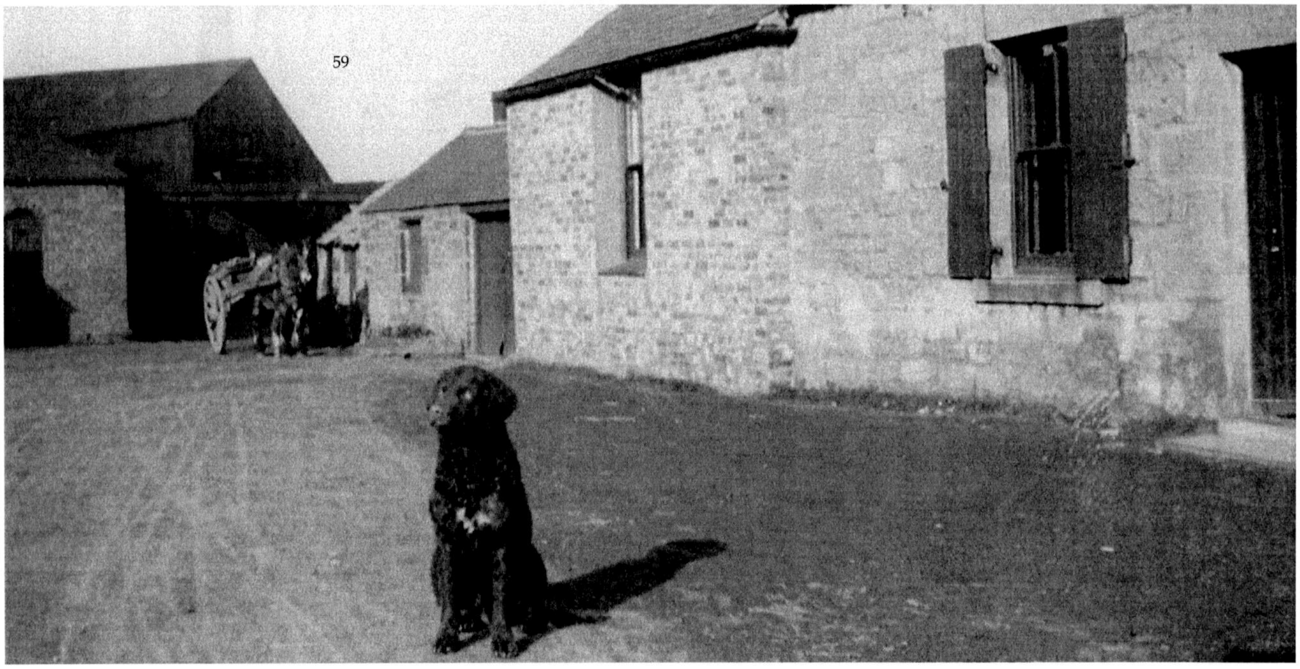

[59]

The pit yard with 'Roy' dated 1905.

The photograph of 'Roy' above, which was taken in the pit yard in 1905, is interesting because the dog's presence would have been banned 15 years later. The then manager Mr. Coverdale S. Anderson issued a decree in 1920 concerning residents keeping dogs.

---

[59] The three photographs above are from Joyce Snaith's collection.

His letter dated April 12th 1920 reads: *Following a strong complaint from the Castle Authorities, regarding the keeping of dogs at Shilbottle, as this is in contravention of the Colliery lease, the workmen are requested to do away with their dogs forthwith, or other proceedings will be taken.*

(Signed – C.S. Anderson.)[60]

Not only were conditions of employment harsh and living conditions primitive by modern standards, the landlord and employer had influences into lifestyle choices. In due course, the residents either ignored the Castle's edict, or it was rescinded, because some of the people spoken to in the course of this study did keep dogs.

The Mine

Longdyke's shaft was sunk around 1844/45 to 25 fathoms to the coal seam which in places was only 28 inches. The mine had a drainage shaft seven fathoms beyond, intended and used as a sump for water which was pumped back to the surface. The pump used was a Bearm pump and this was operated from the surface. The coal shaft was ten and a half feet diameter and had a 40 h.p. engine to raise the coal. The engine shaft was seven and a half feet diameter. There was also a ventilation shaft with a furnace at the top to cause up-draught to remove stale air and create circulation. The outcrop of coal ran west south west and east north east on a line north of the mine shaft, eventually for one and a half miles. In due course, two roadways were driven an equal distance apart, the coal being taken out by hand five yards either side of the line. A railway system of three feet eight inches gauge tracks ran for 2,800 yards underground on 22lb rails. There were 24 underground carriages for transporting the coal in hazel baskets or wooden sided trams, of which there were 36. The colliery eventually had eight ponies underground and two on the surface. The coal was moved in 8cwt tubs or sets, not 10cwt as suggested by the colliery viewer, John Buddle, many years earlier. Wooden props were used, where necessary, to support the six-feet pillars of coal. These were left in place after 'winnings' of coal were removed. Three shifts of miners operated; the fore shift and back shift during which the men hand-hewed the coal. The third shift (night shift) followed and drilled the top stone and shale strata blasting it down to a thickness of two feet six inches, making a roadway six feet wide and four feet eleven inches high. After 50 yards of working, trapdoors to assist ventilation were formed.

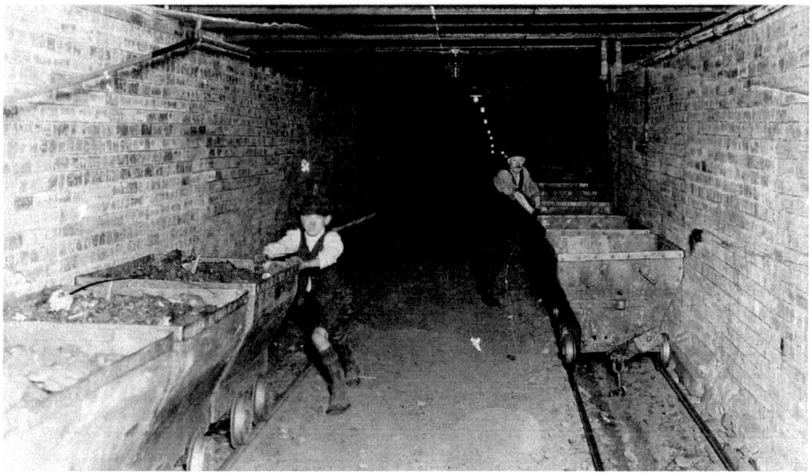

A boy hand putting.[61]

[60] An extract from the Shilbottle Colliery Agreements & Joint Committee ledger, brought into use on or after 5th April 1909, in the archive of Mrs Joyce Snaith.

[61] Photo from Mrs Joyce Snaith's collection. It cannot be stated with certainty that this is underground at Longdyke. If not it is pre-Nationalisation at the Grange Pit.

The coal was 'won' by 'Piece Workers' who were paid 2s 6d per ton.[62] Mr. Harry Air, who started work at Longdyke as a 14 year old in March 1913 wrote: *a siding or flat was made at the outer end of the crossroad on the main or No. 1 winnings … this allowed 'standage' for empty tubs (8cwt) delivered from the shaft bottom by single haulage and the haulage rope was transferred from empty tubs to full tubs according to delivery numbers.*

Safety measures were applied for the control of these tubs (known as sets) as they were coupled together with a shaftey rod or bull trailing behind the load and signalled to the shaft bottom. This shortened the pony haulage or putting to the new siding on No. 2 winning … also No. 2 became the main winning for air intake for both No. 1 and No. 2 which formed an air-split at the crossroads by doors and regulators. This continued until the forming of the 100 yard face either right of No. 1 or to the left of No. 2. It was then that air crossings had to be installed and air-splitting again took place.

The ventilation method – whatever roof stone (or 'canch'[63] *as we called it) was blasted down and packed at the sides of the roadway leaving a space behind this pack for return air with a brattis cloth to help the seal.*

When Longdyke was developed to over half a mile they put another shaft down to coal level. This was known as the air shaft or return and in developing always made air return connections from district to district to this shaft. Thus the first shaft was the inlet for fresh air and the new shaft an outlet for return air thus increasing safety and also making two outlets for manpower. This development or winning continued until sufficient coal was developed to meet the required output for the people employed there, then when the district was worked out or nearing termination further development or winning took place to maintain output.[64]

Candles, squibs and gunpowder had to be purchased by the miners, once a fortnight, from the Co-op. An edict concerning the safe use of explosive shots, which was issued by the manager in 1914, following explosions in other collieries (and one within the memory of many miners at Longdyke in 1892) reads: *When preparing shots no charge of explosives must be taken from the 'caddie' until the hole into which it is to be put is cleaned out ready for that charge. When the hole is cleaned ready for charging the person preparing the shot must bring his 'caddie' to the hole, take out the required charge and place it direct into the hole from the 'caddie'. Then he must take his 'caddie' back to a safe point 'outbyeside' before stemming the hole.*

On no account must any attempt be made to carry explosives exposed in such a way as to be liable to ignition by a candle or other light, and cartridges must not be laid down upon the floor, 'caunch', tub, or other place, before being placed in the hole.[65]

So safety in the use of explosives was a welfare issue for the management and workforce, but also a commercial issue, because death and injury in the mine caused delays and stoppages in production. There was a human and financial cost. In addition, explosive charges were expensive. In 1916 compressed detonators cost 5¼d per pound. A year later the cost had risen to 7½d.

Harry Air continues: *Piece Work was paid by the ton. The tonnage price then, if I remember, was 2s 6d per ton. Each hewer had to fund all his gear and pay for it being sharpened (except for his shovel and wooden crackit).*[66]

---

[62] In 1900, 2s 6d at 2011 values would be worth £11.81. http:/www.thisismoney.co.uk (Historic Inflation Calculator)

[63] 'Caunch' or 'canch' is a mining term for the underground tunnel of stone left immediately beneath where the coal has been removed. The stone-men came in after the hewers to remove the stone and make good the walls and roof supports.

[64] Air, Harry, *Memories of Longdyke Colliery* (1988).

[65] Extracted from the archives of Mrs. Joyce Snaith.

These were carried daily as required, also his clay, candles and squibs and powder. Fuse was provided by the employer but had to be paid for, which was only used when working wet coal. The hewer bought his powder, squibs and candles at the Co-op fortnightly and made his own charges of powder in cartridge form at home, and carried these daily to his working place in a tin canister. Candles and squibs had to be kept separate. The coal was under-curved? With the hand pick, chocked as undercurving? As the hewer had to lie on his crackit while doing so. Next was to hand-drill and blast and all to cast out under two feet four inches in height from five yards either side into his gate and fill the 8cwt tubs, replacing roof-supports in doing so and casting out.

Usually there were three 'putters' to each district, one pony for the four gates to the dip side and two hand putters to the centre and five rise side gates and a boy helper.

Putters were also paid piece-work and paid by the score. 1s 6d per score of five tubs. That is pony putting and 1s 10d per score hand putting. Each tub was 'tokened' by the hewer and putter when being filled and transported out to the siding or flat for main haulage.

All gear required to be sharpened was carried to and from the surface together with the explosives. The tools were sharpened in the blacksmith's shop.

One deputy had charge of each shift. In a district, pre-inspection of the first shift and two-hourly inspections throughout, rules and safety measures and supplies and roadways of all gates to 'plate' up.

Each deputy for each shift carried an oil safety lamp for testing, and at the end of his shift, had to see and lead all men under his charge out from his district.

The coal producers used candles at the working face but travelled to and from their working place with a little glass hand lamp. Whilst working at the coal face they could tell the time by the candle. They had 20 minutes for 'bait', sometimes less, a bottle of water and bread sandwiches. Smoking was prohibited.

The stone or canch men (on night shift) sometimes used oil lamps and sometimes candles. The putters used a little oil lamp called a 'Midgy' and this was trimmed and filled each day and sometimes spare oil had to be carried. Oil torches were used, provided by the employers, on main roadways where the air flow was much greater. Later, carbide lamps were introduced but piece workers had to provide their own.

Wages

The workers' wages had to be drawn between 4pm and 5pm on a Friday and were exceedingly low. In 1908 hand-putters earned 3s 8d per shift,[67] pony-putters 3s 2d. By 1910 the daily rate increased to 5s 4d respectively. Workers hewing coal in wet conditions were paid up to 3d per ton extra depending on whether the wet ran away from their place of work or remained as standing water. Fines of up to 6d per 5cwt tub were imposed for coal tubs which included more than 16lbs stone.

[66] A small three legged stool.

[67] In 1908, 3s 8d = £16.22 at 2011 values.

In his written record Mr. Harry Air included a verse about wages. This was apparently sung by lads from mining families:

'Drillers eleven pence ha'penny
Horse putters eighteen pence.
Hand putters one and ten pence
If they paid their aan expense.
Timber leaders two bob
Deputies half a croon and
The oer-man seven and a tanner,
Just for walking up and doon!'

The Price of Coal

The price of coal per ton 'won' at the coal face in 1911 was:

Singles	2s 2¼d[68]
Doubles	2s 2¾d

By 1917 the price had fallen to:

Singles	1s 11½d
Doubles	2s

The selling price of coal per ton in 1915 and 1916 was 24s 7d, and 25s respectively for best and 12s 6d, and 15s respectively for smalls.[69]

The Workforce

Records show the following workforce at Longdyke[70]:

Year	Underground	Surface
1915	210	26 [71]
1921	289	84
1923	267	98
1925	266	103

[68] In 1911, 2s 2d = £9.38 at 2011 vallues.
[69] The relative value of £1 between 1915 and 1917 at 2011 values is £84.40, £75.58 and £63.94 respectively.
[70] Data extracted from www.dmm.org.uk/company/c011.httm – Durham Mining Museum – Co-operative Wholesale Society.
[71] These figures have been calculated from a hand written schedule in the *Shilbottle Colliery Agreements and Joint Committee ledger*.

Twenty years before the abstract from Mr. Harry Air's account,[72] conditions in Longdyke would have been less sophisticated, but they held sufficient attraction for parties of visitors to enter the pit.

The record of one such visit, as part of the summer programme in 1890 of St James' Young Men's Association from the Church in Alnwick, has survived.[73]

On arrival at the pit, Mr. Roscamp, the engineer ... guided the party' ... he accompanied the group past an 'air compressing engine ... a fan engine for ventilating the mine, a perpendicular pumping engine, pumping 40 gallons per stroke, a horizontal winding engine for drawing the cage up, and also a similar contrivance for working the 200 trams that run on the permanent way to Alnwick Drop ... each tub carries six hundred-weights of coal.[74]

Candles were dealt out among the visitors, who 'ascended a flight of steps and joined the eager throng at the top of the shaft where the cages were busily plying. They are box shaped and restricted to take four men at a time. The tingling of a bell announced our downward departure. In half a minute we were lowered at great velocity 23 fathoms into the mineral world where a lot of cheerful faces dispelled our nervous propensities. A tarry odour ... assailed our nasal organ. Entering a long tunnelled excavation, laid with a tub railway which pervades the whole mine, it was as dark as midnight, the occasional glimmer of a candle lending a feeble light to show the way, for a pretty strong current of air prevented one from exposing his light to any advantage.

Here were situated stables which in every way resemble ordinary horse stalls ... eighteen ponies looking in the pink of condition ... Prince being the head of the stables and had done eighteen years of good service in this starless region.

... we proceeded along the air course down which a refreshing breeze was "draughted" from the shaft of the old pit (a reference to the Keeper's Pit). We then got a capital idea of the coal seam which was 2 feet 4 inches to 2 feet 6 inches.

Retracing our steps, Mr. Roscamp proposed going down 'the dip' the direction in which the strata inclines, to show pumping and workings to the ladies and several others ... while old Mr. Young, whom we joined, was detailed to take the remaining contingent up 'the rise' to the 'whin sill' ... our guide with his oil lamp led the van up a burrow-like course towards the workings.

Passing through two 'fly doors' that regulate the circulation of air, ... we came to ... 'the spout' ... used for pouring the coal from a high point in the seam to which it suddenly rose, down to the tubs. ... we were informed that our whereabouts was close beneath Greenrigg Kennels. The heat was of tropical degree and signs of heavy perspiration and the gradual darkening of complexions were in evidence.

The fumes from the oil lamps and candles were troublesome and it was now becoming hard work to walk at all ... the way being only four feet high. At given points hung a sheet of rough canvas serving as a temporary air-check, and blackening our faces as it brushed over them. A mile journey having been accomplished we reached the whin sill where a cinder coal hewing was being carried on, but not before we had undergone the self-inflicted penalty of crawling 70 yards on our 'hunkers' (bended knees) up a working only 2 and a half feet high. Here the veteran guide gave us an illustration of hewing and, in turn, each of us hewed a piece of 'black diamond' to treasure as a souvenir of our visit.

---

[72] *Ibid* Air, Harry, (1988).

[73] This account made available by Vera Mallon from records held by Bailiffgate Museum, Alnwick.

[74] The reporter seems to have been slightly misinformed.

Mr. Roscamp's party arrived ... who had had the acceptable privilege of driving most of their journey ... conveyed in trains of tubs drawn by Dick and Paddy, two willing ponies, who each showed they were possessed of mettle characteristic of Derby Day.'

This record of the single visit underground is peppered with phrases which reveal the excitement of the author and the mood of his or her companions. For the 'pitmen' the excitement was probably tempered by labour, frightening routines and the daily drudgery of sinking into the dark unknown for hours of hard effort in cramped, damp and hot conditions.

Some of the employees at the mine had surface jobs though, including those who looked after the tramway which transported coal from Longdyke to Alnwick. The tramway ran to the Alnwick Drop, (referred to in the opening paragraph of the visitors' account) and is shown on the map below.

It was an innovative mechanism for moving the coal. Mr. Dixon, the manager appointed in 1902, was responsible for it being brought into use.[76]

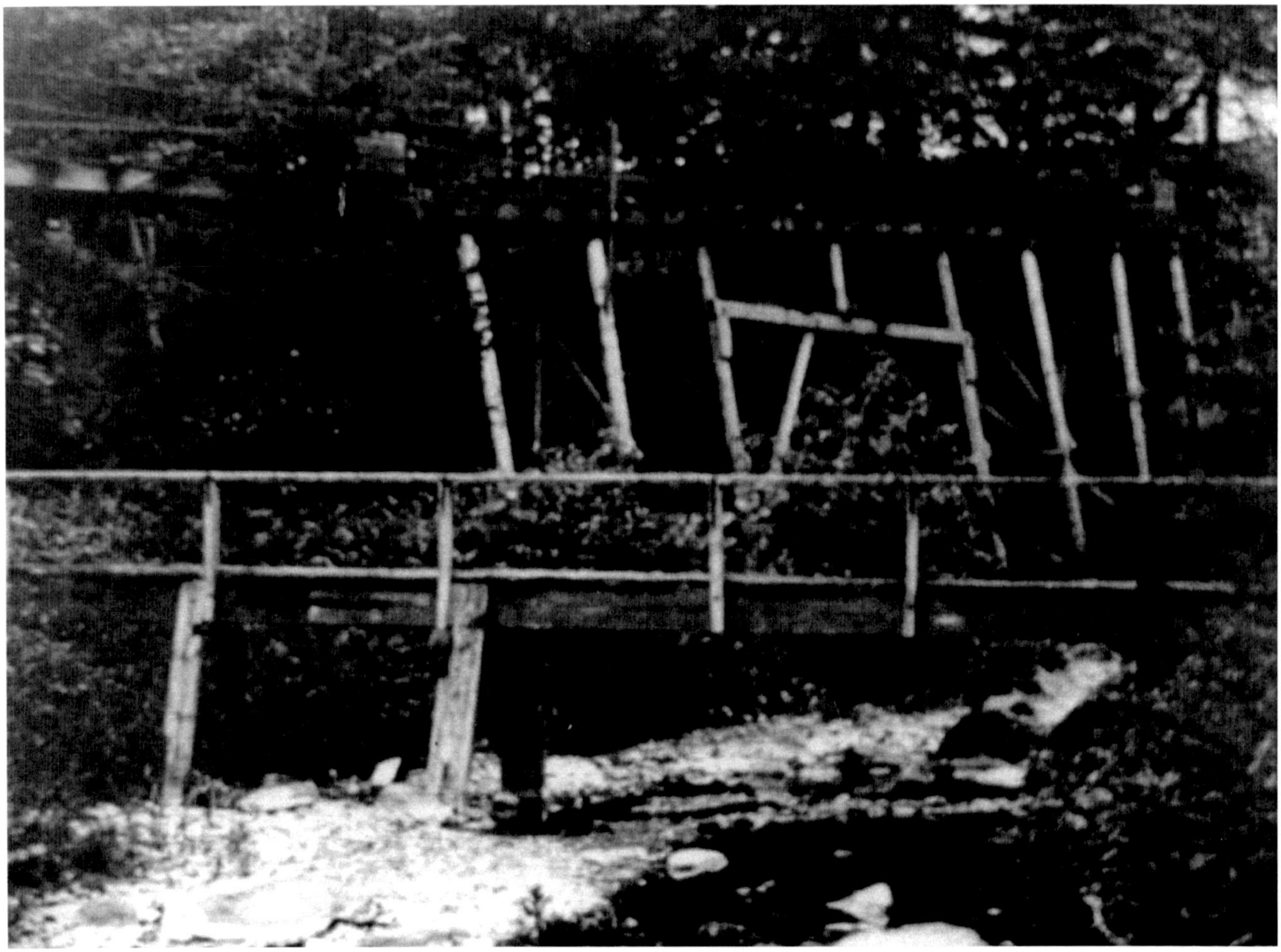

The Longdyke Tramway[77]

[76] According to the record of a speech held by Bailiffgate Museum, Alnwick.
[77] Photograph from Mr. D.P. Dalby's collection.

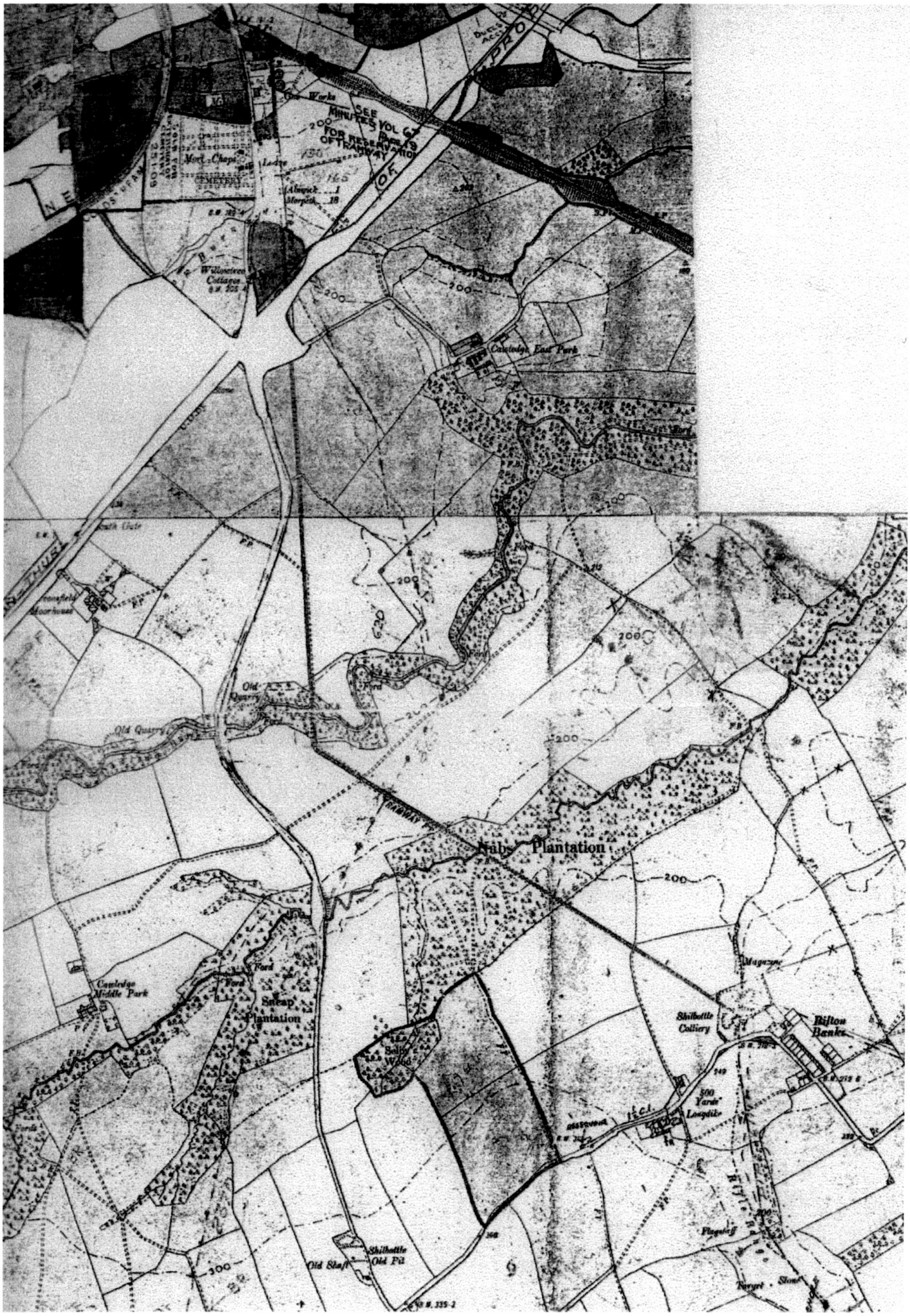

75

[75] From Mr. D.P. Dalby's collection.

Longdyke had two electric turbines made by Greenwood and Batley[78] which generated sufficient electricity to operate the colliery and provide light for 200 yards of the tramway as it left the colliery yard. The trams ran on narrow gauge rails.

79

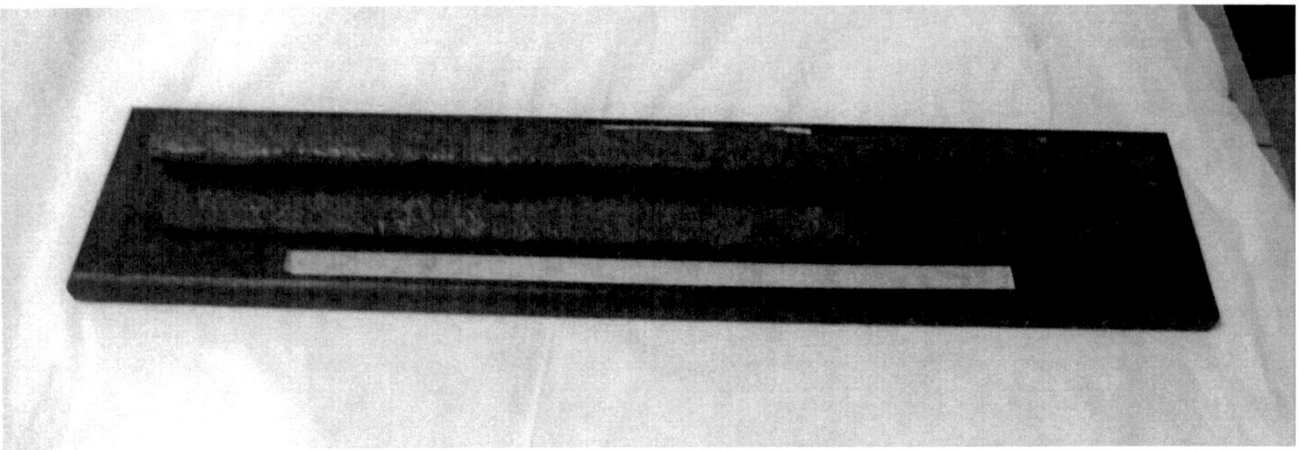

The tramway was controlled by telephone and a two way bell system, with communications along the line to the depot at the gas works on South Road in Alnwick.

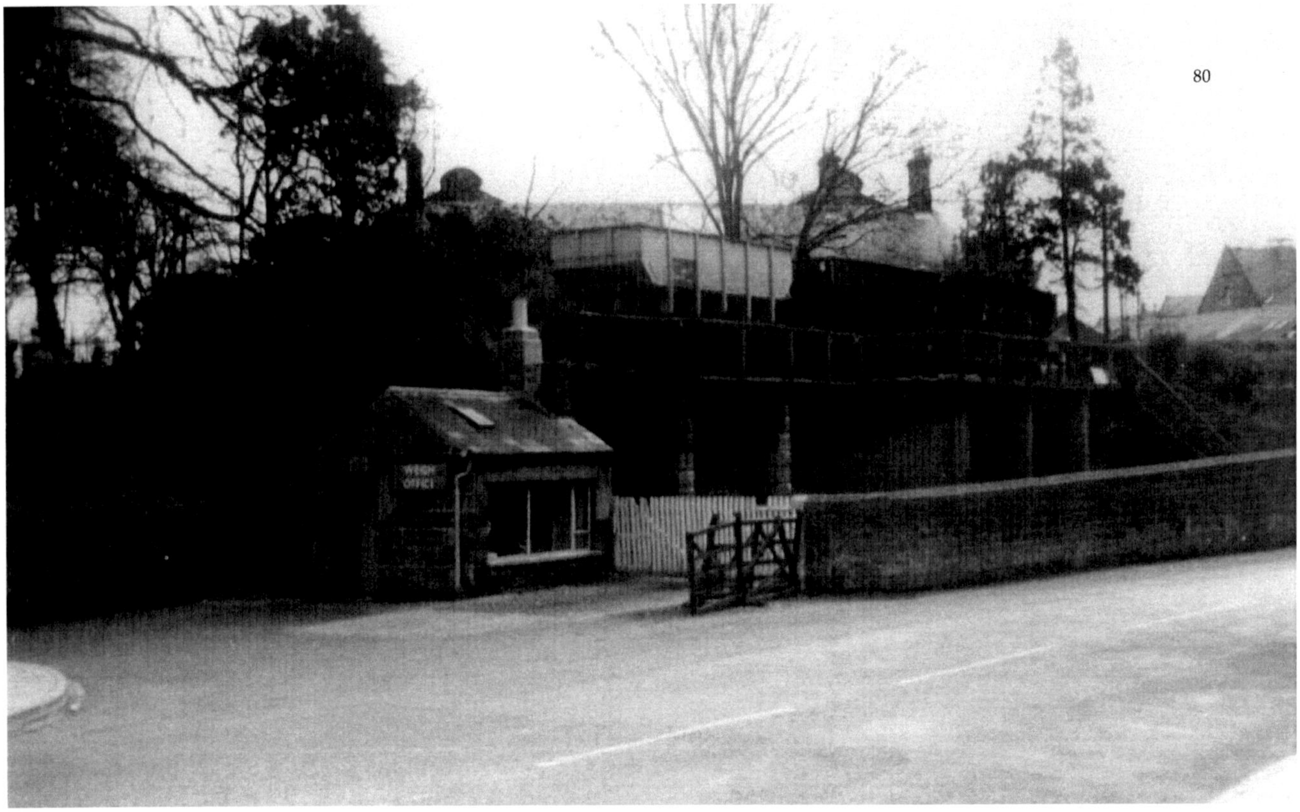
80

This is the site depot at the end of Wagonway Road dating from the British Rail era. More primitive staithes were situated there and at the depot south of Alnwick (where the gas works was situated) during Longdyke's productive years.

[78] Thomas Greenwood and John Batley first set up in Leeds in 1856. Through their Albion Foundry they manufactured all manner of heavy plant including turbines.

[79] A piece of the actual rail, recovered by Mr. Dennis P. Dalby from the 'Callishes' in 1988.

[80] John F. Mallon's photograph reproduced with permission of Vera Mallon.

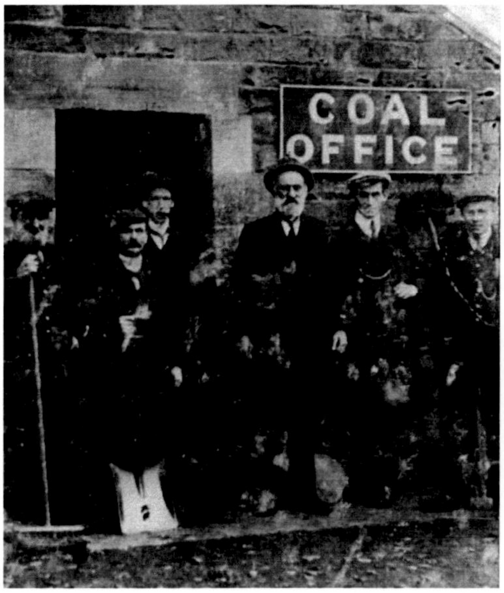

81

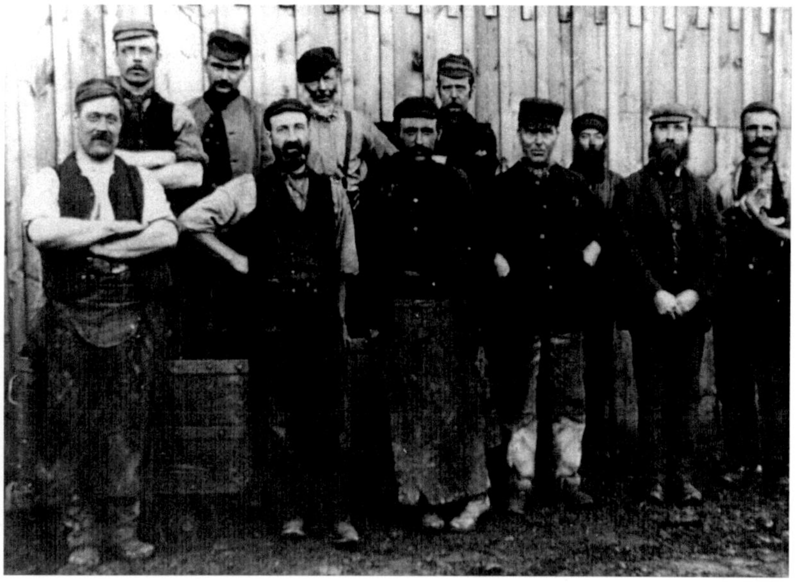

82

Above left: A late 19th or early 20th century photograph of the coal depot and workers.

Above right: Staff of the Shilbottle Coal Company beside two small coal tubs and the wall of the coal depot south of Alnwick.

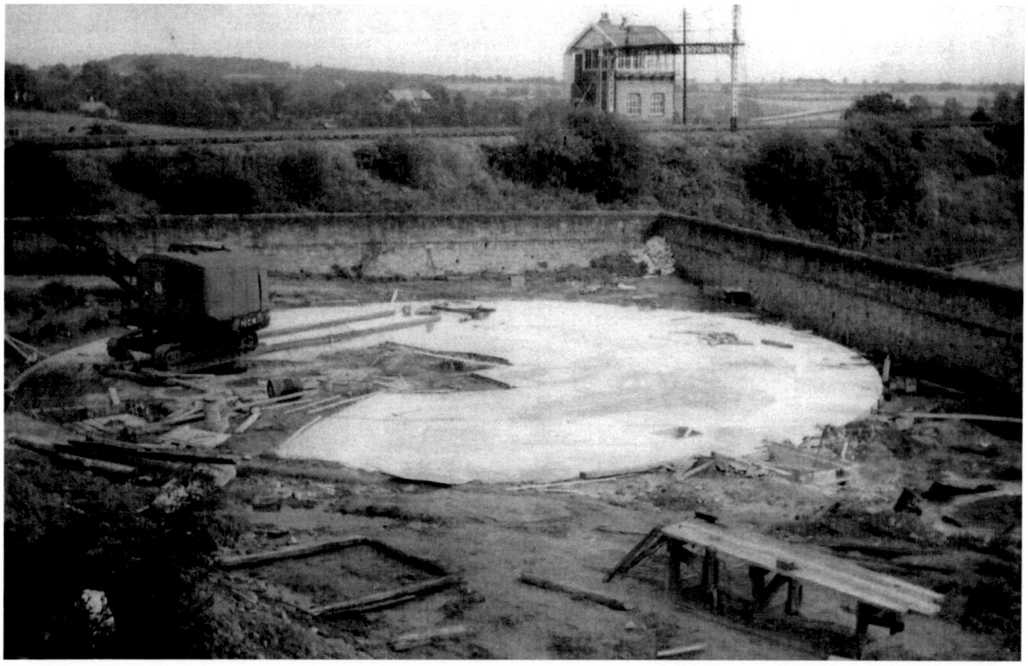

83

Above: The reinforced concrete foundation, in the process of being laid in 1954, for the proposed steel tank gasholder at the gas works site, at Alnwick Depot. The Alnmouth to Alnwick branch line and signal box are visible in the background.

The telephone poles for the tramway were of oak cut from the woods at Swarland.

[81] John F. Mallon's photograph reproduced with permission of Vera Mallon.
[82] Photograph from Mr. D.P. Dalby's collection.
[83] Photograph provided by Mr. Ken Middlemist, from the collection of Mr. D.P. Dalby.

At the colliery end of the line there was a five foot drum driven by electric motors, around which was wound a heavy endless rope. A similar drum was located at the Alnwick depot.

The tubs ran in pairs about 30 or 40 yards apart, usually one steel the other wood, on a narrow two foot steel gauge track. The front and rear of the tubs were fixed to rope guides by special 'shatch' clamps. In the centre, they were attached to a raised bracket which was fitted onto a patent rope clamp with a locating lever. The continuous rope was slotted into the guides and the groove of the clamp. The rope, which was made of steel, was secured by knocking down the lever of the clamp to tighten the rope.

When the tramway was traversing a steep climb, principally when crossing the wooden bridges of the two branches of the Cawledge Burn, there were cable guides. Men were stationed at the most vulnerable locations and their job was to knock the lever, whether it needed it or not, to make sure the rope did not become loose. If this had not been done, the tubs could potentially run wild and any resulting accident would have caused long delays while the damage was being repaired. The tramway went through underground tunnels for short distances near Cawledge Park Farm, requiring two tunnels side-by-side for outward and inward journeys.

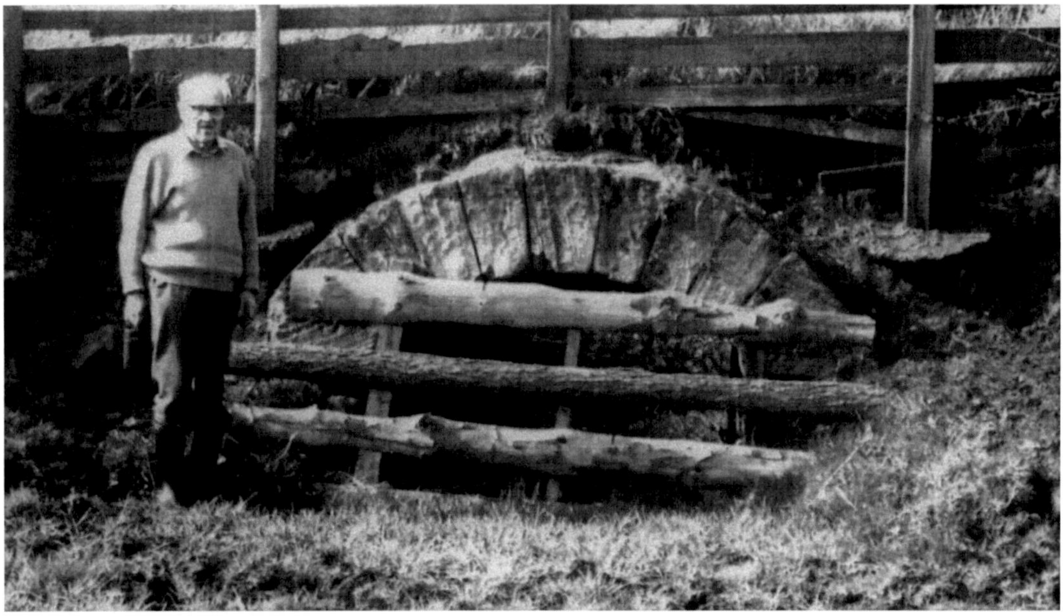

One of the tunnels for the tramway with Mr. Jack Dalby alongside.[84]

At the colliery end of the tramway, returning, empty tubs were knocked free of the steel rope and run down a gentle incline and under the colliery hopper to be re-filled then pushed forward to be once more hitched to the rope, clamped on and made ready to start the journey of some two miles back to the gas works. Each tub carried 4 to 5cwt of coal. On arrival at the gas works, the full tubs went up an incline, over coal hoppers and were then unhitched from the rope by knocking free the clamp lever. The tubs were then emptied into the hoppers. At this stage the coal was loaded into carts or stacked ready to fire the gas ovens.[85]

[84] Photograph from Mr. D.P. Dalby's collection.

[85] Extracted from information supplied by Mr. G. Ternent following an interview with Mr. Dalby and from written records provided by Mr. W.H. Dixon of Shilbottle and Mr. George Baxter of Hipsburn in 1988.

Volume of Coal Production

At its peak, Longdyke was producing approximately 400 tons of coal a day. Only part of this was sent to Alnwick. The bulk was sold at the pithead or exported by sea from Amble.

John Green recalled seeing the names of two steamers which ferried coal from Amble to Aberdeen. These were *Readhill* and *Ferryhill 11*.

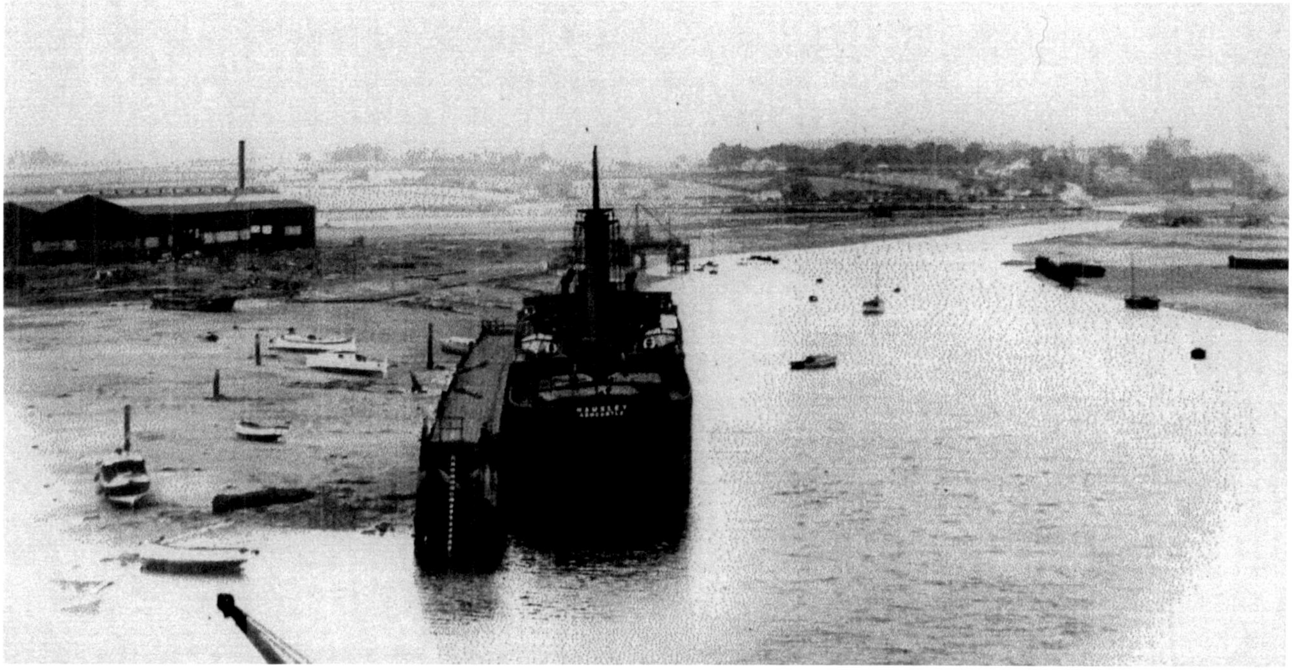

Amble Staithes with Warkworth in the background.

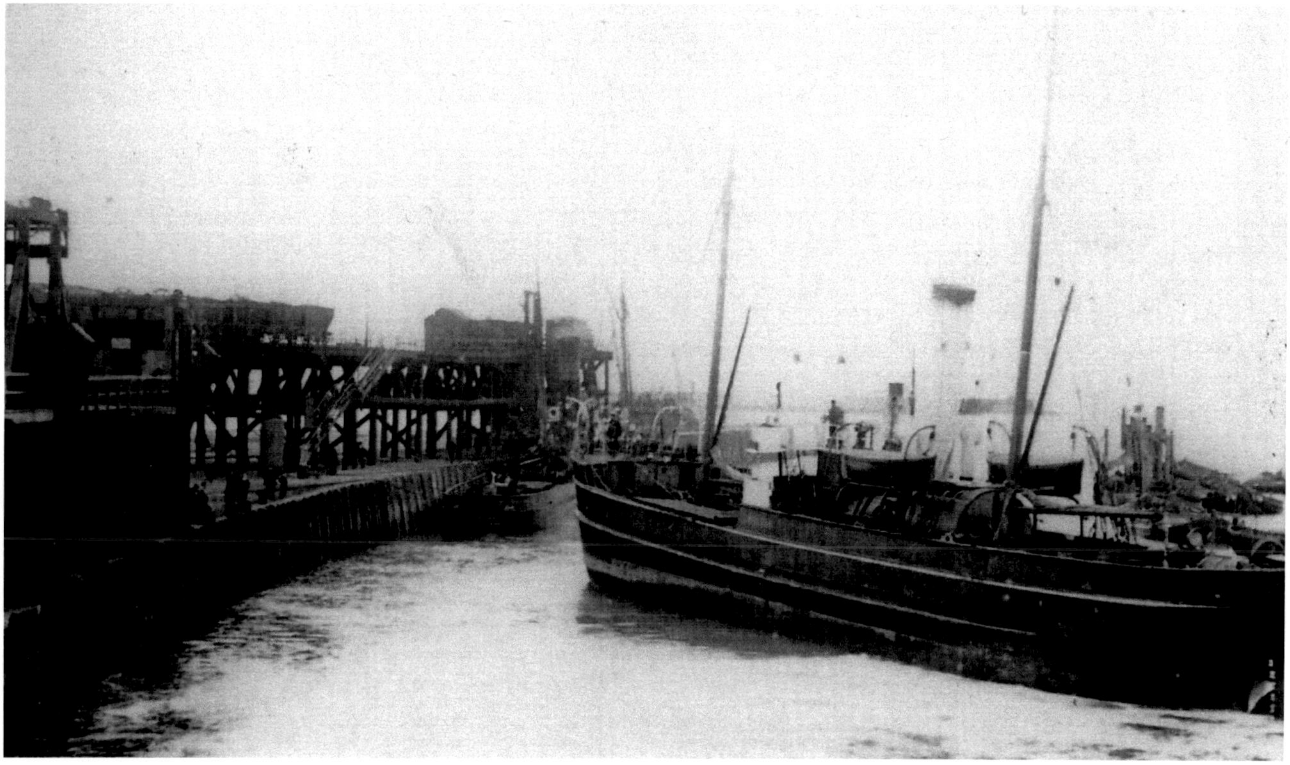

Amble Staithes with a 'collier' approaching.

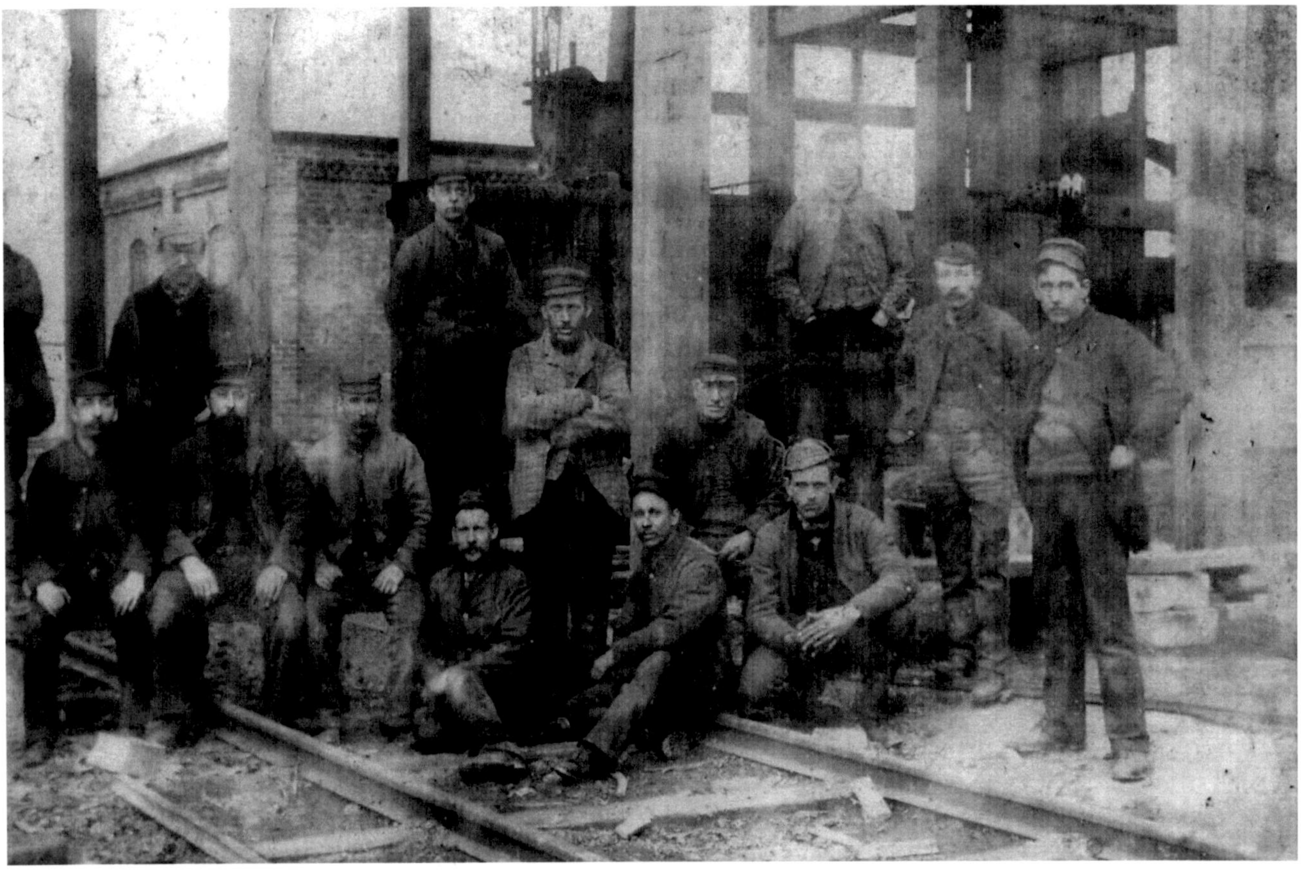

Workmen at Amble Staithes.[86]

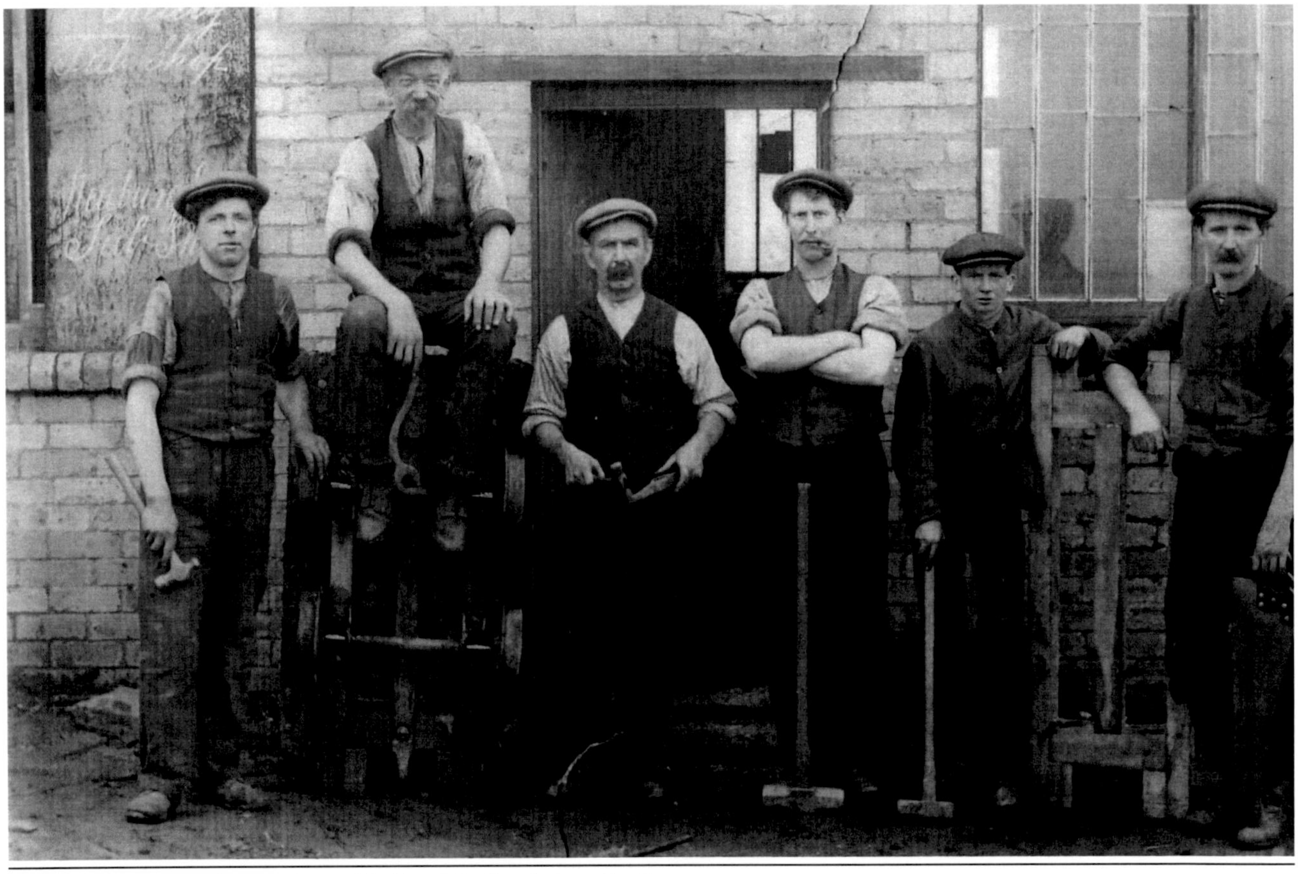

[86] The previous four images from Mr. Ken Middlemist's collection.

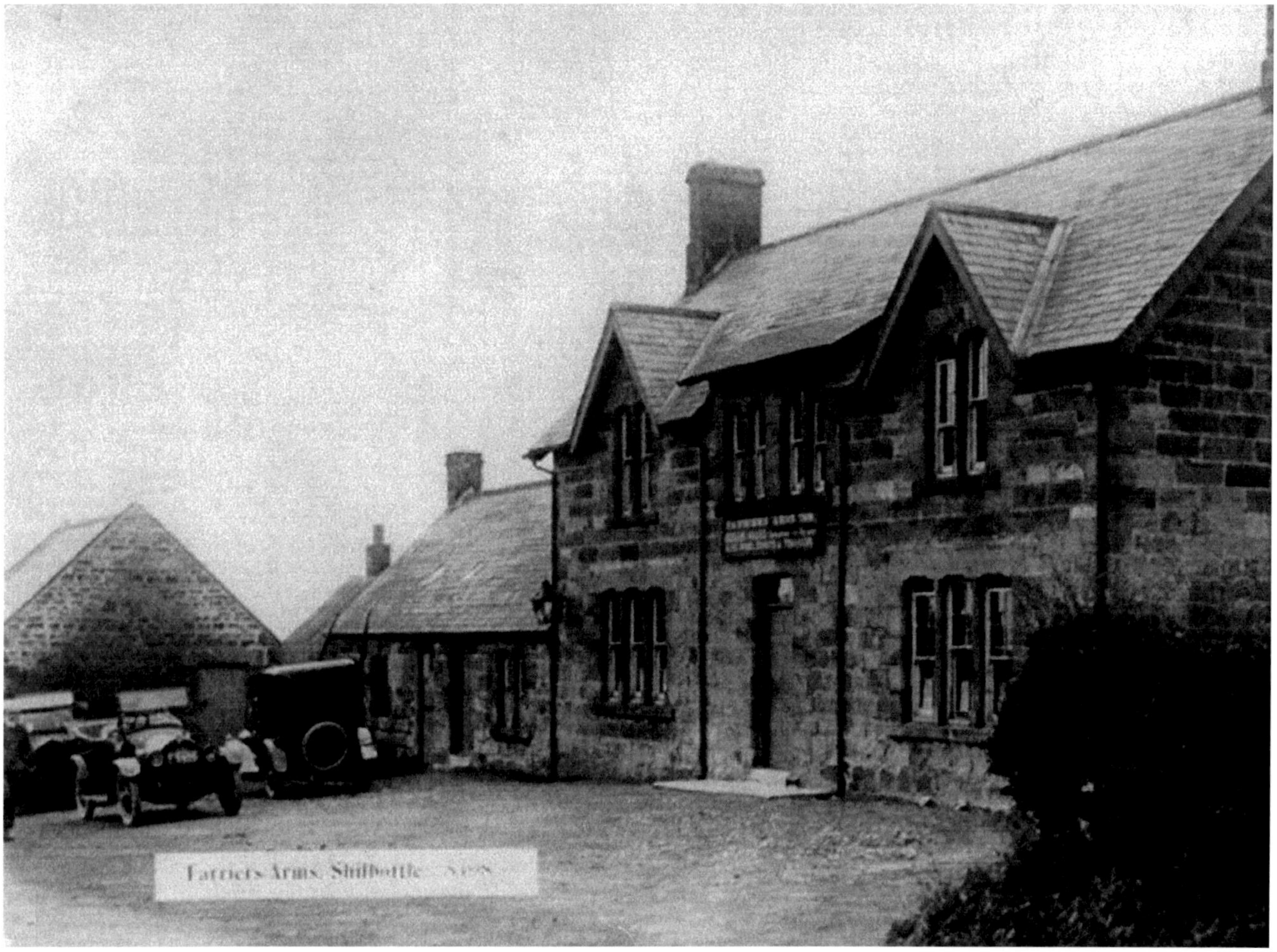

The Farrier's Arms 1908 [87]

The record of a speech given to the colliery officials at their annual dinner at the Farrier's Arms public house in Shilbottle in 1908, by the then manager Mr. Dixon, provides some interesting statistics.[88]

Year	Employees	Tonnage of Coal Produced	Days Worked
1901	182	43,549	236
1906	243	57,928	247
1907	242	67,537	252

In 1907 £20,000 was paid in wages to employees of the colliery, which according to Mr. Dixon was thought to have resulted in *a considerable amount of prosperity in the district.*

The annual dinner was an occasion for residents of Shilbottle Village to join in celebrations and following the supper, the colliery officials *gave a full and fancy dress social in the village schoolroom, which was attended by some hundred and forty people. It was a great success.*

[87] Image provided by Mrs. Elizabeth Haddow.
[88] Extracts of the speech made available by Vera Mallon, from details held by Bailiffgate Museum, Alnwick.

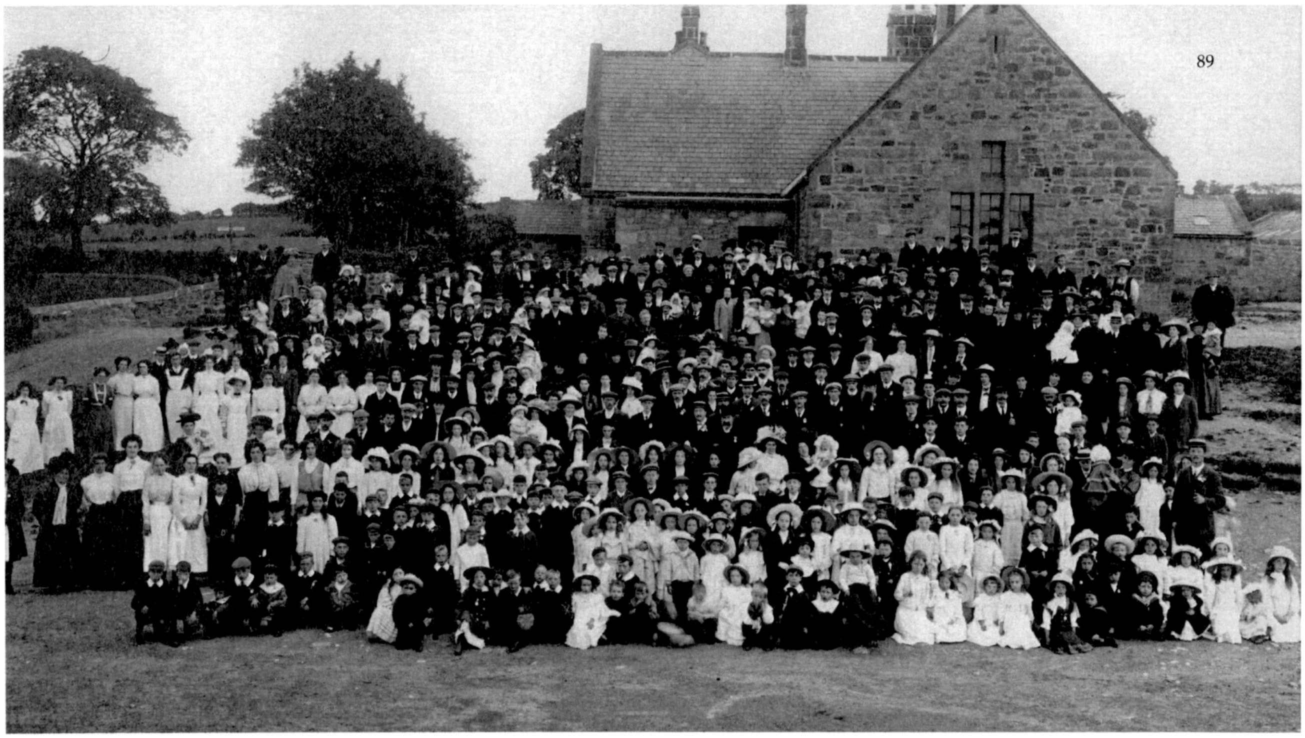

It cannot be stated with certainty that the above image represents the gathering following the officials dinner in 1908, but the location is the school, the period is right, and all residents of the village are in attendance in their finery.

Industrial Relations

Despite the best efforts of the management and officials, unrest among the workforce did occur. John Buddle was the chief negotiator for the mine owners during the 1831-32 miners' strike, taking a hard line on the mine owners' behalf. During this period the plight of the miners was often set to poetry as they sought to publicise their powerlessness and their diminishing potential to earn in difficult and dangerous conditions:

> 'By weight the masters sell your coal, but colliers they compel.
> To work by measure, so much a 'corve',[90] which does not suit them well.
> These corves the masters oft enlarge and make them of great size,
> Which does increase the collier's work and then pull off their price.
> O Britons won't you, them relieve, and better for them provide.'[91]

Hymns were another way of publicising the miners' helplessness:

> 'The Christian collier rises soon, with glory in his soul.
> He prays he might be spared till noon, while working at the coal.
> Then to the pit the collier goes, to earn his daily bread,
> He may be killed for ought he knows, and go to Christ his Head.'[92]

[89] The picture provided by Mr. David Brewis.

[90] A 'Corve' was the basket or bogie into which the coal was placed for delivery out of the mine.

[91] *History Of Coal Mining* ref: NRO 3410/Bell/12/254 held by the NE Mining Institute, Neville Hall, Newcastle-upon-Tyne.

[92] *Ibid* NRO ref: 3410/Bell/12/475

'O Lord hear the poor pitman's cry,
Look down on us with pitying eye,
With heavy bondage we are oppressed
And all our families are distressed.'[93]

The miners prevailed against the mine owners in 1831 when the unity of the employers crumbled, but in 1832 the coal owners stood firm and crushed the union, ensuring that the miners' conditions found little immediate improvement.

Unrest continued throughout the decades. A national movement for improved conditions and wages developed and following months of unrest in 1912, this led to strike action being recommended. At the end of February 1912 representatives of the miners met with the owners of Shilbottle Colliery and the owners agreed to concede a minimum wage. However, the Northumberland Miners' Federation advised that they had no power to allow the men to work without consent of the National Federation. Coal stocks quickly reduced at this time, prices rose and the North Eastern Railway had to curtail goods and passenger services. The rail company also reduced staff working hours. A knock-on effect was that shop keepers were no longer giving credit, which began to impinge on families in mining communities, including Longdyke and Bilton Banks. The manager at Shilbottle took a compassionate view and gave colliery employees permission to scavenge the heaps east of the colliery to obtain what coal they could. The strike did not last too long and the Miners' (Minimum Wage) Bill was passed by the House of Lords on 28th March 1912. On the same day the miners of Shilbottle were invited to resume work. A majority vote on 31st March 1912 (108 for and 47 against) returned the men to their work.

During this period, from at least 1908, the workforce had appointed their spokesman to represent their opinions and discontents to the manager. Mr. Albert Queen was their most vociferous representative and he took up many causes on behalf of the miners. One extreme example relates to the manager Mr. J.A. Dixon deciding to have two unfit miners evicted from their homes, despite long service and also having sons working at the colliery. Mr. Queen wrote to the manager and also initiated correspondence with The Northumberland Mines' Mutual Confident Association's Secretary, Mr. W. Straker at Burt Hall, in Gosforth.

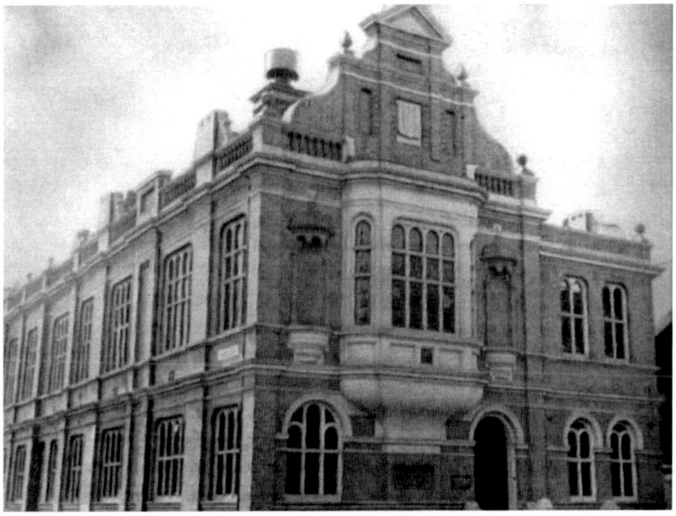

Burt Hall, Gosforth

[93] *Ibid* NRO 3410/Bell/11/28

Mr. Queen's letter is reproduced below.

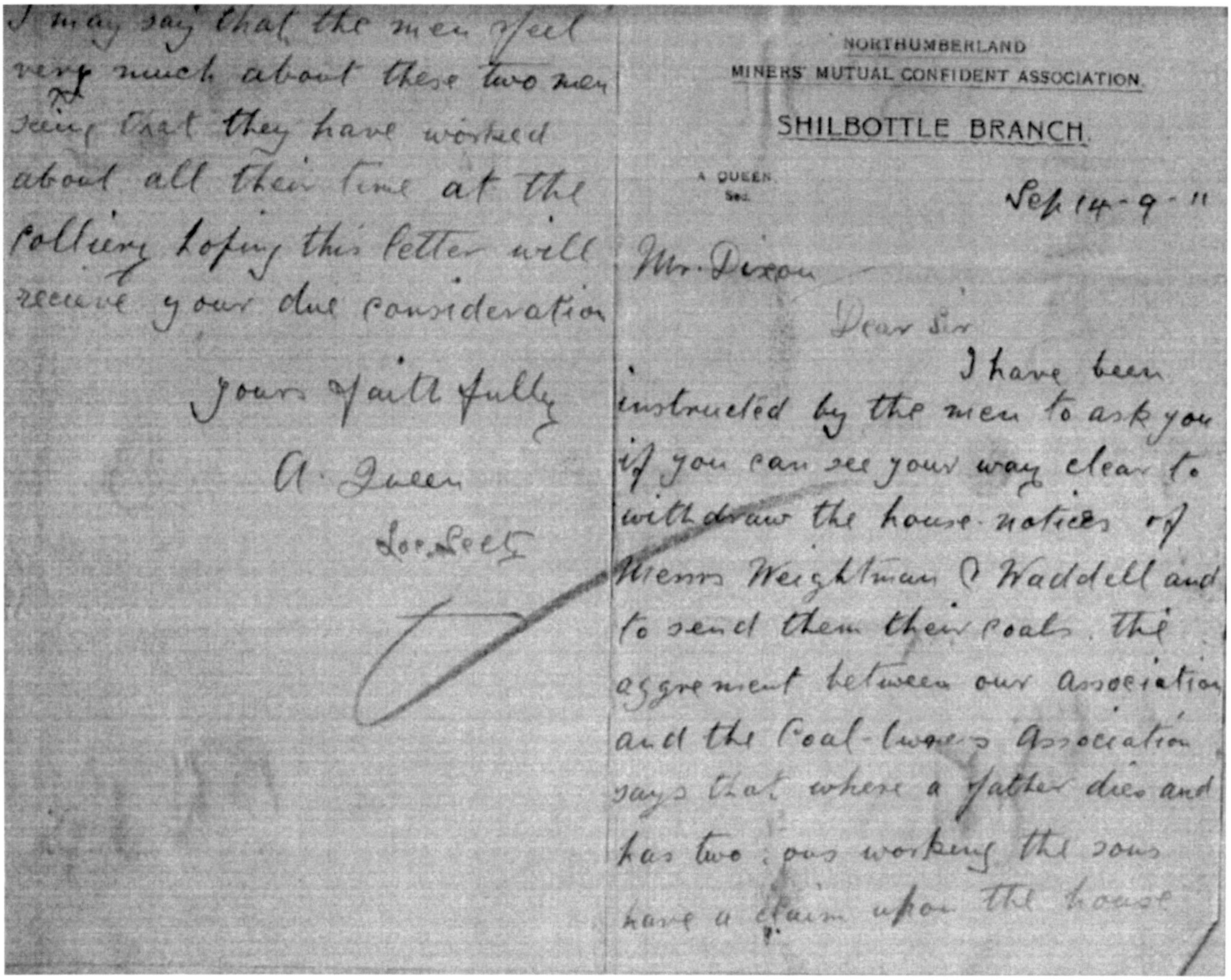
NORTHUMBERLAND
MINERS' MUTUAL CONFIDENT ASSOCIATION.
SHILBOTTLE BRANCH.
A. QUEEN.
Sec.

Sep 14-9-11

Mr. Dixon

Dear Sir

I have been instructed by the men to ask you if you can see your way clear to withdraw the house notices of Messrs Weightman & Waddell and to send them their coals. the aggrement between our Association and the Coal Owners Association says that where a father dies and has two sons working the sons have a claim upon the house

I may say that the men feel very much about these two men seeing that they have worked about all their time at the colliery hoping this letter will receive your due consideration

Yours faithfully

A. Queen

Hon Sec

[94]

Mr. Queen's letter reads –

I have been instructed by the men to ask if you can see your way clear to withdraw the house notices of Messrs Weightman and Waddell and send them their coals. The agreement between our Association and the Coal Owners' Association says that when a father dies and has two sons working the sons have a claim on the house. I may say that the men feel very much about these two men seeing that they have worked about all their time at the colliery. Hoping this letter will receive your due attention.

Yours faithfully,
A. Queen (Hon Sec).'

The Mutual Confident Association's Secretary Mr. W. Straker quickly took up the issue and wrote to Mr. Dixon.

[94] Extracted from *Shilbottle Colliery Agreements and Joint Committee ledger* in the archives of Mrs. Joyce Snaith.

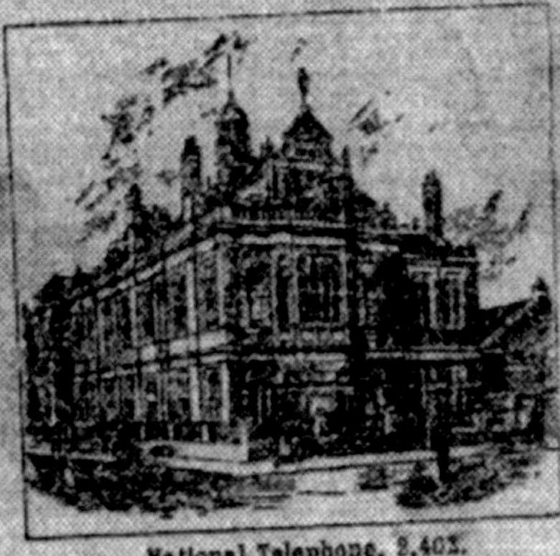
National Telephone, 2,403.

NORTHUMBERLAND MINERS'

Mutual Confident Association.

All enquiries as to Compensation and Law Business to be made to Jos. English.

All Applications for Money, Voting Returns, &c., to be made to W. Hogg.

All business for Executive Committee, Council Meetings, Trustees, and General Enquiry to be made to W. Straker.

All letters as to Financial Matters, business for Joint Committee, Colliery Averages, Applications for Contribution Books, &c., to be sent to J. Cairns.

NOTE.—All separate business to be written on separate paper.

Tel. No.—Mr. Straker..Gosforth, 357.
,, Mr. Cairns....Gosforth, 360.
,, Mr. English..Gosforth, 363.

Burt Hall, Newcastle-on-Tyne,

September 1st 1911.

. Dixon, Esq.,

Manager,

Shilbottle Colliery.

Dear Mr. Dixon,

I have received a letter from our local secretary at Shilbottle regarding two men who have been unable to work for a considerable time but have workers in their families still at the pit and have been required to leave their colliery house. As this is not a general practice throughout Northumberland will you kindly let me know if there is any special reason why you have required these men to vacate their houses. It seems to be a harsh treatmentwhich is unusual for you to meet out to anyone. I am therefore anxious to know what are the principles in the case.. The name of one of the men is Weddell and the other Weightman.

Yours faithfully,

Wm Straker

Secretary.

Wm ''

[95]

---

[95] Extracted from the Archives held by Mrs. Joyce Snaith.

Mr. Straker's letter reads –

'Dixon Esq.,
Manager,
Shilbottle Colliery

Dear Mr. Dixon, I have received a letter from our local secretary regarding two men who have been unable to work for a considerable time but who have workers in their families still at the pit and have been required to leave their colliery house. As this is not a general practice throughout Northumberland will you kindly let me know if there is any special reason why you have required these men to vacate their house. It seems to be a harsh treatment which is unusual for you to meet out to anyone. I am therefore anxious to know what are the principles in the case. The name of one of the men is Waddell and the other is Weightman.

Yours faithfully,
W Straker
Secretary'

The manager met with Albert Queen and Mr. J. Hall on 20th September to consider the case. Pencil jottings on a further notice in the ledger can be interpreted either that written notices were issued about formal dismissal in accordance with local custom or that a compromise was reached in that Mr. Waddell and Weightman were paid compensation but still dismissed, or that both returned to light duties and retained their householder status. The records are not clear but it is clear that Mr. Albert Queen was a worthy advocate. It is also clear that men named Waddell and Weightman continued as pitmen at Longdyke and Shilbottle. They were not resident at Bilton Banks when the properties were condemned in 1937 but by then many miners were already resident in houses in Shilbottle.

John Green, in his account of Longdyke Colliery[96] adds a degree of detail to the accounts provided by Mr. Harry Air. In particular he refers to the sinking of the second shaft in 1919, which he refers to being 500 yards from the main shaft, but towards Spylaw. The shaft was apparently sunk by a Mr. Mallerburn from Alnwick, who was ably assisted by his wife who operated as 'banksman' and 'winch man', and occasionally by Archie Inglis and Stan Douglas, when the shaft got deeper.[97] Mr. Green states also that *... coal was not the only paying product to come out of Longdyke pit. It pumped hundreds of gallons of water out which was sold to the parish's Urban District Council for drinking ...* [it was] *... pumped from the pit to a reservoir which is in a field opposite the Radar Station at the end of Threety,*[98] *then* [flowed] *by gravity to Lesbury, Bilton, Alnmouth and Warkworth.*

In 1916 Longdyke Colliery passed into the ownership of The Co-operative Wholesale Society. Shortly after the end of the Great War in 1918, steps were being taken to establish the mine at Shilbottle Grange. On 13th November 1919 the manager wrote to T. Brodrick Esq., at the Co-operative Wholesale Society headquarters at 1 Balloon Street, Manchester. His letter was in response to a request from Captain Barnet, the Government's representative, who had asked for an estimate of the probable expenditure on the development of what was described as *our new colliery*. The manager's letter was accompanied by

---

[96] Northumberland Archives ref: NRO 2205/2

[97] John Green's account ref: NRO 2205/2

[98] The word 'Threety' is probably derived from the ancient word 'threip' meaning 'no man's land' between two parishes – as in threip-moor between Lesbury and Shilbottle.

complex schedules which showed expenditure up to 30th September 1919, estimated expenditure up to the end of 1920, and estimated total expenditure up to the sinking and development of the Grange Pit. The aim was to provide details *in the event of the Coal Mines being purchased by the State, the value of the New Mines shall be the Capital Expenditure incurred, together with interest at the rate of six percent, per annum, from date of expenditure to date of purchase.* The schedule of expenditure which had already been incurred included capital costs for the engineer's office, petrol store, water courses, workshops, winding house and machinery, steam crane, viaduct, railway, opening quarry, two wagons and workmen's tools. The cost of this completed work at Sturton Grange was £12,527 16s 5d. Predicted costs for sinking the mine, extending roadways, providing pumping gear, power and lighting, cementing the shafts and all that went with developing the mine to 'modern' standards, was £199,935 15s 9d.[99]

Longdyke continued working for almost six further years.

The Dangers of Mining

Day to day injuries underground were common as the black coaldust tattoos on miners' hands, backs and arms bear witness. Mining was a dangerous occupation and whilst the communication of news was slower in the 19th and early part of the 20th century, miners would be aware of myriad disasters elsewhere.

In the 50 years period from 1800 there were on average three colliery disasters every year with a total of 180 recorded in that half century. Some were close to hand too, at Hartley, Wallsend, Westmoor and Killingworth. During this same period 3,486 men and boys were killed or injured underground. During the next half century the situation was worse, with 59,580 serious injuries and deaths.[100] Longdyke was not exempt.

The Durham Mining Museum lists the following incomplete details of men and boys who were killed at Longdyke between 1881 and 1923:[101]

Name	Age	Date of death	Cause
J. Wrigglesworth	40	1st Apr 1881	Fall of stone
Frederick Weightman	14	17th Jun 1881	Fall of stone
Charles Taylor	44	29th Jan 1892	Explosion
Thomas Ternent	54	9th Dec 1901	Fall of stone
George Foster/Selby	39	18th Jun 1905	Fall of stone
Thomas Newton	26	16th Jun 1906	Fall of stone
John Storey	25	19th April 1911	Fall of stone
William Taylor	60	21st Jan 1915	Crushed by tubs
John Shell	16	26th Sep 1916	Crush injury
Martin Ryan	28	24th Oct 1917	Fall of stone
William Rogers Pringle	20	17th Jun 1920	Pneumonia[102]
James Skinner	32	24th Jan 1921	Entangled
William Alexander Mitcheson	48	7th Aug 1922	Fall of stone
J. Ternent	44	26th Mar 1923	Gas explosion
Lancelot Wilkinson Chicken	46	28th Apr 1925	Fall of stone

[99] This information extracted from papers provided by Mr. Adrian Ions.
[100] http://www.cmhrc.co.uk/site.literature/minersday/index.html
[101] www.dmm.org.uk/colliery/s015
[102] Listed by Durham Mining Museum – but death considered by coroner's jury to be not related to an injury three years previously.

From 5th July, 1898 Shilbottle Colliery was admitted as a member of the Northumberland Coal Owners Mutual Protection Association and from their records and other sources, it has been possible, except for the two earliest deaths, to ascertain the circumstances leading to the men being killed.

Mr. J. Wrigglesworth

The precise details of 40 year old Mr. Wrigglesworth's death on 1st April 1881 are unknown but he died through being buried under a fall of stone.

Frederick Weightman

On 17th June 1881 14 year old Frederick Weightman was also killed by a fall of stone. It has been established that he was a 'putter' and he is thought to have been the nephew of 28 year old Thomas Weightman, who was resident in Shilbottle.

Charles Taylor

Charles Taylor, aged 44 years, died in an explosion on 29th January 1892. This occurred when he: ... *a stone-man, who was acting as a charge-man in the driving of a stone drift, had charged three holes, two with gelatine on the right hand side of the face and the third with gunpowder on the left. Ordinary fuses were being used and after lighting the fuses attached to the gelatine shots, he attempted to light the fuse of the gunpowder shot. He had some difficulty with this so he retired, being under the impression that the fuse had not caught. The two gelatine shots went off and he immediately went into the place to light the gunpowder shot, when it exploded. He received injuries from the flying stones from which he died within a few days.*[103]

Thomas Ternent

On 9th December 1901, Thomas Ternent, aged 54, was removing some of his clothes about three yards from the face, preparatory to commencing work, when some stone suddenly fell from slips in the roof. The place had been examined an hour and a half previously by the deputy, who detected one slip, but considered the roof secure. Mr. Ternent left a dependent widow, two daughters aged 17 and 10, and two sons aged 8 and 5.

In calculating what compensation, if any, the deceased's family would be paid, the weekly wage over three years, plus the value of free coal was drawn into the equation. Mr. Ternent's coal allowance was worked out at £13 per year and the salary lost through his death, over a three year period £266. 4s 0d. His widow, Mary was awarded £300 compensation.

Mr. Thomas Ternent's gravestone can be seen in Shilbottle Church Yard.

George Foster

Also known as George Selby, George Foster, aged 39, died on 16th June 1905. He had been employed as a 'stone-man' and was killed by a fall of stone. He left a widow and three sons aged 13, 10 and 7, all of whom were wholly dependent on him. The claim for £236. 12s 0d was fully accepted and that sum paid to his widow.

Thomas Newton

Also known as Thomas Davison, Thomas Newton, aged 25, a 'shifter', died on 16th June 1905 following a fall of stone. *The shaft siding, which lay above the seam being worked, had been in the course of enlargement for two years. Side-stone was worked off on occasions when the pit was idle. The road, when finished, was about*

[103] http://www.dmm.org.uk/names/a1892-04.htm

12 feet wide and 10 feet high. The sides were principally post with blue metal at top and bottom. The jacks in the stone were blackened with dust. On the day of the accident a shift of three deputies had worked at the place from 2 a.m. to 10 a.m. They were visited both by the under-manager and overman.

At 10 a.m. deceased men and others commenced their shift, and while the deceased men filled loose stones into tubs a stone-man prepared a shot about 18 feet from the place where the stone fell, and this shot was fired at noon charged with 1lb. of powder. It did not do much work, but may have helped loosen the stone. After returning, after the shot, the overman made an examination and then work was resumed. In about 20 minutes a mass of the post fell from the side and caught the deceased, who were filling stones. The fall came away at jacks and there was a slip at the bottom. It gave no warning, but any slight sound might not have been heard owing to the noise proceeding from pumps working in the shaft and water falling therein. The Local Inspectors reported, 'we are of the opinion the occurrence has been a pure accident.'

Mr. Newton, a single man, lived with his stepfather and mother and they were paid the sum of £236.12s 0d compensation.

John Storey

Aged 25, John Storey, a deputy, died on 19th April 1911, from injuries received on 5th December 1910. Mr. Storey's spine was fractured through a fall of stone. He was a single man. His father was under-manager and the compensation paid in this case was £70 (a reduced sum because a weekly payment of £6. 8s 4d had been made between the accident and the date of John Storey's death).

William Taylor

Hewer, William Taylor, aged 60 was killed on 21st January 1915. Mr. Taylor was crushed by coal tubs. His widow was paid £333. 9s 0d compensation.

John Shell

Aged 16 and a horse-putter, John Shell died on 26th September 1916. Young John Shells' death was a result of injuries alleged to have been received on 22nd September, when his right leg and foot were crushed by a tub. The coroner returned a verdict that death resulted from inflammation of the ankle and septic poisoning, accelerated by shock. There was insufficient evidence to establish how the septic poisoning occurred, but it was accepted that the shock occurred through an accident whilst he was working at the colliery. The claim was resisted by the insurers when they first heard it on 14th October 1916, but at a later hearing, after pleading from the family's solicitor Mr. Weir, the sum of £20 was awarded *without prejudice.*

William Rogers Pringle

Aged 20 and a putter, William Rogers Pringle died on 17th June 1920. Mr. Pringle's family claimed that William's death was due to a hand injury on 17th January 1917 which occurred when a tub was upset on him. A post mortem examination revealed that Mr. Pringle died from septic bronchi-pneumonia, the result of bronchiestas which showed that his death was not related to the accident three years previously. His family's claim for £143. 12s 0d compensation was resisted.

James Skinner

Aged 33, James Skinner, a surface worker, died on 24th January 1922. The circumstances were that his clothing got caught in a revolving shaft. The coroner found the shaft to be dangerous. He ordered the same to be protected by adequate fencing. The deceased left a widow of 32 and two sons aged 2 and 1. Mr. Skinner's coffin was provided by the colliery and his widow was paid £300 compensation.

William Alexander Mitcheson

Aged 48 and a hewer, William Alexander Mitcheson died on 7th August 1922. Mr. Mitcheson died as a result of injuries received on 13th July of that year, when a fall of stone fractured his spine. He left a widow, sons of 20, 11, 7 and 5, and a daughter aged 8. His widow was paid £295. 13s 4d compensation.

Mr. J. Ternant[104]

44 years and a 'stoneman', Mr. J. Ternant died on 26th March 1923 as a result of injuries received on 23rd February of that year. The coroner found that Mr. Ternant died from blood poisoning, the result of burns caused by an explosion of fire-damp in Shilbottle Colliery, where he and a man named Thomas May were working. The jury found also that the explosion had been caused by a naked light lit by Mr. Ternant or by his colleague Thomas May. The family's claim for £595. 8s 0d compensation was therefore turned down.

Mr. Thomas May's claim for compensation was also turned down because – *May was warned that there was gas present in the working place and in spite of this two partly burned candles were found in the working place These candles were found by the stoneman who brought him out after the accident.*

Lancelot Wilkinson Chicken

Aged 46 and a deputy, Lancelot Wilkinson Chicken was killed on 28th April 1925 by a fall of stone. Mr. Chicken left a widow, four daughters aged between 22 and 8 and a son of 19. His widow was paid £448. 10s 0d compensation.

The registers, which run to nine, 6 inch thick volumes of records and minutes of the Northumberland Coal Owners Mutual Protection Association provide tangible proof, if any were needed, of the hazards of coal mining. The index alone, with single spaced, typed entries is an inch thick. Each line in the book provides a statistic and marks the loss of a life, or serious injury through industrial accident, giving rise to a claim for compensation but not all injuries resulted in a record being made or a claim being submitted. Only six claims for non-fatal injuries were recorded up to 1922.

On 3rd August 1908 hewer R.J. Thompson, aged 51, claimed for compensation, but his claim was rejected on the basis that he had contributed to his injury through serious and wilful misconduct by riding on the set. The colliery doctor reported to the insurers that Thompson's injury was neither serious nor permanent.

Thomas Shield, aged 40, a horse keeper, claimed in respect of an injury to his knee. The colliery doctor, Thomas Beattie, found him to be suffering from extensive osteoarthritis which was aggravated by his injury. He was capable of light work, but as none was available, he accepted £225 compensation.

John Hannon, aged 20, claimed in respect of an injury alleged to have occurred on 29th January 1915, when he stated he had slipped on an unsound surface. This was also resisted when the colliery doctor found that Hannon suffered from a condition called 'varicocele' which was not caused by the accident.

On 1st November 1915, Frank Queen, a hewer aged 60, was blinded in one eye and was awarded £60.

---

[104] It is probable that this is the incorrect spelling of Mr. Ternent's surname.

On 16th March 1916 S. Rennison was adjudged to have contributed to his injuries by disobeying orders and riding on an engine set, jumping out when the engine was in motion, thus contributing to his injury. His claim was resisted.

On 1st March 1922, S. Appleton, aged 44 claimed in respect of an injury to his wrist which was sustained whilst working on the screens. He was found to have a dislocation of the carpal bone which rendered him permanently disabled. He was paid compensation of 16s per week.

There would have been more accidents involving injury than those recorded because the work was hard and physically demanding, requiring risk taking, ingenuity, strength of purpose and brute force in sometimes the most hostile of environments.[105]

A short, fictitious story *Mekin it Safe*, about an underground fatality, is included in the appendices. It uses 'pitmatic' prose in an attempt to capture Northumbrian dialect, whilst also trying to portray a sense of loyalty, stoicism and practical, commonsense-solidarity among the workforce, even in adversity.[106]

When accidents occurred and there was any hope (or need of further treatment) casualties from the pit would most likely be taken to Alnwick Infirmary, which is shown below with a pit ambulance outside.

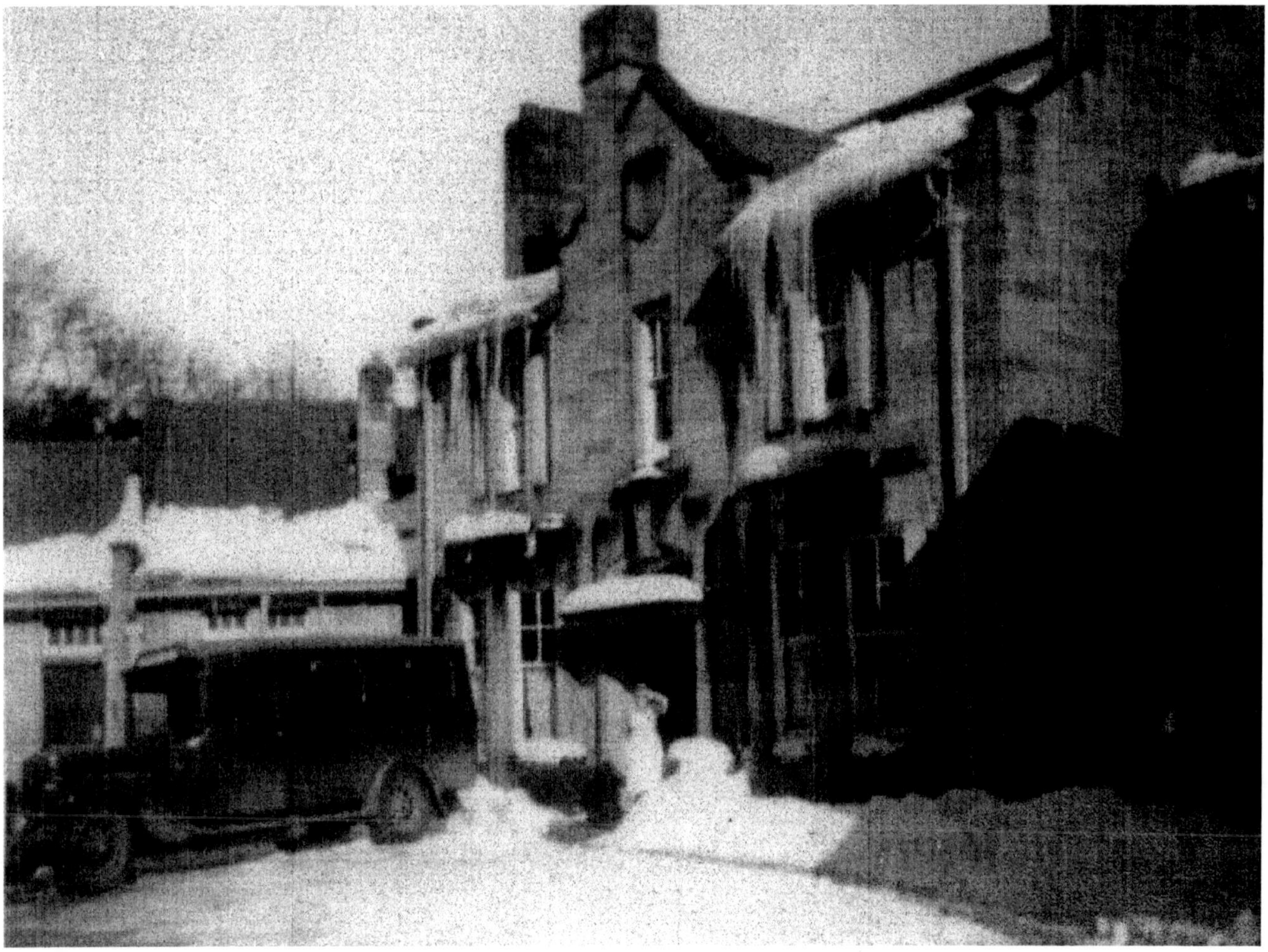

[105] The index to the minutes of the meetings of the Northumberland Coal Owners Mutual Association show six further fatalities and three non-fatal injuries, which were subject of claims by Shilbottle Colliery workmen between 1936 and 1940.
[106] 'Mekin in Safe', by the author, won the 2010 Dialect Prose competition in the Northumbrian Gathering at Morpeth. Appendix 2.

Below is the Whittle Colliery Welfare ambulance, an Austin 6 Registration Number JR984, which was usually driven by Alexander Waters.[107]

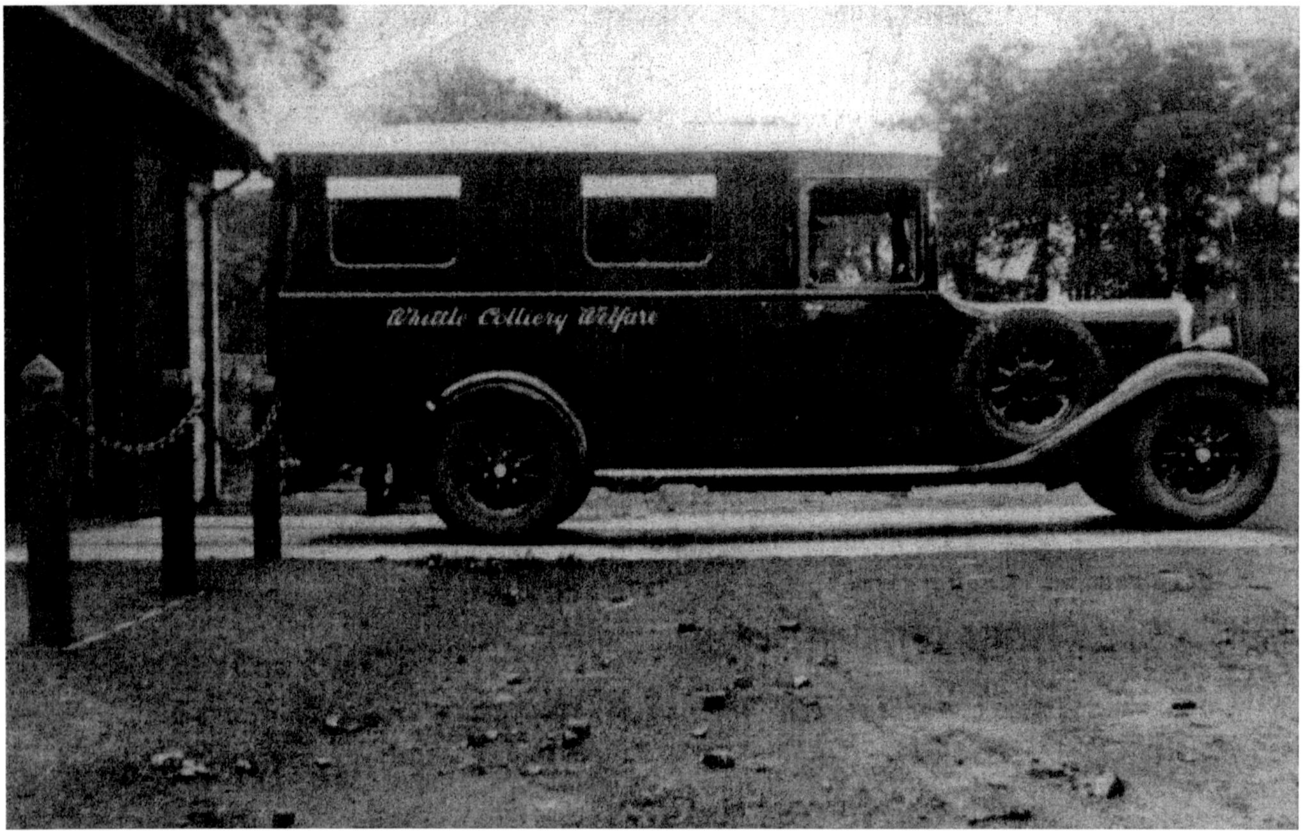

It is not known whether the ambulance, or one like it, was ever used to transport injured workers from Longdyke – but the vehicle's status as a rescue vehicle is of importance and is of historical interest – hence the inclusion here. Some former residents have suggested that the 'rescue charabanc' had been converted from the manager's private motor for use during the war and in emergencies.

The Managers of Longdyke Colliery

During its lifetime Longdyke was managed by at least five managers. Those known were:[108]

Nichol Cheeseman, Bilton Banks. He is named as manager on the share release document which was issued when the colliery was proposing to move from the private ownership of Messrs. R.S. Garwood, J.T. Garwood and H.A. Paynter to public ownership in the name of The Shilbottle Coal Company.

William Alexander Ritson, born 1852. He obtained his manager's certificate of competency on 4th March 1875. The 1881 census puts him at Longdyke as manager. He is shown to be with his wife and two infant sons, a baby daughter, two servants and his cousin. Eleven years later he and his family were at Crumpsall in Manchester.

John Roscamp, born in 1840 at Wingate. He qualified as manager on 26th March 1873 at Acomb. In 1880 Mr. Roscamp was resident near Pickering in Yorkshire and was manager at Longdyke from 1884. He was

[107] Both of these photographs were supplied by Mr. Adrian Ions.

[108] Information extracted from Durham Minning Museum's website www.dmm.org.uk/wjoswho/a507.htm

still in post in 1896 and during this period lived at Bilton Banks with his wife two daughters and later one son.

Joseph A. Dixon, qualified as a manager on 2nd March 1897 and was manager from 1902. He remained in post until the beginning of the Great War in 1914.

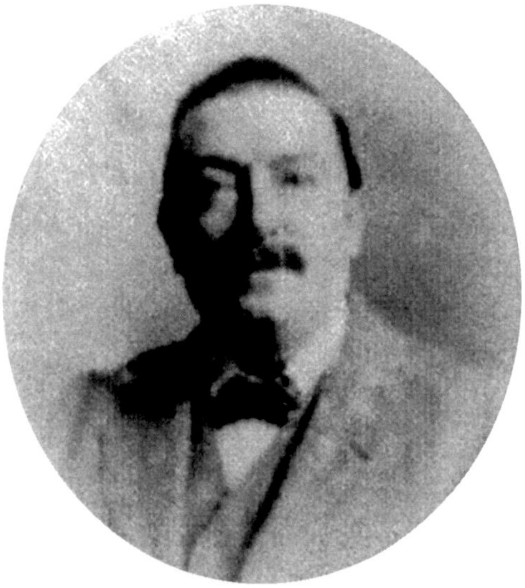

Joseph A. Dixon

Coverdale Smith Anderson, who obtained his manager's certificate in 1910, followed Mr. Dixon. Born in Shilbottle in 1887 he began working at the colliery as a labourer and progressed to be under-manager in his twenties, later becoming manager. Additionally, from 1922, he had managed the Shilbottle Beacon Quarry. He remained in post as manager of Longdyke, Framlington and Whittle until the mine closed in 1925. He oversaw the sinking of the Grange Pit at Shilbottle. He moved from Longdyke to the manager's house at Shilbottle Grange and assumed responsibility for managing the colliery there, remaining at Shilbottle until 1944.

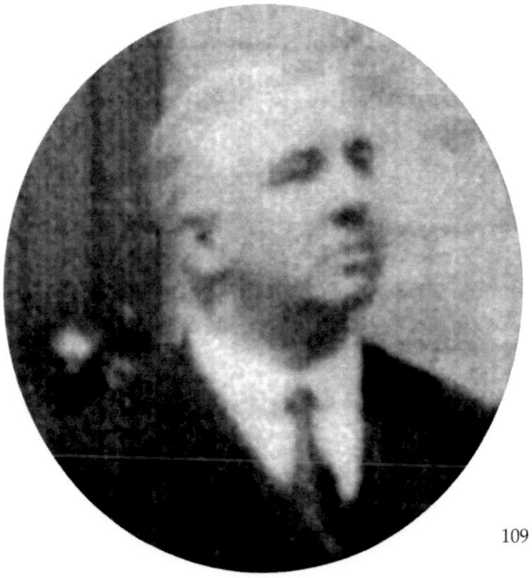
[109]

Coverdale Smith Anderson

[109] This image has been cropped from a photograph (donated by Mr. Kenneth Willcox) of the Shilbottle football team which won the CWS Cup at Silvertown in 1933.

The End of Coal Production at Longdyke

The colliery was abandoned on 19th August 1925. On Saturday 23rd May 1926, The *Alnwick and County Gazette and Guardian* published this photograph.

The article was entitled:

LAST OF SHILBOTTLE PIT PONIES BROUGHT TO BANK
FAITHFUL WORKERS NINE YEARS DOWN PIT – DANCED WHEN THEY SAW DAYLIGHT AGAIN.

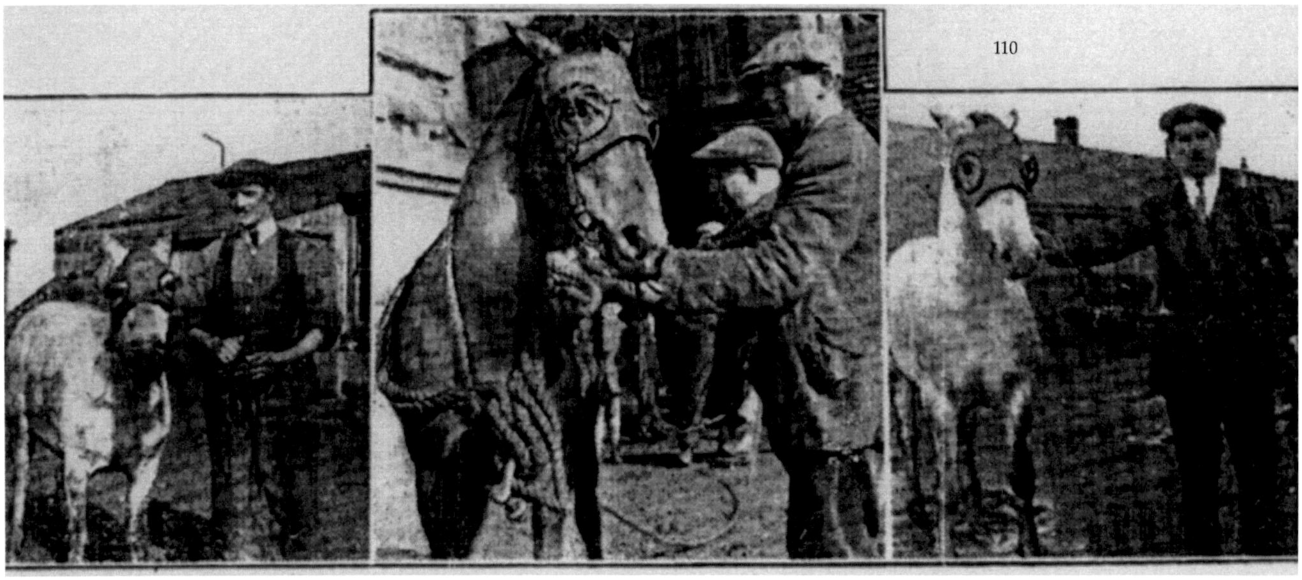
[110]

The newspaper's reporter recorded what he described as *a historic event at Old Shilbottle Pit, which has now been closed. Practically the last act in stripping the colliery was the bringing to bank of the ponies which have so long done valuable work below. The services of these animals, also the use of steam, will be entirely dispensed with under the new arrangements, since the Grange Pit, recently opened, is being worked entirely by electricity. It is about a mile distant from the Old Pit, and is the property of the Wholesale Co-operative Society.*

It is pleasing to record that the shutting down of the old mine has not put anyone out of employment, the men – numbering about 150[111] *– having been taken into the Grange Pit. Very good houses have been erected on the spot for their accommodation, and others are in the process of construction.*

The pit ponies now released from the industry are largely of the Shetland breed which has been found particularly suitable for underground work. Among the above photos, the one on the left shows a little Shetland pony in charge of Mr. G.V. Taylor, electrician attendant at the colliery. The animal had been down the pit for about nine years and has now been sold.

The picture in the centre is that of a larger pony, not one of the Shetlands, which were small enough to be raised to bank on the cage. It was too big to be brought up by this means. Therefore a rope net was used and is seen in the photo coiled about its body and neck. Mr. Alfred Pearson, carter, is holding the pony, and Mr. Andrew Tweedy, shafts-man, is standing by. This animal also had been about nine years down the pit.

---

[110] Details provided by Vera Mallon, from archive material obtained from the Bailiffgate Museum, Alnwick, with grateful thanks also to the *Northumberland Gazette*, Alnwick.
[111] This figure does not equate with the 369 employees quoted earlier.

The pony shown in the other photo is a Shetland, and it is held by Mr. Andrew Punton, check-weighman. It had been 'down below for a good many years. Ten ponies in all were employed in the pit. On reaching the surface all looked in the pink of condition. In fact, the greatest care has been taken of them.

It will be noticed that in the photos all the animals are wearing a species of visor, as worn in the mine. It is made of leather with steel guards covering their eyes.

On being raised to the upper air the animals seemed to go frantic with delight, dancing about on their hind legs, pawing the air and indulging in other evidence of joy. It may be stated that for some weeks after being brought into daylight the eye-sight of pit animals is at least weak.'

Bilton Banks – the village

Between the sinking of Longdyke Colliery in the sixth decade of the 19th century and the 1881 census, the village of Bilton Banks was built. The exact date of the houses being constructed has not been established, but two firm clues are available. The first is to be found in the report of Frederick Richard Wilson, the sanitary inspector, in 1874. He is referring to poor sanitation in the village of Shilbottle, in which he states – *the present prosperity of the pit (Longdyke) has caused a demand for houses and too much crowding for want of them. ... the dwellings are of a very unsanitary kind ... rotten old privies, choked drains and water not fit for drinking.*

Following this report of 1874, to alleviate the housing shortage, the new village of Bilton Banks was constructed near the colliery. This comprised 19 houses in a long row and seven (often six homes) in a short row. There was also a much larger house, set apart for the manager.[112]

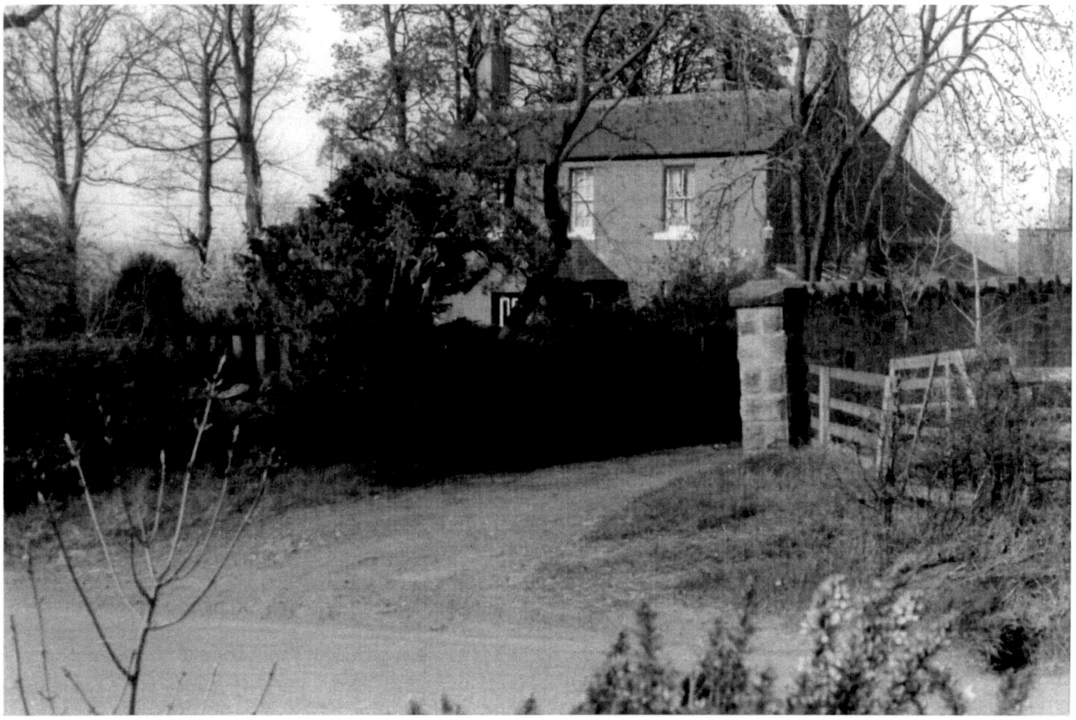

113

The Manager's House.

[112] Jermy, *ibid* p. 21.
[113] Photograph from Mr. D.P. Dalby's collection.

The baptismal records for St. James' Church in Shilbottle provide the second clue and help confirm that the houses at Bilton Banks were built just after 1874. Each year between 1813 and 1873 the average number of men who brought their children to be baptised and who declared their occupation to be miner, was five. In 1874 the annual figure increased to 16. The following year it was 26. In 1878 two miners, bringing their children for baptism gave their addresses as Longdyke, which could mean that they either lived in one of the farm buildings there, or the name Bilton Banks had yet to be adopted.

The first references to Bilton Banks, as recorded place of abode in the Shilbottle register was on 11th August 1878. This was for Sarah Egdell, whose father Edward was a colliery blacksmith. Interestingly, the parish records for Lesbury have an earlier record, also for Egdell. This is for the baptism of Agnes, the daughter of Edward and Mary Ann Egdell, engineer of Bilton Banks. The first miner to appear in the Lesbury records is for Robert, the son of William and Elizabeth Little, miner of Bilton Banks.[114] This record is followed each year with between 4 and 8 miners, resident at Bilton Banks, presenting their children for baptism at Shilbottle. One was mining engineer, William Alexander Ritson, with his wife Mary Ann, bringing their child Lizzie, born on 4th August 1882 for baptism on 7th August 1882. From 23rd July 1882, following a change of parish boundaries, the baptism of miners' children at Lesbury is also more common, but not as common as it is for Shilbottle.

Prior to the construction of the houses, all miners employed at Longdyke travelled into work from Alnwick, Shilbottle, Alnmouth, Warkworth and other nearby villages, usually walking there and back. Return journeys of seven miles were not uncommon so the levels of fitness, and subsequent exhaustion at the end of a shift of labour, must have been considerable. Once the houses at Bilton Banks were occupied, up to one third of the workforce at Longdyke lived on the doorstep of the colliery. Up to 38 men and boys from the village worked as miners.[115] Much of the sandstone for the houses was quarried from Spylaw, a hundred yards up the bank. The medical officer of health, who inspected the houses in 1937, came to the view that the bricks used in the houses were hand-made.

There were two rows of houses built in parallel. The Long Row had 19 dwellings in a stepped, terrace which was set back about 60 feet from the Alnwick to Alnmouth road. The land between the front of the dwellings and the roadway provided gardens for the inhabitants.

The Short Row, comprising seven houses, (two houses later being altered to form a single dwelling) was behind. The gardens for these houses faced east towards the coast. In the roadway between the houses, earth closet 'privies' were positioned. These were up to 30 feet from the houses. The dwelling houses were designed back to back, so that a single chimney stack accommodated flue outlets from adjoining houses. The house at the most south-easterly end of the Long Row, which completed the row, whilst attached to its neighbour, had its own chimney stack. A single water supply, in the form of a stand-pipe, was situated at the foot of the Short Row a distance from the houses of between 30 and 150 feet depending on the house's position in the row. There was no street lighting until 1919/1920.

Mr. Green states: *His house* [the manager, Mr. Anderson's] *had electric light for years, carried by wires from the pit, so it was not a big job to run wires up the 'Raa' and string them on poles that were fastened to the shutters,*

---

[114] The Lesbury records show three families living at Bilton Banks in 1761-62 (Richardson, Huntley and Taylor). There are also two single women – but there are no miners until 1877 and here the address is Longdyke for the family of Scott on 17th September when their daughter Isabella was presented for baptism.

[115] 1881 – 30 workers, 1891 – 38 workers, 1901 – 37 workers. Data extracted from census records for these periods.

five of them in all, spaced out so they really lit up the place ... We must have been the first village round about to be flood-lighted. One of the lights, it so happened, was on our lavatory and gave me a little social standing. It was known as 'John Green's' light among my friends.[116] For light indoors, paraffin lamps and candles were used by the residents.

The dwellings were all of similar design with minimal exceptions. Houses 1 to 13 in the Long Row were built of random or rubble stone, with brickwork on some upper walls. All chimney stacks were finished in brick. Houses 14 to 19 were all built with bricks. The Short Row houses were all constructed from random sandstone.

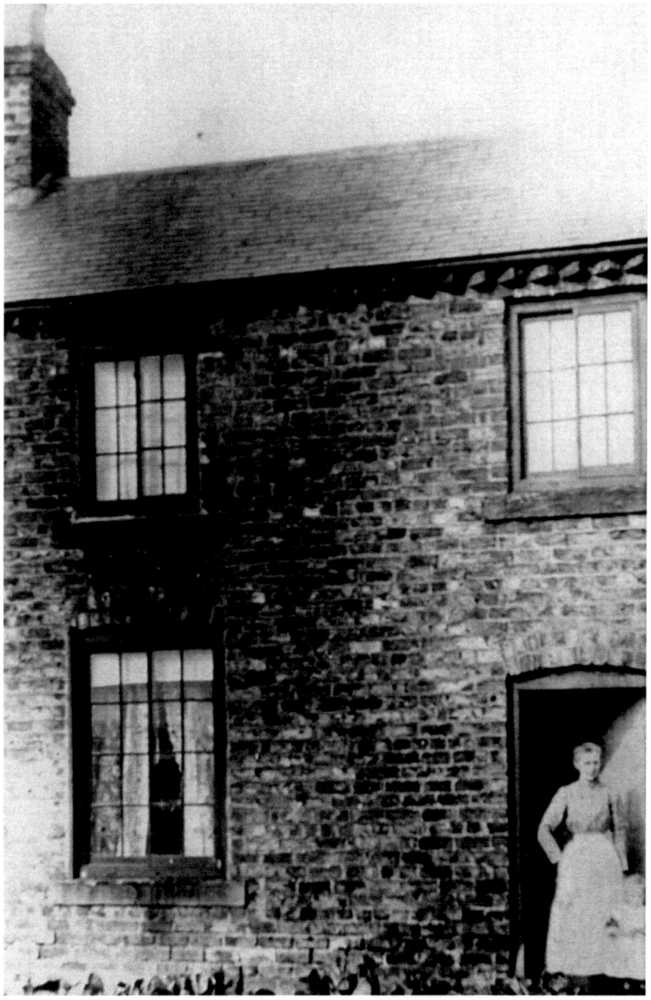
117

This photograph shows the construction and style of the properties.

The ground floor of the dwellings comprised a single living room which provided approximately 13 feet by 8 feet of flooring which was made from solid concrete or in some houses, wooden boards. Depending on the position in the row, to the left or right of the front entrance, which was accessed from the garden, was a living room. This had a window facing onto the gardens. The fireplace, with a metal range, was on the wall opposite the staircase. This was on the wall adjacent to the neighbour's living room, which meant that chimney breasts were back to back.

---

[116] See John Green's account – Northumberland Archives, ref: NRO 2205/2.
[117] Photograph from Mr. D.P. Dalby's collection.

A door, formerly the back door, led into a small pantry with a marble cold slab and later an add-on scullery/wash house which had a corrugated iron or asbestos roof. The scullery or wash house was down a short step. In the corner was a boiler. There was no bath and with the exception of 4 Short Row, until the addition of the scullery, there was no sink. When the scullery was added, next to it was fitted a wooden drainage board.

The ceilings were fractionally over 8 feet high and these were roughly brushed smooth, some coated in distemper.

The door from the front garden led immediately to a steep flight of stairs. There were 12 risers on 8 inch stair boards leading to two bedrooms on the upper floor. The room immediately accessed from the staircase was L shaped and was substantially smaller than the other bedroom. The larger, rectangular bedroom had a fireplace situated on the same wall and immediately above the downstairs range.

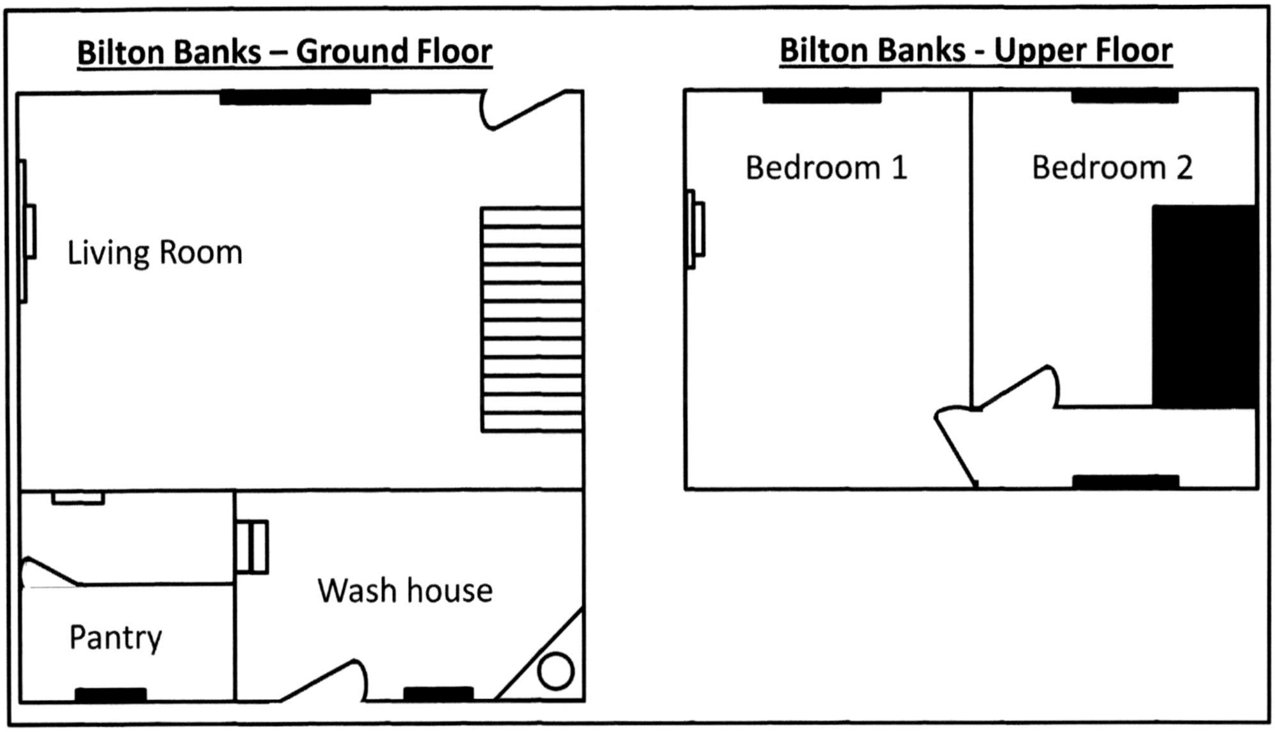

Above: The approximate lay-out of the dwellings at Bilton Banks – the adjoining house being the mirror image.

The steps led from the front door up to the passage on the upper floor connecting bedrooms one and two.

The step leading to the passage at the pantry from the scullery/wash house had originally been the back entrance to the house.

The bedroom windows faced towards the garden and the flooring in the bedrooms was wooden boards.

The external earth closet 'privies' were situated across the lane. The 'privies' were up two steps and consisted of a wooden seat with a hole in it. Under the hole was positioned a large galvanised bucket. Toilet paper (according to some former residents) was often torn up newspaper or the wrappings from apples or other fruits which had been purchased from shops or travelling salesmen.

Beyond the enclosed 'netties', and adjoining them, were rectangular 'middens' into which ashes and household waste was emptied awaiting weekly collection by the 'night soil men' with their shovels and their horses and carts. The regular coal, delivered from the pit as a 'perk' for service, but in lieu of higher wages, was not kept under cover. It was piled in the street.

Un-drained, uneven, compressed clay provided a walkway at the rear of the houses. One gulley for rainwater was shared by two houses, but each house had its own rain barrel. There was no footpath near the roadway and no dividing walls between houses making it possible to walk from the top of the rows to the bottom without impediment.

Two of the houses in the Short Row, numbers 4 and 6, were slightly bigger. Number 6 was officially designated the Under-manager's house and this had four bedrooms.

Housing Act, 1925 Survey

Former residents of Bilton Banks[118] have commented about occasionally seeing rats, bugs and beetles around the houses at 'The Old Pit'. Sadie Rennison, for example, (whose account comes later) spoke of returning from an evening's dancing as a teenager, and going next door to her friend's house. She was told to watch out on the stairs because at night the cockroaches came out. The warning was too late. Sadie heard them crunching underfoot. Generally, the householder's aim was to keep vermin at bay and for those living in houses with concrete, rather than wooden floors, this was slightly easier.

Despite the best efforts of people at this time (and many were exceptionally 'house-proud'), between the First and Second World Wars, infectious diseases in the general population were very common. Indeed, the medical officer of health, Doctor Scott Purves of Alnwick, regularly reported to Alnwick Rural District Council's Health and Housing Committee, and his reports provided details of births and deaths and minimal fluctuations in the number of people in the population. His reports also drew attention to any outbreaks of infectious and contagious diseases such as measles, scarlet fever and chicken pox.

Where appropriate, he reported deaths arising from diphtheria and pulmonary tuberculosis which were significantly associated with poverty and deprivation.

Poor sanitation, over-crowding, inefficient water supply, facilities for bathing and pest control, and inferior housing were all subject of comment in the medical officer's frequent reports.

The government too were concerned with the nation's health and the passing of Housing Acts by Parliament also led to the Rural District Council in Alnwick, developing their own protocols and eventually drafting bye laws which set out the standard for housing for residents and particularly *the working classes.*

It was against this background that on 11th January 1937 Alnwick Council gave notice of proposed entry to the 25 dwelling houses at Bilton Banks for the purposes of survey and inspection under Section 127 of the Housing Act, 1925. Clearance Notices were not confined to Bilton Banks.

[118] Sylvia Johnson (formerly Purvis, née Punton), Ronnie Knox, Esther Shell (née Stewart), Sadie Rennison (née Swordy).

The Alnwick and County Gazette for May 29th 1937 (and others) reports similar evaluations being conducted across the region, including Craster, Dunston, High Hazon and Radcliffe. The newspaper later reported orders for demolition being confirmed in notices issued by the clerk to the RDC Mr. Richard Rothwell, of dozens of defective properties.

The council's notice in respect of the houses at Bilton Banks was addressed to his Grace, the Duke of Northumberland, the owner of houses at Bilton Banks, through his agent Beresford Pierce. The notice was issued by Doctor Scott Purves, who was then resident at Bondgate Without, Alnwick. His notice indicated that two days after its issue, he would enter the houses at Bilton Banks, on 13th January 1937, between 9.30am and 5pm, for the purposes of inspection and evaluation. The notice obviously carried with it a legal right of entry and provided minimal warning to the residents. When he carried out his survey, Doctor Purves was very diligent and the record shows that he used a finely printed questionnaire to ensure that each dwelling was equally considered. His survey documents were completed in a tiny but readable, forward sloping script with a fine nib pen.

He took particular note of the window sizes and compared this with floor space as a percentage, from which he further calculated opportunities for natural lighting and ventilation. He made judgements about rising damp, evenness of walls, smoothness of ceilings, stability of floor-boarding, the state of window sashes, safety measures on the staircase, appropriateness of the oven and bathing and hygiene facilities, the latter of which were mostly entirely absent. On 13th February 1937, Doctor Purves, and his associate Mr. Oswald M. Farrell, Sanitary Inspector, who accompanied him during the survey, submitted their report to the council's Health and Housing Committee. The report, which was accompanied by an introductory statement, is of a condemnatory nature. It is, however, worth passing comment on the nature of Doctor Purves' diligence.

His 'working document' on house number 15 in the Long Row, related to the property then occupied by Mr. J.R. Punton and his family.

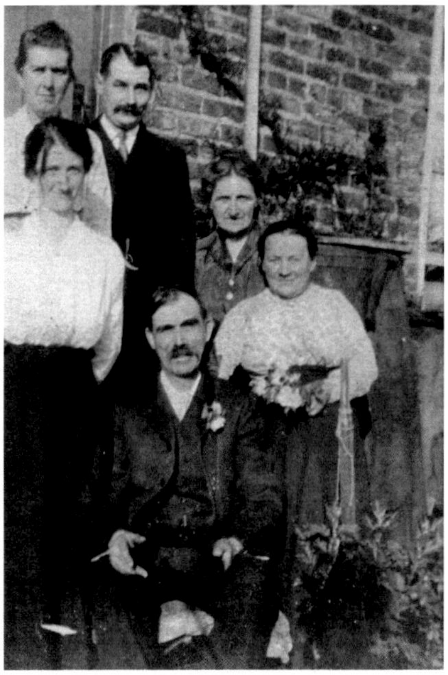

Above: James Robert Punton, standing at the back with his wife Eleanor, was born at Bilton Banks. He is pictured here with his neighbours and friends in 1920.

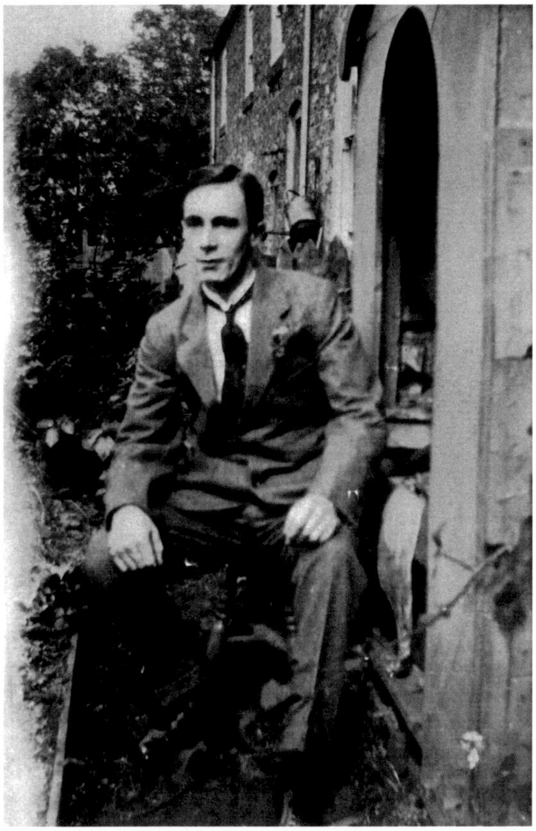
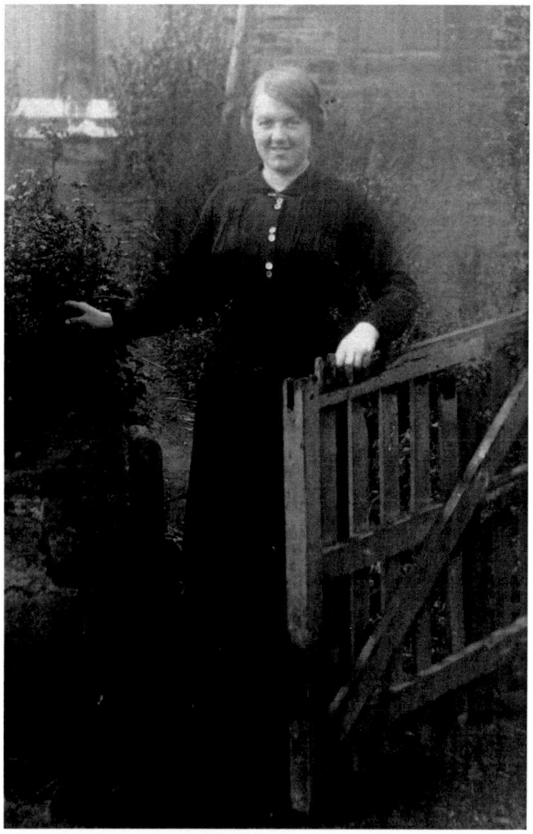

James Robert Punton Jnr (Bob) and his 'sister' Jane Ann Air at Bilton Banks pictured in 1920.

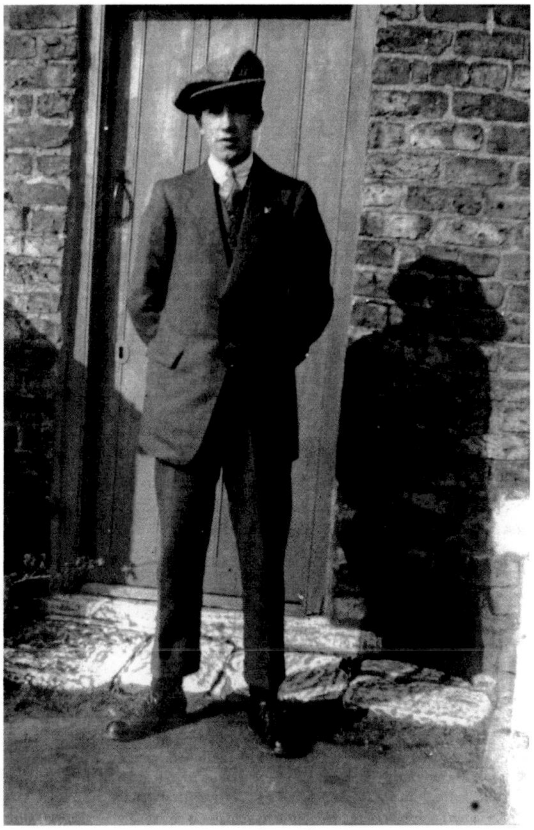
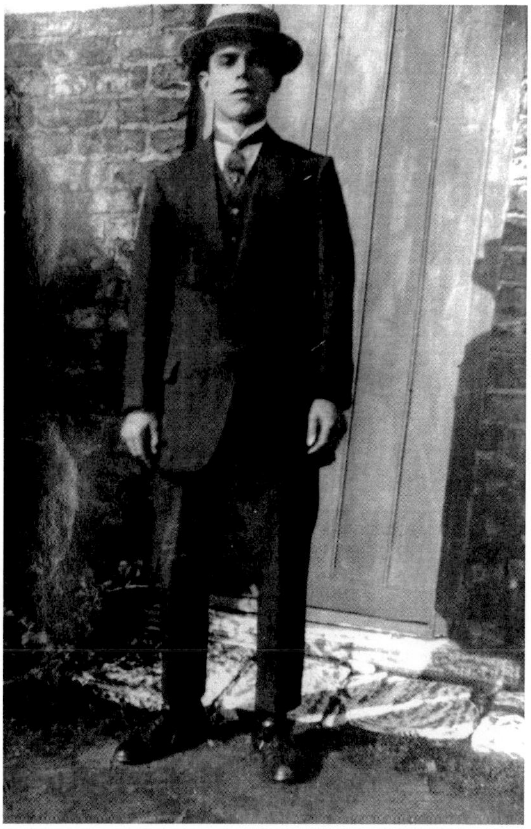

Joe and Richard Lillico Punton pictured in 1920 at Bilton Banks. All three Punton sons worked at Longdyke.

The medical officer's report on Mr. Punton's house is pretty typical. It shows details of flaws found in the house as follows:

Ground Floor
Walls damp
Ceiling uneven
Pantry damp

1st Floor (bed1)
Floors shaky
Walls uneven
Ceiling cracked

1st Floor (bed 2)
Walls uneven
Ceiling cracked
Floors uneven

Staircase
Badly lit
Steep 8″ treads
Dangerous 12″ risers

Ventilation
Bad

Roof
Fair – blue slate

General
No damp-course
Slight damp penetration to walls
Dilapidated midden
No sink
Paving/cobbles un-drained and defective
Windows badly fitted
Plaster cracked and damp
Cooking range useable[119]

Walls
Stone weathered
Brick worn/weathered
Rising damp

Doctor Purves' papers include his estimate of the current value of the house (in 1937), which he put at £50. He itemised his estimate of the likely cost of effecting repairs to each house, including for example, refitting the stairs (for £6 0s 0d), modifying the windows (for £3 10s 0d), inserting additional floor joists and making good the floors, fitting skirting boards, re-framing doors, leading water into the house, which in total, for house number 15 in the Long Row, came to £75 3s 0d.

He ended his report on house number 15, as he did for others in the Rows, by asking a rhetorical, pre-ordained, legally framed question: *Is the dwelling dangerous or injurious to health of the inhabitants, of the area, by reason of the bad arrangements of the house or narrowness or bad arrangement of the street in the area?*

Answer *Yes.*

His answer, in respect of house number 15 – and all the others in the rows, justified him coming to the view in 1937 that the miners' houses at Bilton Banks should be condemned and the occupants re-housed.

The following table showing occupier, number of day rooms and bedrooms in each house and the persons living there, has been extracted from Doctor Purves' report.

[119] This wasn't the case in houses 1, 2, 4, 6, 14, 19–23 where the range was considered obsolete.

The final column in the table shows that the council were advised too, that the 'tied' houses were rent free, and made available to colliery employees for services rendered.

Long Row			**Day**	**Beds**	**Over 10**	**Under 10**	**Rent Nil**
1	Bilton Banks	A. Boyd	1	2	2	0	Services
2	do	J. Taylor	1	2	2	0	do
3	do	J. Stewart	1	2	3	0	do
4	do	J. Snaith	1	2	2	2	do
5	do	T. Lorimer	1	2	2	2	do
6	do	J. Anderson	1	2	4	2	do
7	do	W. Edgar	1	2	4	2	do
8	do	J. Wilson	1	2	2	1	do
9	do	D. Stones	1	2	2		do
10	do	R. Straughan	1	2	2	2	do
11	do	J. Knox	1	2	4	2	do
12	do	E. Stuart	1	2	2	3	do
13	do	R.L. Punton	1	2	2	1	do
14	do	J. Gillen	1	2	3	2	do
15	do	J. Punton	1	2	4	0	do
16	do	E. Rennison	1	2	2	2	do
17	do	J. Swordy	1	2	4	0	do
18	do	D. Brooks	1	2	2	4	do
19	do	J. Shell	1	2	2	1	do
Short Row							
1	Bilton Banks	G. Douglas	1	2	5	2	do
2	do	W. Porteous	1	2	3	0	do
3	do	E. Taylor	1	2	7	1	do
4	do	Cockburn	1	4	9	0	do
5	do	McVitae	1	2	6	0	do
6	do	J. Douglas	2	4	8	0	do

In fact, it took almost 18 years for all of the properties to be vacated.

Brian Egdell remembers his father, in 1955, using bricks from the demolished houses at Bilton Banks to build a garage in the garden at Garden Terrace in Shilbottle.

Audrey Bell (née Snaith) believes her family home at Bilton Banks was the last to be demolished. That was in 1959.

Former residents, some of whom are listed in the table shown above, have provided verbal or written accounts of what life was like in the Rows.

Life in Bilton Banks

When not at work, or resting after work, the miners relished the environment around their homes. Gardening played a significant part in their life, partly through the necessity of growing their own vegetables to supplement their diet, and partly because working on their land, in fresh north Northumberland air was a blessing to be savoured after hours underground.

Being located in and around farmland, there was an accessible supply of manure to fertilise the vegetable plots, which whilst narrow, in some places extended to 60 feet, depending on the situation of the houses on Bilton Bank. The variety of produce grown was extensive: early and late potatoes, white and Swede turnips, beetroot, carrots, onions, leeks, cabbages, salad crops, peas and beans – and when space permitted a smattering of flowers. Some enthusiastic gardeners had their own greenhouses (as can be seen below).[120] Many kept hens, geese and pigs.

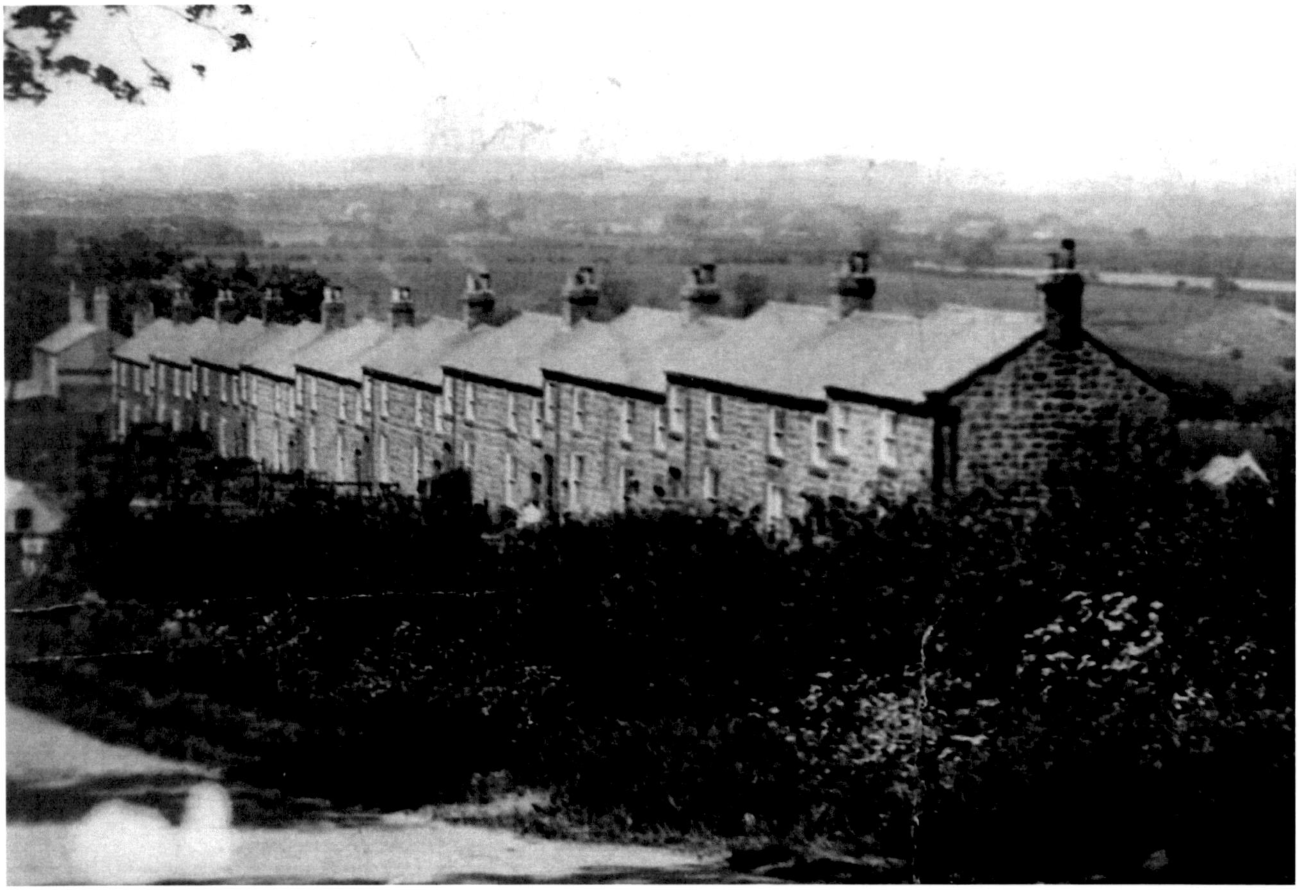

[120] John Taylor's greenhouse is partially visible on the extreme left of the above image.

Sadie Rennison (née Swordy) recalls – *For recreation there was a reading room on the green. It was an oblong building, its dimensions being approximately six yards by five yards. The entrance door had a window adjacent to it and on the wall opposite there was a fireplace. To the right of the door was a concrete stage with a short flight of steps for amateur performances and the occasional concert.*

The reading room was used by the men for dominoes and cards. Whist drives were also held there. The women gathered to make mats on large frames and canvases, both 'proggy' and 'clippy' being produced through communal labour, with much chatter. Some were finished as flat as carpets.[121]

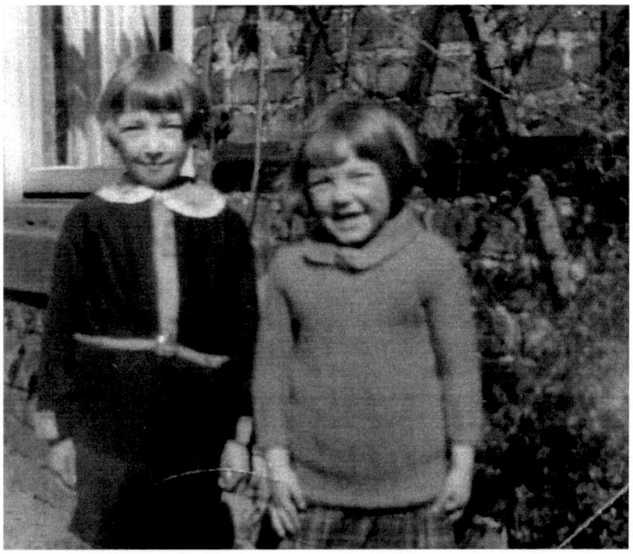

Betty Swordy with her sister Sadie Rennison, 1932.

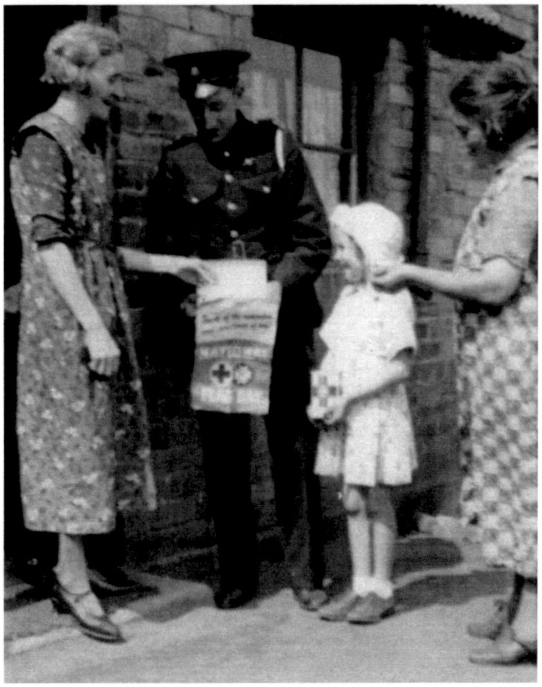

Esther Stewart, aged about 6 with her father James, in Red Cross uniform. Katie Knox is on the left and Ethel Stuart is on the right.

[121] According to Esther Shell (née Stewart)'s account during an interview on October 2011, her 'mother's mats were renowned for being as flat as carpets.'

Throughout his lifetime Mr. Joe Knox, Katie's husband, (who in 1937 lived at 11 Long Row) was renowned, and ahead of his time, for taking photographs.

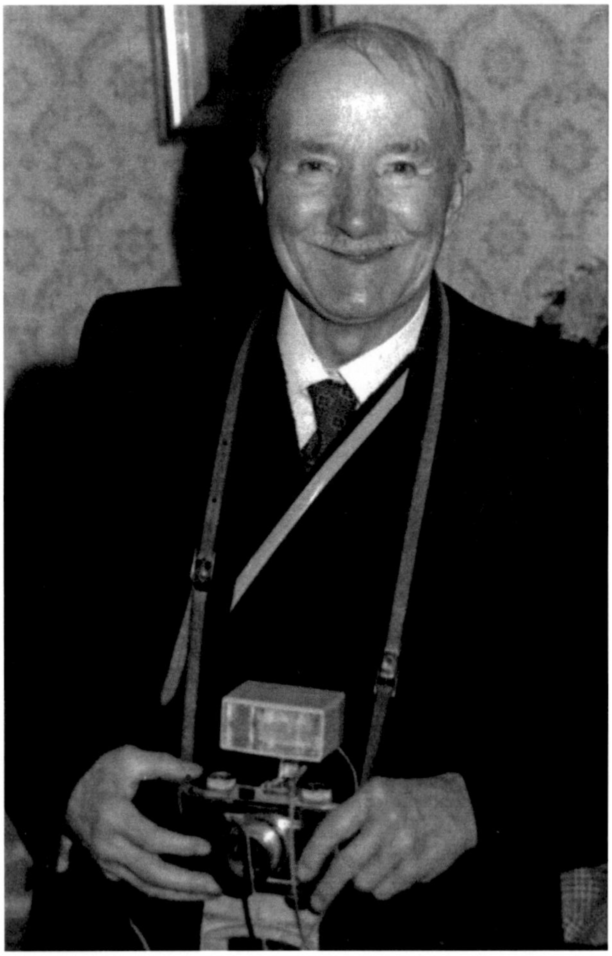

Joe Knox (seen above), with his beloved camera, at a wedding reception. He took the photograph below of Esther Stewart and won a *Journal* newspaper competition with it in 1940.

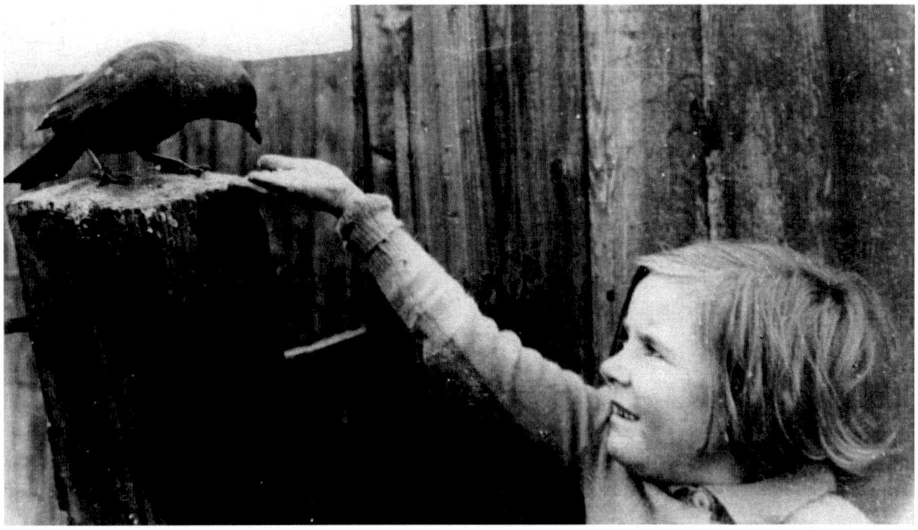

Esther, aged about six is feeding a jackdaw at Bilton Banks.

The quality of the original photograph is so clear it is possible to discern the darn in Esther's cardigan.

In addition to large vegetable plots, some of the men had allotments beneath the manager's house. John Green's brief history refers to the CWS wagons calling at the manager's house to collect vegetables grown by the manager's two gardeners. The wagons went from there to sell the produce around the 'Raas.'

The grocer used to sell the manager's apples, two or three for a penny and good they were too, but I never had a penny. I had to get my apples the other way.

The Douglas family were more entrepreneurial. They had a small-holding above the Long Row.

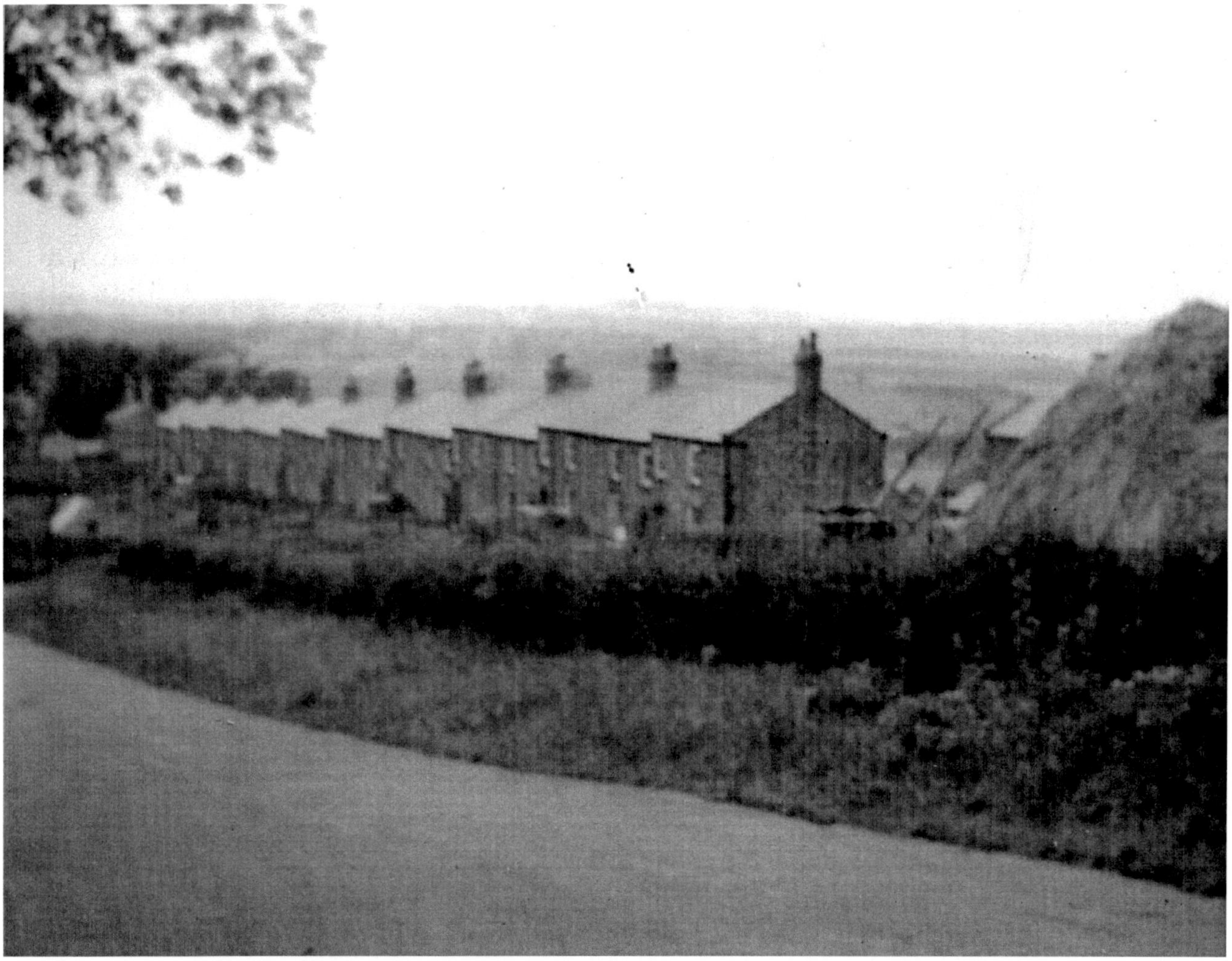

The Douglas family's haystack and horse cart is visible in this image.[122]

Religion had its place. Edward Anderson, Coverdale Smith Anderson's father, was a Great Western Methodist local preacher, both at Shilbottle and Felton. *It was common for him to walk to Felton and back to deliver a sermon and take the service. (He was also a herbalist who collected his herbs from the hedgerows. He made and sold medicines and endeavoured to 'doctor' anyone who wanted to tell him their ailments.)*[123]

In the 1930s the Anglican vicar of Shilbottle was Rev'd William Robson. He was followed by Rev'd John Simpson and Rev'd Harry Gordon Cutter. After the Second World War came Rev'd William Hume.

---

[122] Photograph from Sadie Rennison's collection.
[123] Extracted from Leslie Anderson Varty's written account.

Around his time, Sunday School at Bilton Banks was being led for a period by Alice Scott, a former resident of Bilton Banks who had moved to Shilbottle.

Entertainment

Quoits, for out-of-doors activities, were stored in the reading room. The game, with its characteristic metallic clank when the quoits collided on the ground, was played by the men on the green outside the reading room.

On one occasion at least, Bert May, who had his own dancing school in Alnwick, came to the reading room, on the invitation of John Swordy, to perform his tap-dancing routine. His daughter, Sadie Rennison recalls that Bert's tap shoes were specially constructed with loose ebony soles to accentuate the tap.

Domestic Routines

The women had particular routines. For example each Friday they brushed the earth ground across to the middens and scrubbed the steps with yellow Donkey stone.[124] The rationale behind this was that because there were no street lights, at least the outline of the steps was clearly delineated and visible in twilight and darkness. The saying was that *more people pass the house than come in,*[125] so a good impression needed to be created.

The women rolled up and dusted their home-made mats, swilled the street and polished their black range cookers. After shift, they 'dadded'[126] their men-folk's clothes against the wall to dust them off before drying them in front of the fireside range.

John Green relates an occasion when a prankster created early morning confusion.

All the houses had rain barrels outside the back door, fitted with a lid to keep out the dust etc. And every housewife cleaned the boots and put them out to dry on these lids. You didn't dry leather boots in front of a fire and … in summer time the boots never went inside the house, the men just sat on the back door step and put them on when they needed them. Well, one morning, the night shift got the blame. As they finished work at 1am, some joker started at the bottom of the Row and worked his way up to the top, shuffling all the boots like dominoes, then went quietly to bed. When the first shift, which started at 4am, came for their boots – Ahem! – they were two hours late … and the 'Raa' was a seething mass of men … some never got their right boots back.[127]

Judging from the image of John Green opposite, it is not hard to imagine that he knew more about the early morning boot-shuffling, than he divulged in his story.

---

[124] This was a chalk-like powdered stone mixed with bleach and water and set into a mould, often carrying a stamped on 'donkey' emblem.

[125] Extract from Smith, Ken and Jean, 'The Great Northern Miners' Donkey Stone and Dadding, (Newcastle: Tyne Bridge Publishing), p. 128.

[126] 'Dadded': a Northumbrian term – particularly in mining communities, for beating or pounding a garment to release dust and debris.

[127] Green, Northumberland Archives ref: NRO 2205/2

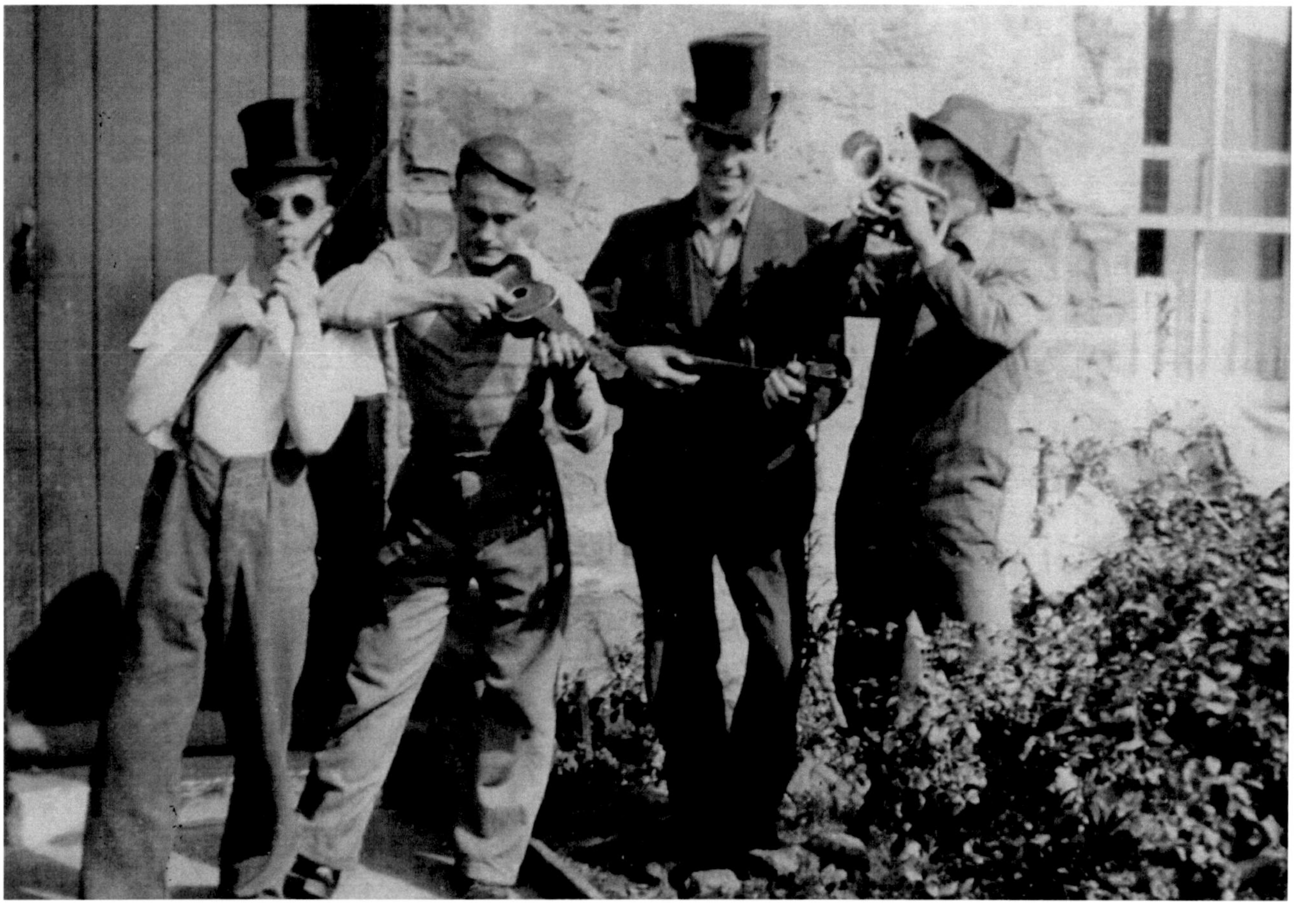

John Green (second left with the ukulele) with his mates at Bilton Banks.

Leslie Anderson Varty, who was born at Bilton Banks in 1917, wrote of another joker from an earlier time.[128]

A friend of my father – who was something of an athlete although a small man ... he lived with his wife and family about the middle of the street and next door to him lived an excitable Scots woman who believed in the occult. Sometimes as Bob (or 'Peg' as he was known) was on night shift, he would of course go to bed during the day and when the 'spirit' moved him, he would cover his head and shoulders with a sheet and drop down through the trap door into the Scot's woman's house to pretend he was a ghost! Needless to say she didn't see the funny side, but all the village was aware of what he had done and enjoyed the joke.

Sadie Rennison's account of more serious matters continues – *It was hard work for the women. Each day they boiled the water in the 'set-pot' at the back side of the large fire, ready for their men returning from the pit to have their baths in front of the fire in a big zinc bath. The clothes horse, with towels or a sheet, was put round to preserve decency. The water had to be got from the stand-pipe. Andy Arnott made a wooden device; we called a set-square.*

We stepped inside the square of wood, dropped it on top of the buckets we had in each hand, with the bucket handles either side of the side-woods to stop them from banging against our legs and spilling as we walked.

The women spent time cooking and baking their own bread, often twice a week. Their utensils were commonly cast steel or enamelled pots and pans.

---

[128] From a written account sent to the author by his son, Leslie Ian Varty.

On washing days, mother used a handle on a paddle on top of the wash tub to swish the clothes back and forward. I usually had to help and she insisted on 140 swishes back and forward each way and there was no cheating or slacking. Mind, her routines paid off, because her clothes always came out spotless.

Bowel movement was another thing. Each day dad used to ask each one of us kids in turn "Have you been to the toilet?" Unless our answer was yes, we got dosed with castor oil which mam kept in the big press in the living room; either that or it was Epsom Salts.

Audrey Bell recalls her mother using 'Oxydol' washing powder and 'Whitlow' which was added whilst boiling, and she recalled carbolic soap being commonly used for scrubbing. She also remembered her parents administering to her Scott's Emulsion, Malt, Viral and Parishes Food tonic as supplements, whether she wanted them or needed them or not.

Leslie Anderson Varty, referring to earlier times, continues: *Life was very simple. We bathed once a week in a tin bath in front of the living room fire ... our mothers did the family wash once a week and that was normally on a Monday. Water was put into a 'poss-tub' with washing soda and then beaten with a 'Dolly' or poss-stick, until judged clean. They were then put through the mangle which was clamped to the side of the poss-tub. Clothes were either wool or cotton (and when older) I wore woollen shorts and long-johns. Boys did not possess underpants, vests or pyjamas so at least that lightened the washing load.*

Everyone washed in the living room or in the wash house (since my father was a master shifter and we had a wash house). My mother would light a coal fire under the set pot and put buckets of water into the cast iron, built-in container. The whole thing was a brick erection about three feet high with a fireplace at the bottom on bars and the cast iron pot sat directly above the fire.

Most families only had one change of clothes so we changed usually after bathing ... we must have had a good healthy smell.

Most homes had the living smell of bread baking or food cooking, damp washing drying round the fire, 'Brasso' and lead-polish from the fireside range, smoke belching up the chimney and warm bodies.

The rabbit catcher came on a Friday. Roger Harrison, who lived there as a youngster at a later stage, from 1935, contended that his – *mother made the best rabbit pie in Bilton Banks. There were five of us and we all got a leg!*[129]

Roger Harrison's account continues: *Rabbit pies, with pastry crusts, were most commonly made and the fillings were not always purchased. Sometimes though, rabbit was roasted like chicken and stuffed with sage and onion. The kidneys were often favoured and fought over.*

Sadie Rennison's account continues: *Sometimes a bit of steak was bought to go with the rabbit or a piece of bacon was added. Mince was common and it was also usual for the labourer in the house – often dad – to get the biggest portion. On Saturday we sometimes had tinned salmon; on Sunday it was a roast – beef or lamb, with vegetables. All the women seemed to bake on a Sunday – apple tarts, date tarts, egg custard tarts and cakes, also scones. We kids weren't allowed to bake in case we spoiled anything. Food was precious and couldn't be wasted. Mother made*

[129] Smith, *ibid* 'The Garage Colliery' p. 113.

130

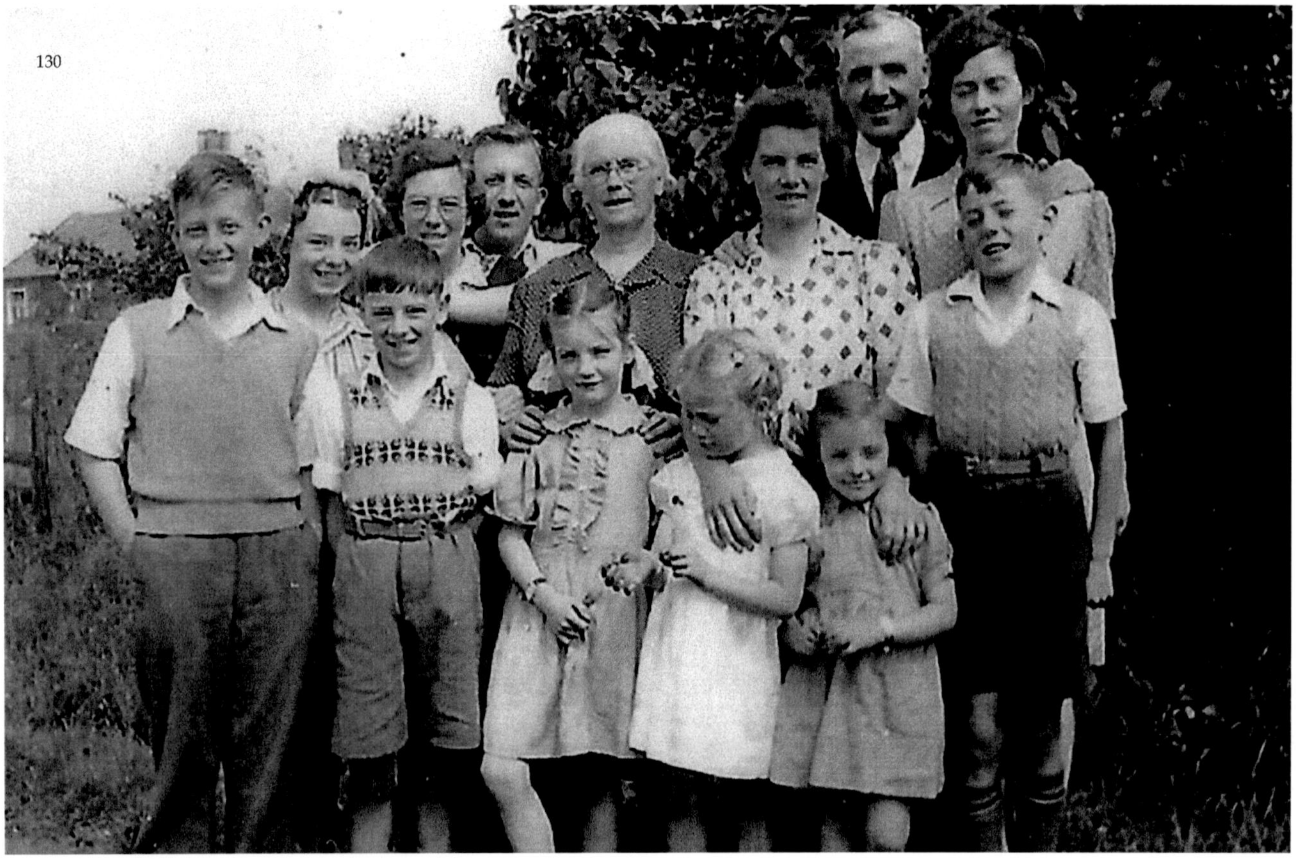

This photograph, taken in 1949, shows Roger Harrison on the extreme left. The others left to right are Margaret Baird, Ormond Baird, Jean Baird, Harry Harrison, Margaret Mavin, Roger's granny Collinson, Kathleen Harrison, Roger's mother Robertina (Robin) Harrison, Edith Mavin, Charlie Mavin, Constance Mavin and Gordon Harrison.

round scones for the tea but finished off the pastry with a big, square girdle scone which was cut up for bait on Mondays. We would have tinned fruit, jelly and custard – and bread and butter to make it go further.

Leslie Anderson Varty's account continues: *My diet, as a youngster would make the average dietician turn in his/her grave. A typical day's food – Breakfast (at 7.30) fried bacon in fat, with egg and possibly tomatoes, home made bread and butter and tea. Dinner (remember DINNER was always in the middle of the day)...boiled beef, pork, pork or mutton chops (Roast was for Sundays only),vegetables and Yorkshire puddings or dumplings. Rice or sago puddings or fruit and cream followed. Supper – sausages, bread tea or something else cooked.*

Sadie Rennison's account complements John Varty's. *Milky puddings were popular – rice, sago, tapioca. At night on a Sunday we had bubble and squeak for supper – 'left-overs' with fried onion, and mock fish (made from egg, potato and onion). For bait for school we had sandwiches (except for scones on Mondays). It was home-made bread with beetroot, paste, 'drippen'*[131] *with tomato sauce. We took a metal flask of tea which we left it at Mary Ann Edwards at the concretes.*[132] *We also went to Arnott's house. Betty, my sister, couldn't pronounce her name properly and called her 'Arney'. She put our flask on the range stove for us, keeping it warm until we went there for our bait. 'Arney' would make our bait sometimes – boiled eggs, cold rice pudding with a spot of jam for afters. She was like a mother to us.*[133]

---

[130] From Roger Harrison's collection.

Doreen Ions (née Stuart) recalls:[134] *My dad never took anything but mam's bread for his bait with jam on when he went to the pit. He took tea in a bottle which was cold by the time he drank it.*

Sadie Rennison's adds: *Scraps and vegetable peelings went to the compost heap although peelings from apples often got consumed on the way. Hazel nuts, rosehips, brambles, wild strawberries and mushrooms were collected from the fields and hedgerows. Fruit was gathered when in season and preserved and bottled in Killiner jars which had a glass top and was placed inside a metal screw on lid and made secure with a rubber seal.*

Like any housing estate, internal furnishings varied and we have no precise way of knowing what home conditions were like when the houses at Bilton Banks were first occupied. However a paper, entitled *The Coal Miners of Durham and Northumberland: their Habits and Diseases*, by Robert Wilson M.D., presented to the Newcastle meeting of the British Association in 1863, provides a general insight. *They* [the miners] *live in villages … the houses built end to end … single rows and double rows … a front door and a back door, divided into two principal apartments. … the fire range is large, and fitted with an oven and boiler for a constant supply of hot water. They have a plentiful supply of small coal and the fire is never allowed to go out from one end of the year to another. Generally the houses are clean and comfortably furnished; a four-post bed; and eight day clock and a mahogany chest of drawers, have always been and still are considered the essentials of a well fitted house …* [in some there will be] *home made cages containing every variety of the finch tribe; in another a trombone, cornet or violin …* [but whatever the state of the house] *if he* [the miner] *is to enjoy the privilege of living in a pit village, he must work.*[135]

At a later time (between 1920s and 1950), and certainly within the memory of former residents of Bilton Banks, whilst the male occupants of school leaving age undoubtedly had to work in the mine, the home making situation was different.

The floors of the houses were covered in thick brown lino with a Hessian back, and either coarse fibre mats or 'proggy' or 'hooky' mats, home-made from cut up, old clothing and forged into patterns on sacking which, during production, was kept taut in a large wooden frame.

Some households (in the 1930s) had stair carpets, with metal retaining rods on the risers. Downstairs curtains were often of Chenille and generally thicker than the cotton ones at the upstairs windows. They were retained on wood poles or brass rods with hooks, or sprung wires.

Furniture was either specifically bought for the properties or handed down from generation to generation, the more established families having double and three quarter, iron-framed beds (often two in the larger bedroom, with a third bed in the smaller room) with woollen blankets, flannelette sheets and quilted or heavy eider down covers. Some households had honeycomb cotton material with tassels as bed-covers. Bedroom furniture comprised dressing tables and tall-boy sets of drawers, often an ottoman blanket chest or metal 'kist'. In many houses the parents slept downstairs in the living room, which would also be furnished with settees, arm chairs, a 'chaise longue' and fire-side stools. 'Posher' families sometimes had a piano.

---

[131] 'Drippen' was the essence of meat, congealed with fat, which came from the cooked meat.

[132] 'The Concretes' was the rather disparaging local name given to the houses built from concrete blocks in Colliers Close in Shilbottle village.

[133] This account is based on an interview with Sadie Rennison, of Lynemouth – aged 86 in 2011.

[134] Based on Doreen Ions' written recollection and an interview carried out in October 2011.

[135] NEIMME: Wilson, Robert, M.D. *Transactions of Tyneside Naturalist Club 1863–64 Vol. VI* – p. 200.

In the 1920s and later, clothes were hung on hooks on a rack near or behind the doors, or stored in deep drawers known as 'presses.' There was often a small table on which to stand a jug of water and a bowl for washing.

Margery Slater remembers her family (the Egdell's) having one of the first horn radios.

Indoor lighting was provided by candles or paraffin lamps, often one hanging from the ceiling on an adjustable chain; another with a domed glass cover, clipped to the wall.

Esther Shell recalls the family table in the living room doubling as an Anderson air raid shelter. During the week this would most commonly be covered with flexible lino but at the weekends it was smartened up with a white cloth.

Margery Slater remembered her mother warming the beds with a hot oven shelf wrapped in a towel or blanket. In some houses, cutlery could be solid silver for Sundays; more often it was *commoner tin stuff* for every-day use.

Leslie Anderson Varty recalling the 1920s states – *Boys and girls wore dresses up to the age of about 3 or 4. At that age boys were 'breached' i.e. put in short trousers.*

Commenting on the children's activities, Mr. Varty states: *One of our games was with the local doctor's chauffer. Remember in those days (1921+) cars were very rare. My uncle (as colliery manager) had a Model T Ford and a few people had motorcycles (the under-manager and my other uncle the colliery surveyor, each had a Harley Davidson). The doctor's chauffer wore a uniform, peaked cap, long boots and goggles (open car). We kids used to run up to the car and pretend to touch it at which he would chase us. This was one of the highlights of our week.*

Doors were never locked and I well remember visiting neighbours' houses with my pot or bowl whenever they had anything tasty – soup etc. Of course other children did the same to our mother.

Esther Shell (née Stewart) recalls[136] – *'Granny Douglas' house at the bottom of short row (number 6) had been the deputy manager's house so it was bigger. She kept one bedroom shelved out and stored jam and bottled fruit there. She doled it out to the families when their stocks ran out.*

Her house was the only one which had water direct into the scullery from a large, metal rain barrel. Drinking water still had to be got from a standpipe.

They kept pigs, ducks, hens, geese, turkeys. When a pig was being slaughtered, granny Stoddard from Lucker (near Belford) came to help. The whole pig was used and everybody in the village got something. I watched at first then got told to help. I was shown how to butcher the pig including scraping 'the muck' out the intestines with the back of a knife, soaking them clean in salty water. The intestines were needed for making the black and white puddings.

Esther Shell also recalled the severe snow storm of 1947 when the whole of Bilton Banks was cut off for three weeks. *The kids walked to school down the long field and the snow was so deep we could step over the T bar on the top of telegraph poles.*

---

[136] Based on an interview in October 2011.

Henry Brewis, in his book *A Stroll in the Country,*[137] refers to another storm in 1958 which necessitated the use of the Short Row as a billet for his sheep. *Well, I'll tell y. For several days until Mother Nature relented, until the sleet abated, till the dry breeze blew, till the sun struggled through again, every sheep we had, spent those terrible few days billeted in The Short Raa at Bilton Banks. There were sheep in the kitchen, the front rooms, upstairs in the bedrooms, even the odd one stuffed into a netty. And most of 'em survived among the dust and peeling flowery wallpaper.*

Esther Shell also recollected that: *Granny Douglas was the midwife for the village and delivered most of the babies in her time.*

Doctor McLeod came in his car when folk were sick. His assistant, a Russian gentleman, whose name sounded like 'Kulkdin' was very caring and when somebody was sick he would sometimes stay overnight until they got through the crisis.

John Green recorded: *... it was a very close knit community. More than that, nearly everybody was inter-related – cousin marrying cousin etc. Besides this it was very class conscious. You knew what shelf you were on. In descending order – manager, overman, deputies, then workers, even these having a scale – hewer, stone-man, pony putters, then hand putters, and shifters being the lowest. ... even on bank this applied, the banksman being king.*[138]

The table of residents, shown earlier, reveals the number of people under the age of ten who were resident in the village. The photograph below captures a few of them taken, around 1940.

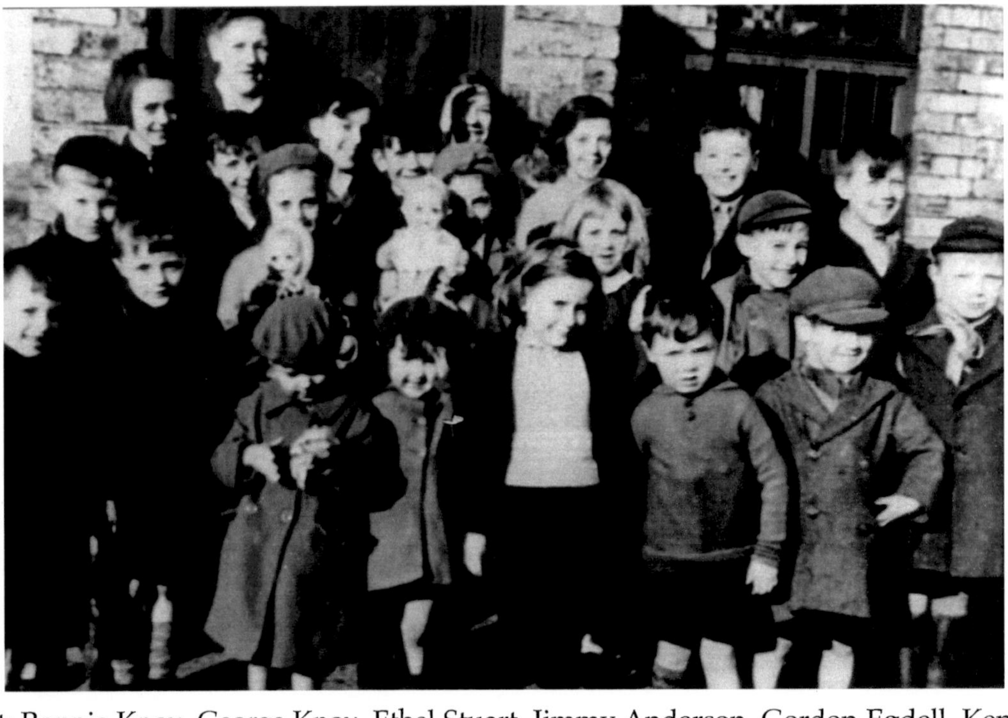

Left to right: Ronnie Knox, George Knox, Ethel Stuart, Jimmy Anderson, Gordon Egdell, Kenneth Knox, Mildred Egdell, Joe Knox, Molly Stuart, Ethel Stuart, John Douglas, Sadie Rennison, Nina Knox, Esther Stewart, Margaret Pattinson, Mildred Egdell. Billy Pattison, Ronnie Rennison, Irwin Lorrimor, George Douglas, Billy Anderson, Henry Wilson.

[137] Brewis, Henry, *A Stroll in the Country,* (Newcastle: Powdene Publishing, 1999) pp. 94–95.

[138] Green, NRO 2205/2.

[139] Photograph from Ronnie Knox's collection, taken by his father.

Doreen Ions' account continues: *Water was heated in a 'set-pot' in the scullery (wash house) for bathing and for washing clothes ... and water from the rain barrel outside was used for handwashing and some household tasks. Sometimes in the winter we had to break the ice before we could get any water.*

We didn't have a bathroom, so had to bathe in a tin tub in front of the living room fire. It was a walk across a dirt track behind the house to reach the row of 'netties'. (It wasn't uncommon for a brick to be removed in the communal wall between the 'netties' so that conversation between those in adjoining 'middens' could continue.)[140] *We used cold ash from the fire in the wooden container (in the same way that soil is used in outside latrines) and the contents were removed and cleaned out once a week by someone from the council.*[141]

If somebody was going to Alnwick to shop, they would ask their neighbours if they wanted something brought back for them. It was quite a walk to get the bus because we had to go as far as the Keeper's Cottage on the Alnwick Road, not far from the Callishes. My sister and I had to walk there and back every day as we went to school in Alnwick. At home we played happily around the houses with skipping ropes and ball games and we made stilts with tin cans. The lads made 'boggies' with old pram wheels and a plank of wood and rope for steering. We had an iron ring for 'booling' and spinning tops. On Sundays in the summer we would walk to the beach at Alnmouth.

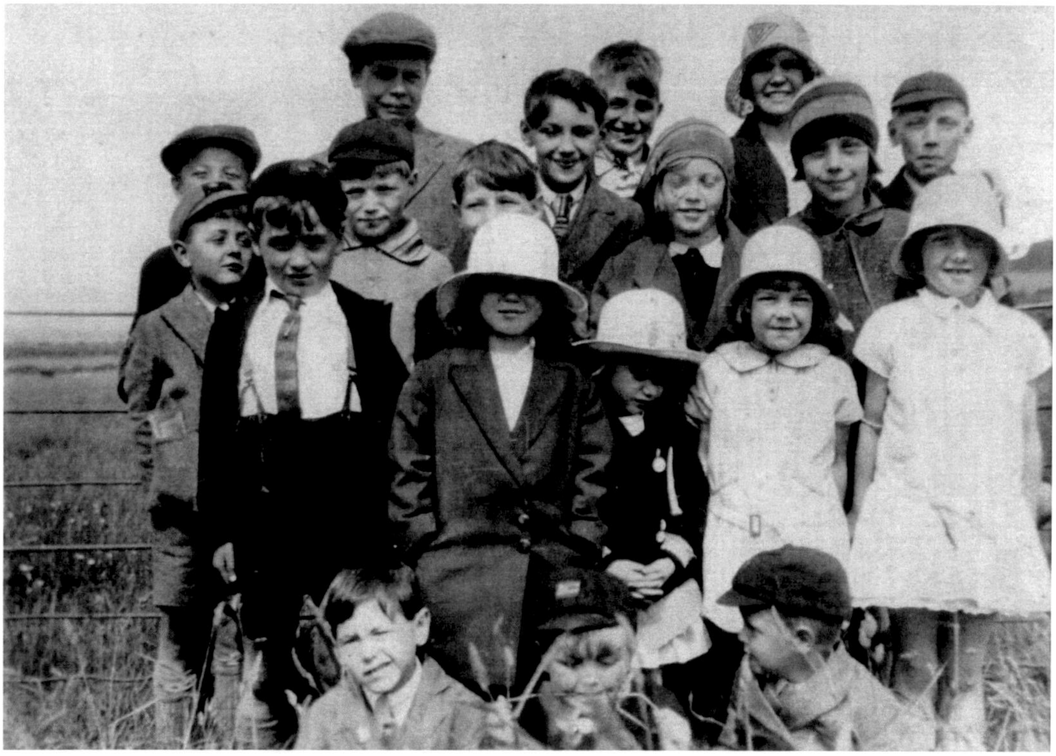

This photograph,[142] taken in 1931 is of a Sunday School outing at Easter. Not all of the children were from Bilton Banks, but most were.

Back row, left to right: Billy Porteus, Johnnie Stewart, Winnie Scott (Teacher); middle row: Jim Swordy, Willie Gillon, Dickie Punton, Aidan Knox, Florrie Knox, May Porteus, Cecil Weightman; front row standing: Norman Snaith, Lance Weightman, Jean Mossop, Maisie Gillon, Sadie Swordy, Betty Swordy; front row sitting: Ken Punton, Brian Weightman, Bobby Snaith.

140 Additional information following a conversation with Carol Hope (née Inglis).

141 According to Sadie Rennison's recollection, the midden man (in the 1930s) was old Mr. Pearson, who took his 'bait' in the reading room opposite Sadie's house.

142 Photograph from the author's collection – originally supplied by Sadie Rennison.

Sadie Rennison continues – *We had bazookas that we blew in to make a tune, maybe a penny whistle, paper and combs to hum through and old tins to drum on with sticks. We would march around like a band making a right din. Dad played the mouth organ and sometimes for a laugh, Ella Arnott would put it in the gap in the living room window to let it blow its own tune in the wind.*

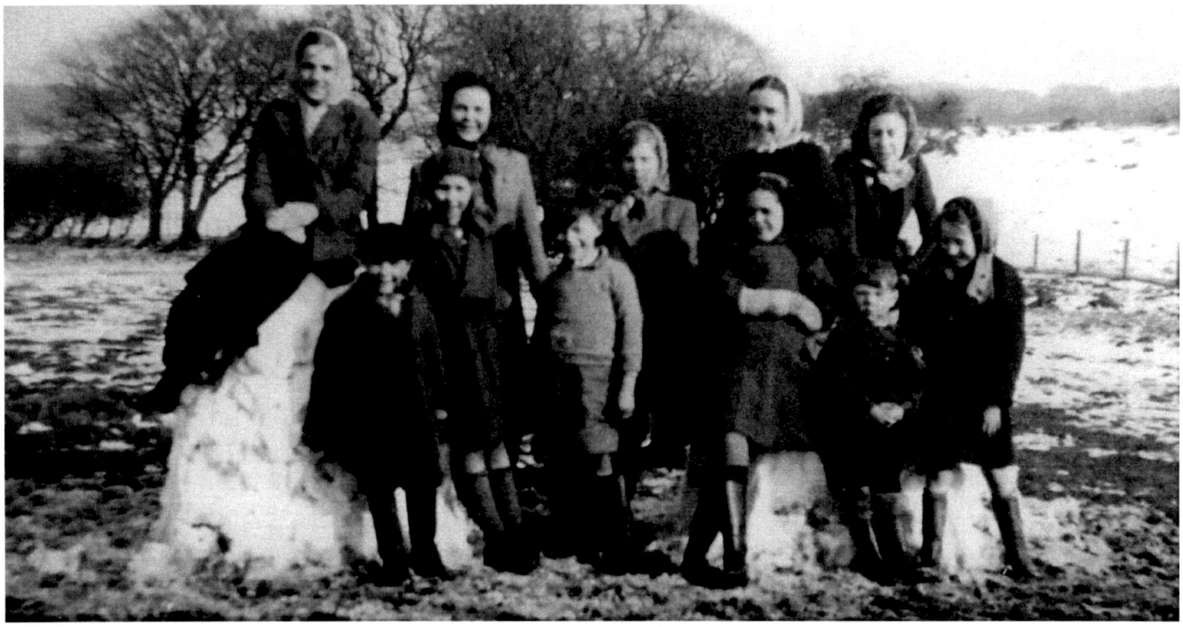

Back row, left to right: Mary Anderson, Audrey Snaith, Ethel Stuart, Esther Stewart; front row: ?, Eileen Snaith, Win Straughan, Doreen Stewart, Clive Straughan, Betty Stewart.[143]

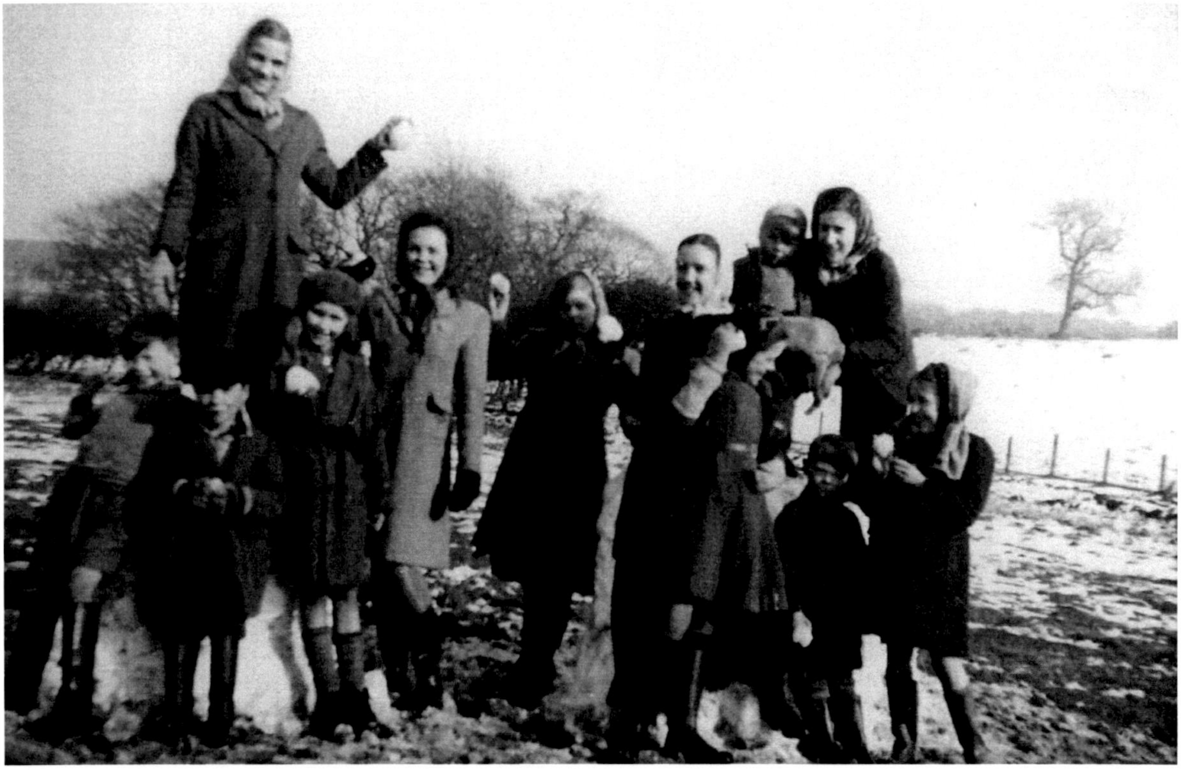

The addition here is the child Thomas Gray – and a dog![144]

[143] Photograph from Esther Shell (née Stewart) taken 1944.
[144] Photograph from Esther Shell (née Stewart) taken 1944.

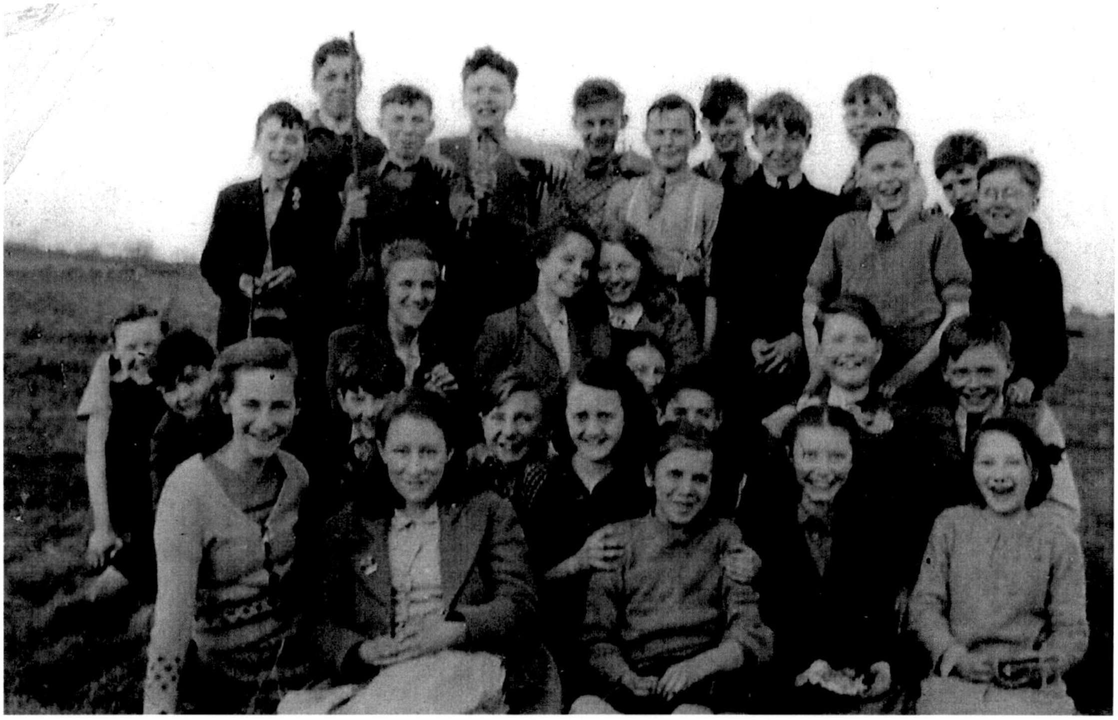

This group comprises a combination of Shilbottle and Bilton Banks youngsters.[145]

Top row, left to right: ?, Billy Pattinson, Harry Stewart, Ivan Robertson, Roger Harrison, Robin Wilson, Basil Scott, Brian Wilson, John Mather, Oswald Crisp, Billy Henderson, Brian Hall; middle row: Malcolm Lloyd, ?, Mary Anderson, Shirley Thompson, Joan Douglas, ?, Ian Nicholson, Jackie May; front row: Brenda Goodfellow, Hazel Pooley, George Tomlinson, Winnie Thompson, Alison Ogle, Edna Burton, Margaret Lorimer.

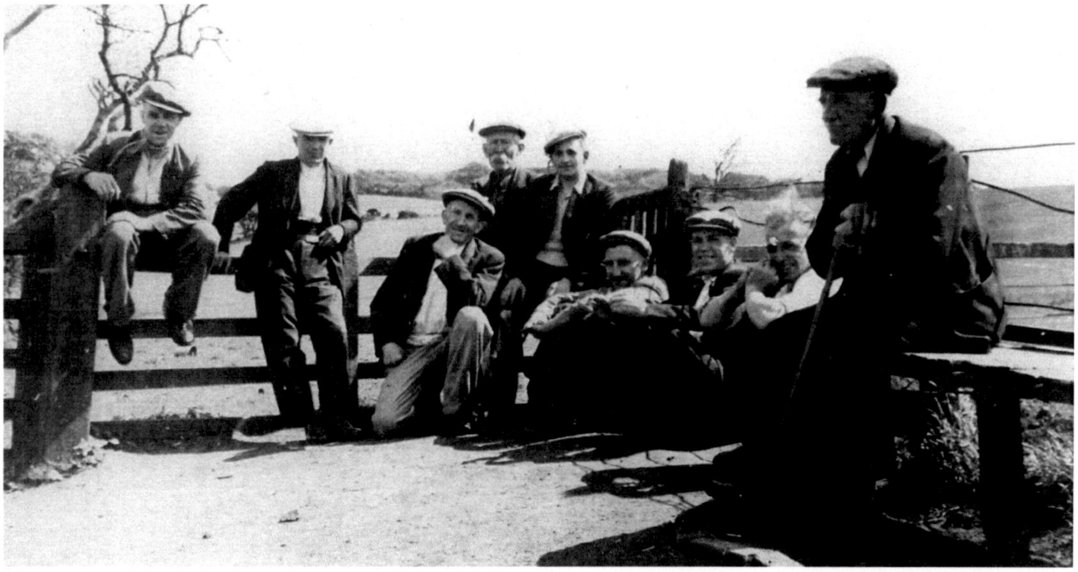

Left to right: Joe Pattinson, Johnnie Wilson, Jim Stewart (senior), Mr. Wood (father of Peg Douglas; grandfather of George Douglas),Verdun Straker, Jim Stewart (junior) Jim Douglas, Jack Douglas, and Ned Wheatley.[146]

[145] Photograph provided by Ronnie Knox. Names provided by Mary Anderson.
[146] Photograph, 1939, from Esther Shell (née Stewart) with complementary additions and name details from Mr. Raymond Straker.

The People of Bilton Banks and Longdyke

In any social history there are gaps which arise because information has not been unearthed; photographs have not been located; the researcher has failed to explore fruitful avenues of enquiry; or has been selective in his or her methodology. But even with an incomplete history it is possible to provide a picture of the people of Bilton Banks and Longdyke, many of whom speak fondly of the place they came from as 'home'.

So, acknowledging there will be gaping holes, the following pays tribute to lives past, people who mattered and people who contributed much to our collective memories.

Family historians will note the prevalence of their family names in the census data. Particular family names stand out because they have been recorded in Anglican and other records for generations. These include Burrell, Jeffrey, Riddell, Weightman and Wilson. Nearer to present day, it is names known to the researcher like Chrisp, Green, Patton, Punton, Straker and Ternent which are prominent.

It is clear that there were characters and people of special talent, who in a different generation would have had better opportunities to excel and find fulfilment beyond the dangers and extremes of tunnelling underground.

During the early days, most of the children of Shilbottle, whose fathers worked at Longdyke, received their primary education at the Church of England school at the west end of Shilbottle village.

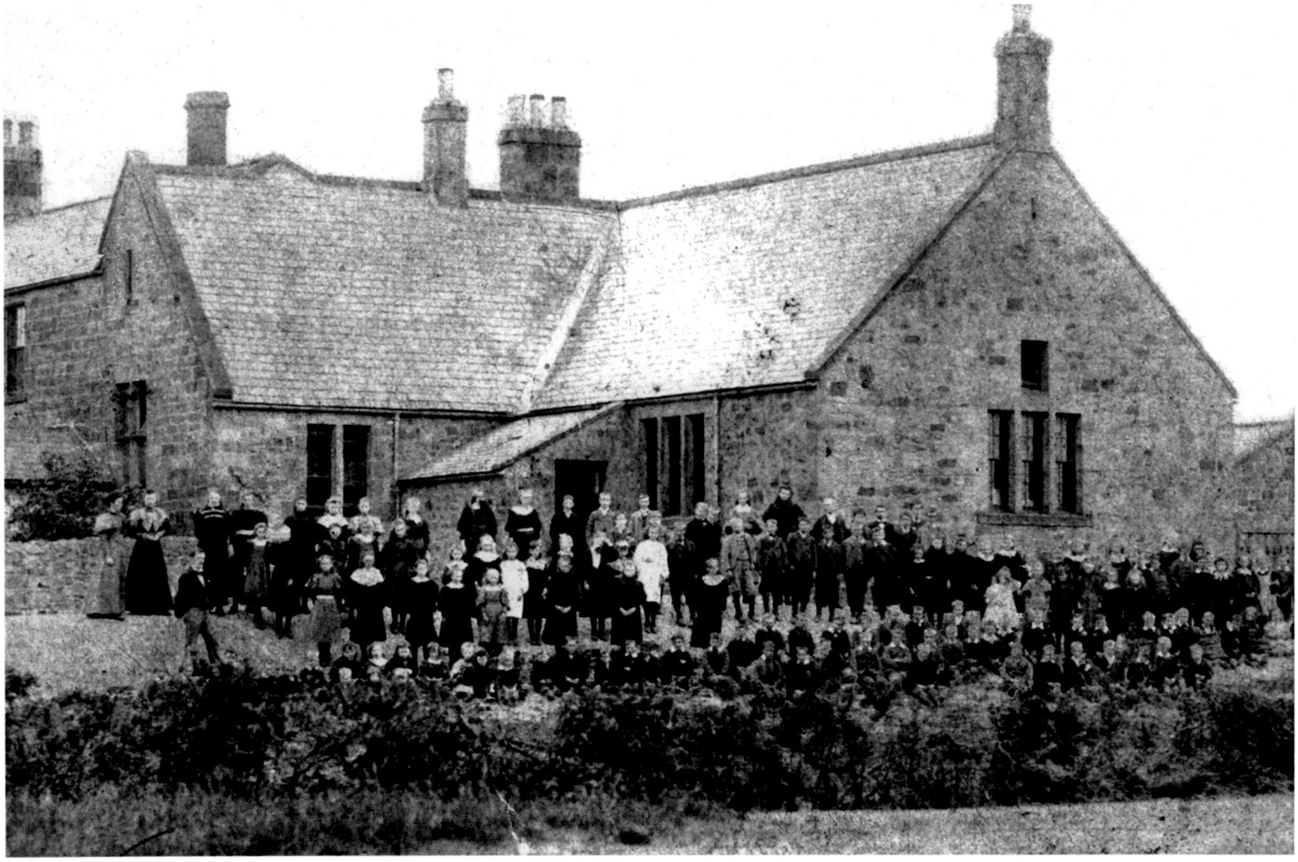

Shilbottle Church School *circa* 1900.

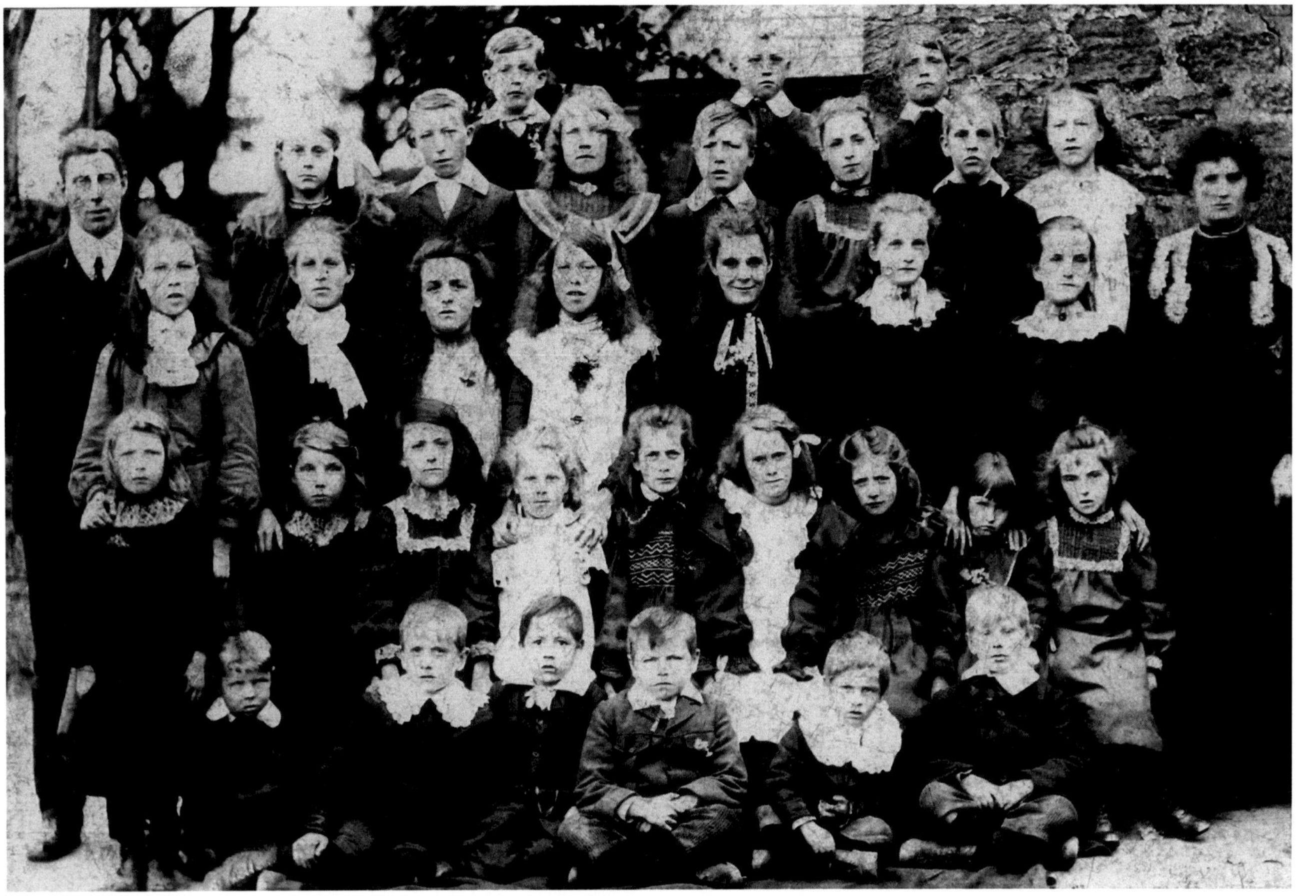

The Village School *circa* 1904.

Many children who excelled came from families who couldn't afford to send them forward to the grammar school. But going down the pit at fourteen or younger, didn't stop them from excelling in other fields. Joe Knox for example, whose camera captured some of the images shown throughout this text, was a man with a keen eye and special talent.

Oscar Green wrote poetry which revealed his command of language, his humour and his discerning eye.[147]

'There was an old lady of Alnwick,
whose statistic were something titanic,
now whenever she,
had baked beans for tea,
'mongst the neighbours
she caused quite a panic.'

[147] William Oscar Green 1917–1983

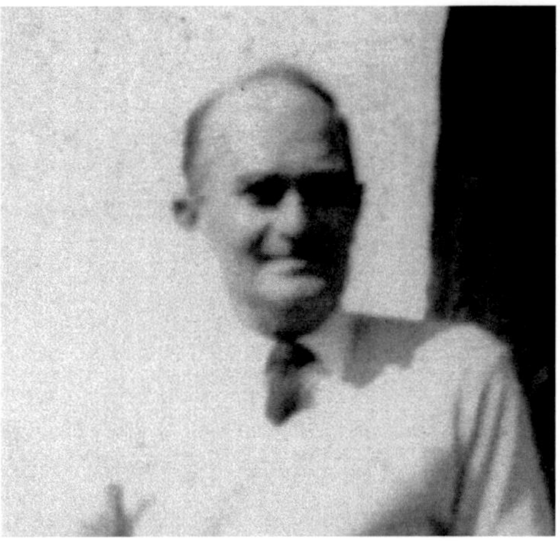

148

Oscar Green

As we have noted, Oscar's brother, John Green, wrote accounts of mining at Longdyke and of life in the village of Bilton Banks. As a young man he was an accomplished footballer as well as an amateur historian.

Mr. Harry Air, as we have seen, progressed through every level of coal mine production to hold the position of 'Overman' at Shilbottle Grange Pit. Mr. Air had a mind for fine detail and a concise way of expressing himself.

Roger Harrison, from a later era, invented mining machinery, started his own business and diversified to provide residential nursing care in a purposely adapted hotel at Whitley Bay.

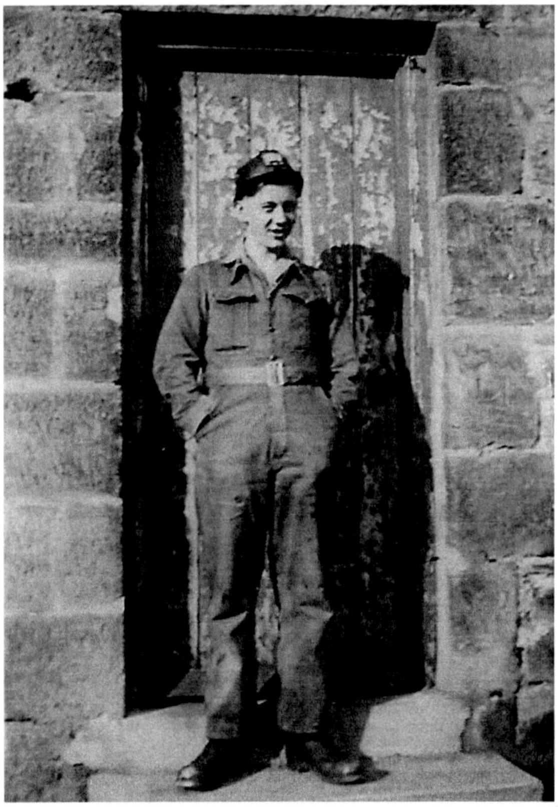

Roger Harrison aged 16

[148] From Mr. Billy McKnight's collection.

The women showed entrepreneurial skills too. Granny Douglas (Peg) ran a small retail business from her home at the top of the Short Row. Most learned how to make mats and the best of their hard existence. Many married from the village and went on to forge successful lives with their families. Gwen Inglis and Winnie Straker were often at the centre of village activities, supporting the sporting prowess of their husbands and children. Some ladies survived early widow-hood brought on by industrial diseases and disaster, and some moved on to new places – London, New Zealand and elsewhere.

Gardening and vegetable growing has been mentioned earlier as a pleasurable and important outdoor activity for miners. So was sport, particularly football.

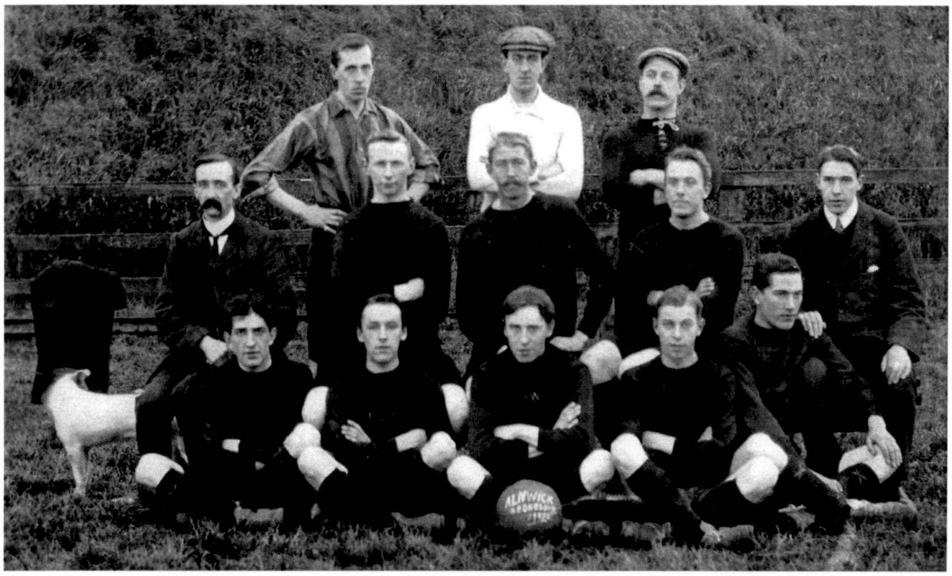
[149]

The team which participated as Alnwick Wednesday 1902-03

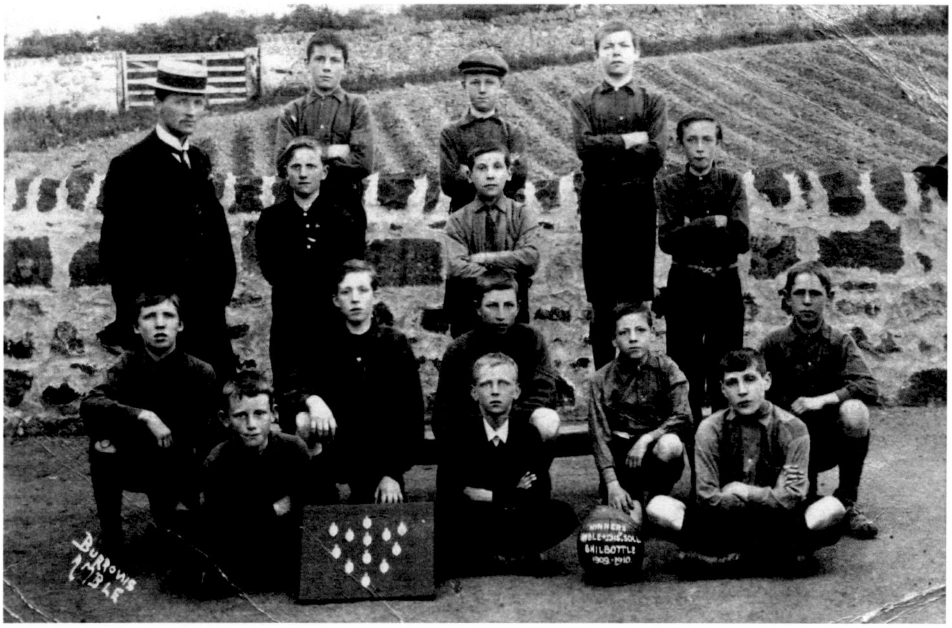
[150]

The winning Shilbottle team of the Amble and District school league 1909-1910. Harry Stewart on the extreme left, his brother Johnnie on the extreme right.

[149] Photograph from the author's collection.
[150] Photograph from the author's collection.

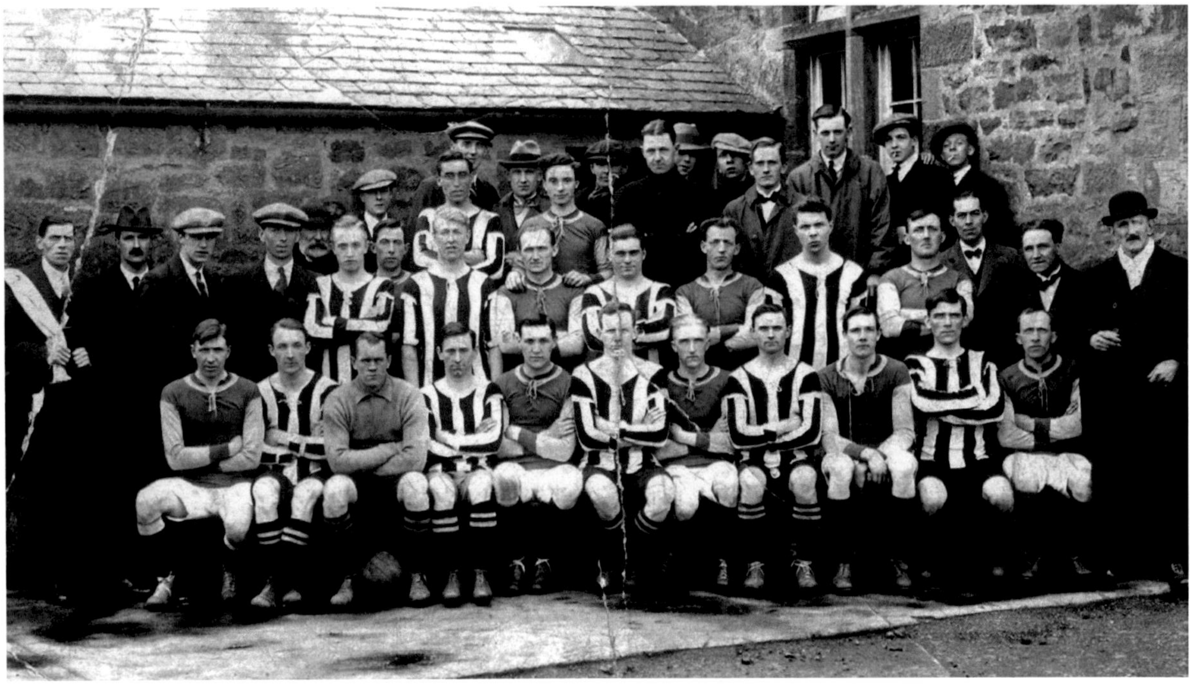

151

Shilbottle's football team in 1915. Johnnie Stewart seated on extreme left.

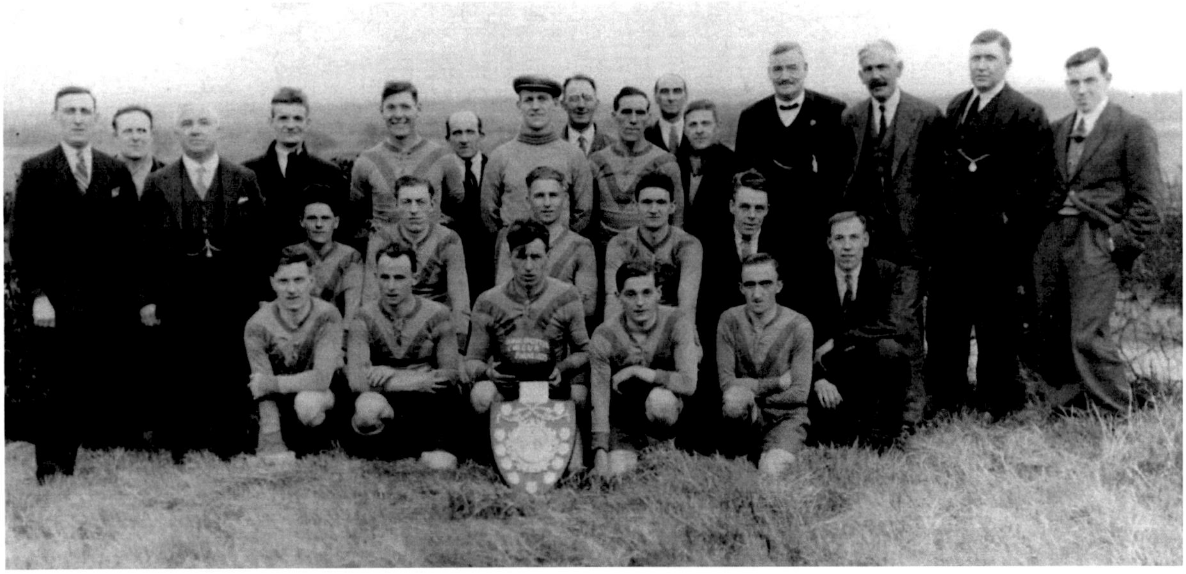

152

Shilbottle's team after winning the CWS Cup final in 1934 with the colliery manager Mr. Coverdale Anderson 3rd from the left.

Back row, left to right: J. Toward, Ned Sim, Mr. Coverdale Anderson, R. Trotter, Harry Wood, J. Tully, Sam Buglass, A. Allen, Jack Wilson, J.W. Ternent, Tom Baxter, A. Moffat, J.J. Stewart, J. Thompson; middle row, left to right: Jim Madden, Mark Swan, G. Batey, R. Slater, Joe Pattinson, W. Casson; Front Row, – kneeling left to right: J. Brown, T. Bell, Tom Hodgson, W. Green, A. Graham.

Discerning eyes will note the degree of continuity in these pictures (and a certain family bias), schoolboy players becoming adult players and then committee members.

---

151 Photograph from the author's collection.

152 Photograph from the author's collection.

Singing too was popular but not always entirely seriously as the image taken in 1914 outside the Shilbottle Parish Room shows.

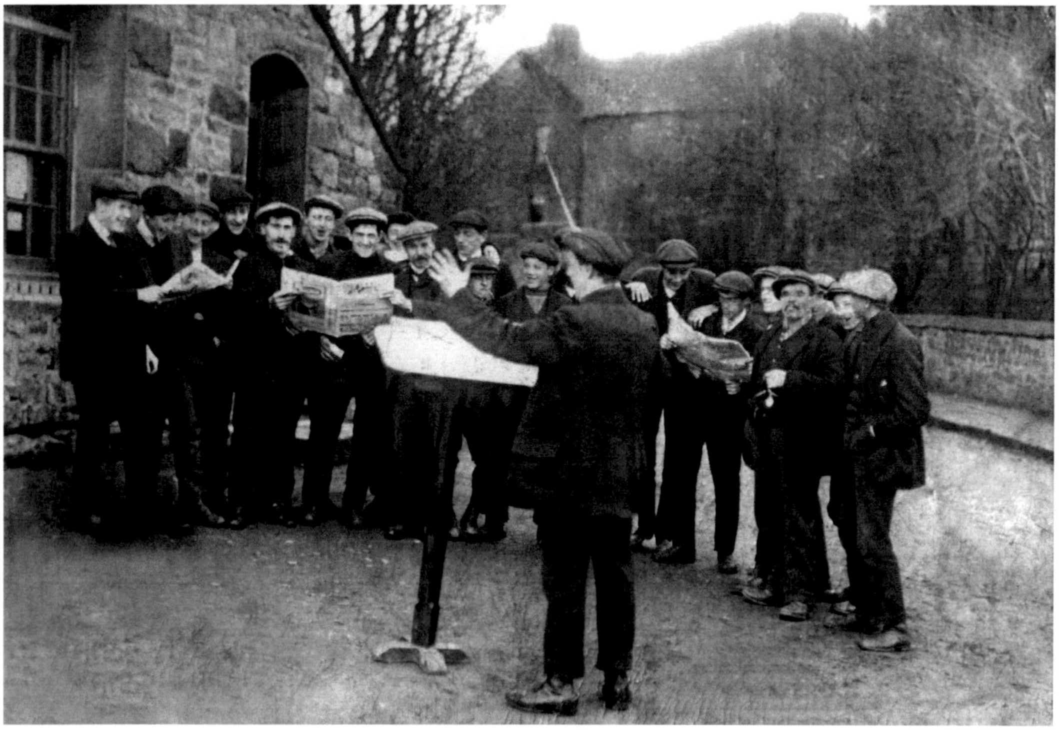

153

Johnnie Stewart is second from the left; Ned Donaldson is to his right. The 'conductor' is John Swordy. The men were all probably employed at Longdyke Colliery.

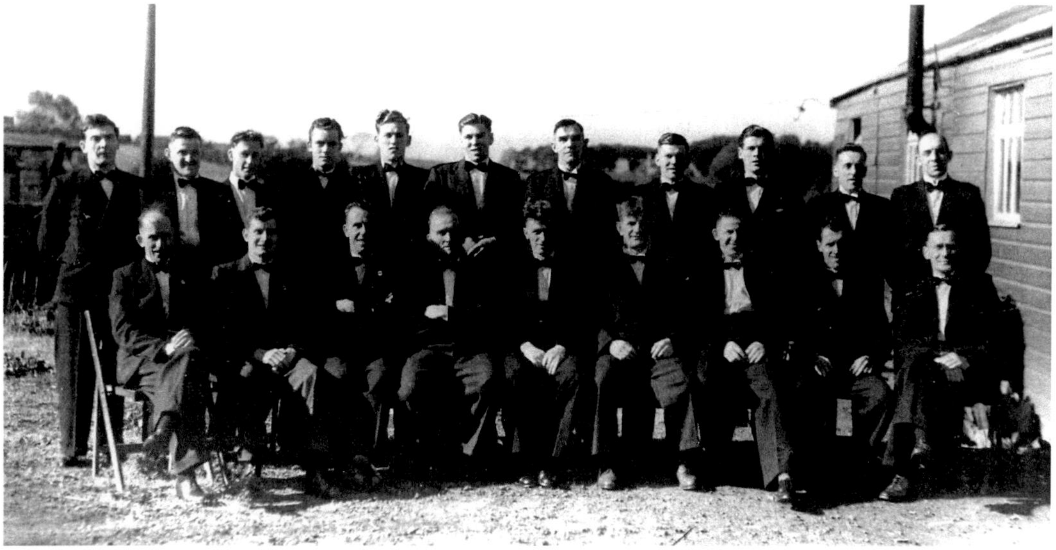

154

This more formal image of Shilbottle choir is taken in the 1950s and includes some former residents of the houses at Bilton Banks.

Back row, left to right: Tom Pearson, Thomas Ternent, ? Bill Gray, Tom Gray, Dick Punton, Jackie Gray, Tommy Prentice, Ernie Rennison, Jimmy Buglass; front row, left to right: Jackie Agnew, Alf James, Bob Hall, Geordie Easton, Norman Henderson (choir master), Bob Trotter, Jimmy Ternent, Brent Snaith.

[153] Photograph from the author's collection.
[154] Photograph provided by Mr. Tom Pattinson.

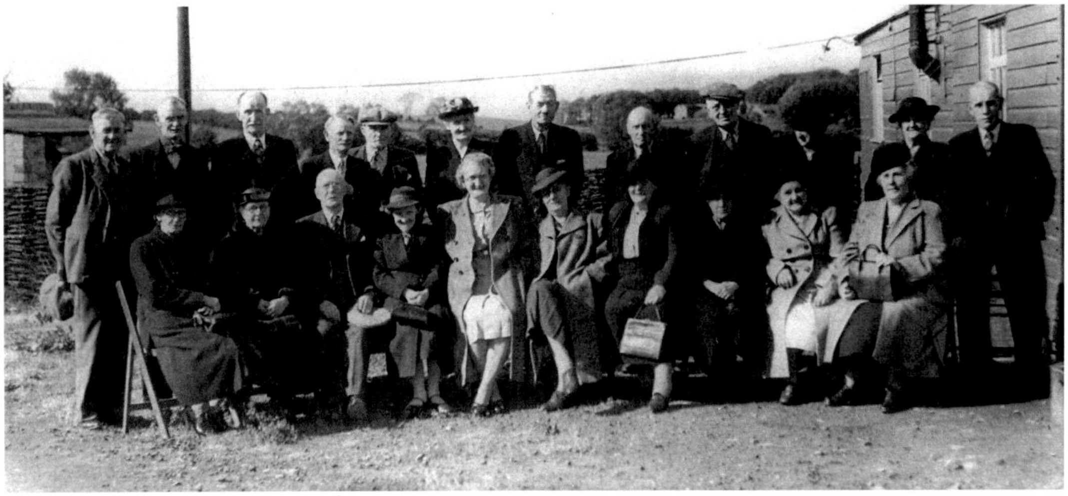

155

Taken at the same location and including former residents of Bilton Banks including – Back row: Mr. Middlemist, C. Billanie, Mrs. Murray, Tom Baxter, Mr. Willcox; front row: Mrs. Brand, Mary Weightman, Mrs. Knox, and Alice Baxter.[156]

Stepping back a few decades, the Great European conflict of the First World War, between 1914 and 1918, saw a number of miners from Longdyke volunteering for service.

The Iron and Coal Trades Review newspaper for 30th July 1915 reported: *Whole regiments had been recruited from colliery districts and there was one regiment in which every private was a pit-man, every officer was connected with a colliery and the commanding officer himself was one of H M Inspectors of Mines. On the whole miners have contributed 250,000 men to the new armies.*

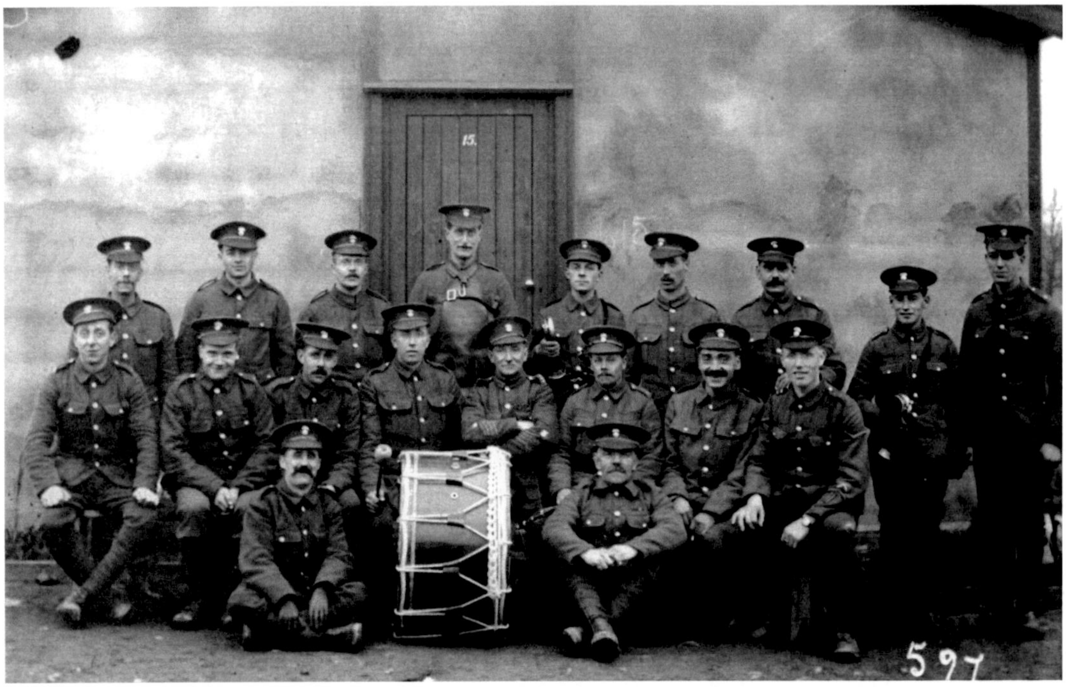

A contingent of local men who joined the Fusiliers – this image was taken at Catterick on 17th December 1916 with Johnnie Stewart in the centre, with the big drum.

[155] Photograph provided by Mr. Tom Pattinson.

[156] Extracted from the Shilbottle Colliery Agreements and Joint Committee ledger in the archive of Mrs Joyce Snaith

More than a third of the workforce at Longdyke went to war. Many did not return including:

Robert Baxter	George W. Buglass	Thomas Charlton
Robert Green	Joseph R. Hall	John Hindhaugh
George Slater	John Smails	William Smails
James Thompson	Alexander J. Tweedy	Thomas H. Weightman
Brian B. Weightman	Robert C. Weightman	James J. Wilson
Mossman Wilson	William Wilson	Martin Young

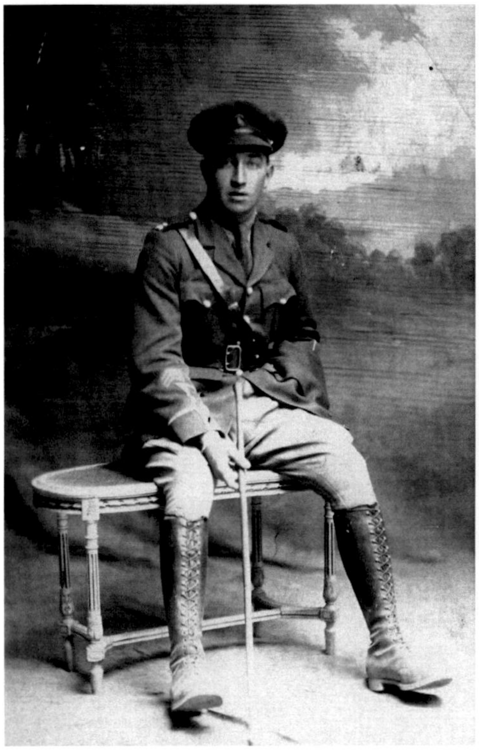

Henry (Harry) Stewart

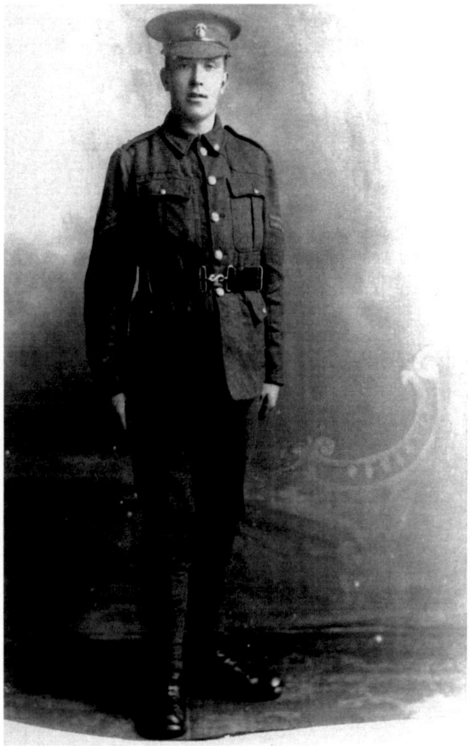

John James (Johnnie) Stewart

Harry Stewart and his older brother John James Stewart, who were both miners at Longdyke Pit, went with the 7th Battalion Northumberland Fusiliers to France. John James (the author's grandfather) returned injured. Harry was physically unscathed but was killed by a fall of stone in Shilbottle Pit on 8th November 1934. Joe Knox, the cameraman, whose photograph is featured earlier, was with him when the stone collapsed. Harry and Johnnie Stewart's father, Storey Stewart was also a miner at Longdyke.

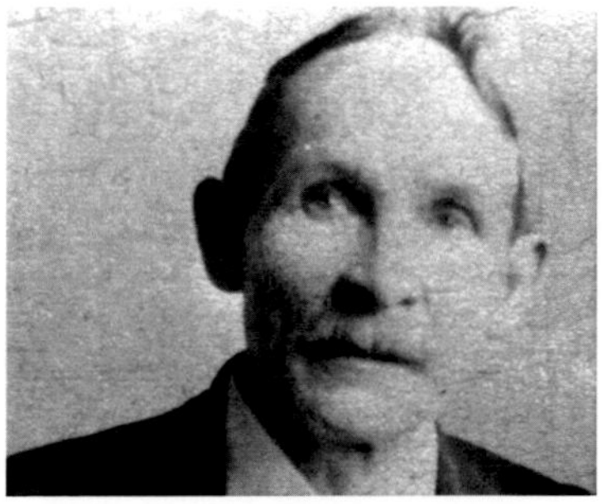
[157]

Storey Stewart *circa* 1919

[157] Above three photographs from the author's collection.

The name of Knox resounds around Shilbottle and there are many branches of the family. Below are the descendants of Thomas Knox, who had families to his first and second wives. William, the second son to his first wife had fifteen children including George born in 1898 and Margaret born 1900. George and Dora lived first in the Rows at Bilton Banks and then in the Colliery Yard.

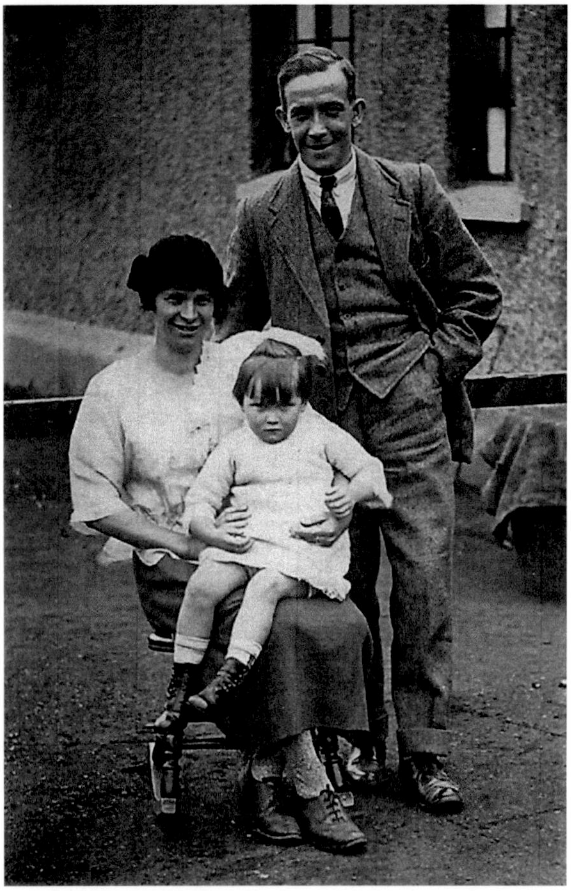

Nora (née Egdell) and George Knox, with their daughter Florrie at Colliers Close, Shilbottle, 1923.

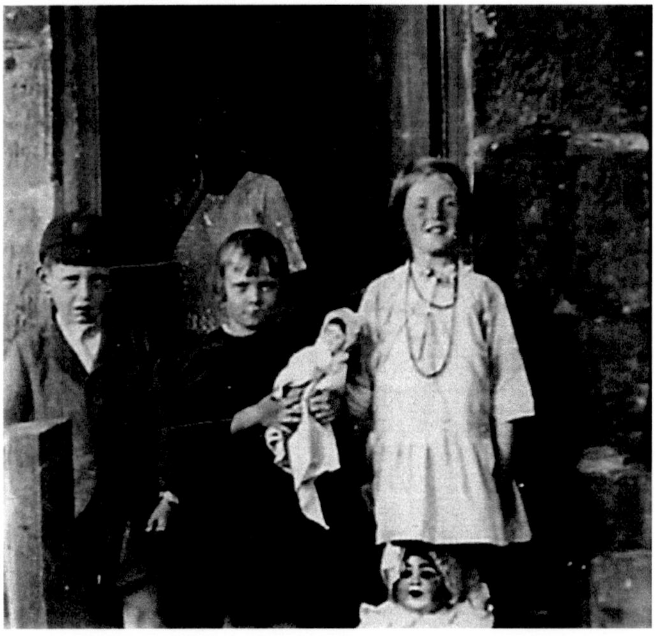

Florrie with her doll and friends: Dora in the doorway in 1926.

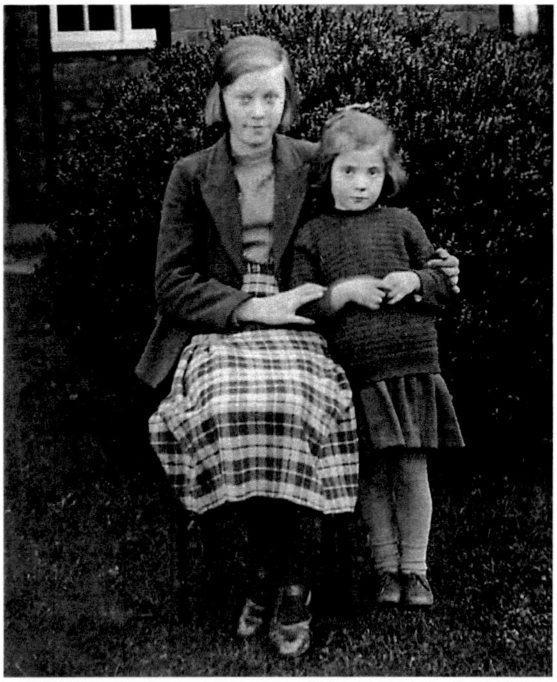

Florrie Knox with her sister Nina at Shilbottle School 1931.

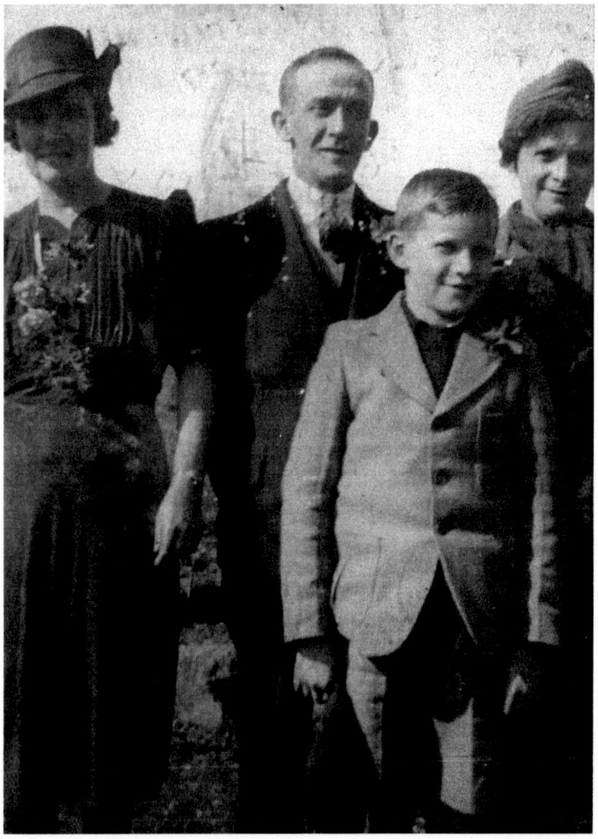

[158]

Margaret Mercel (née Knox, formerly Bowart), George Knox, and George Knox (Jnr.) and Dora Knox in 1941 at Collier's Cottage, Bilton Banks prior to the marriage of Florrie Knox to her cousin George Bowart. Dora Knox was formerly one of the Egdell 'clan', whose family lived in the Long Row.

[158] The four photographs above provided by Peter Bowart. Both the ladies in the last photograph were his grandmothers. See John Green's earlier references to close-knit communities.

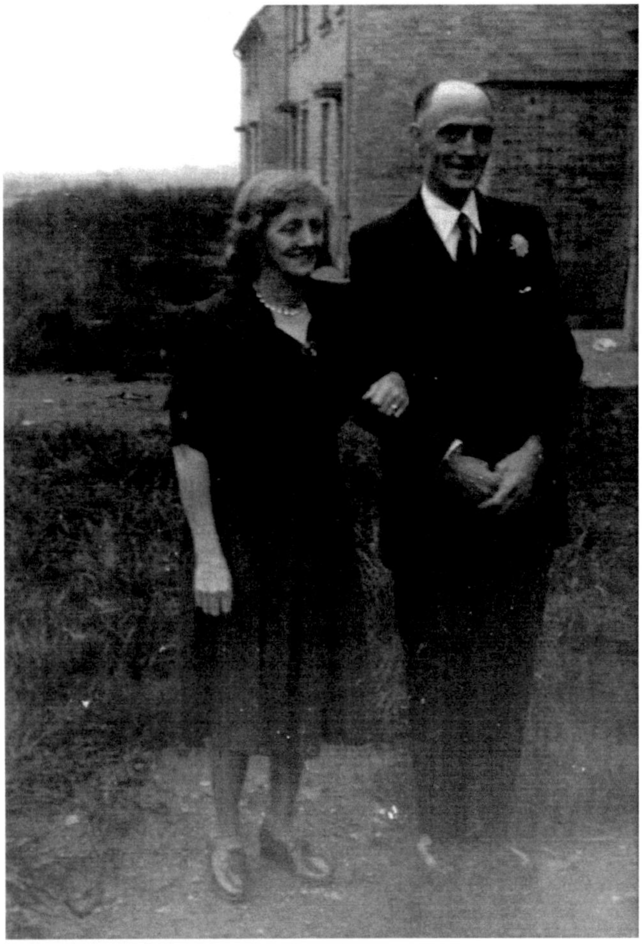

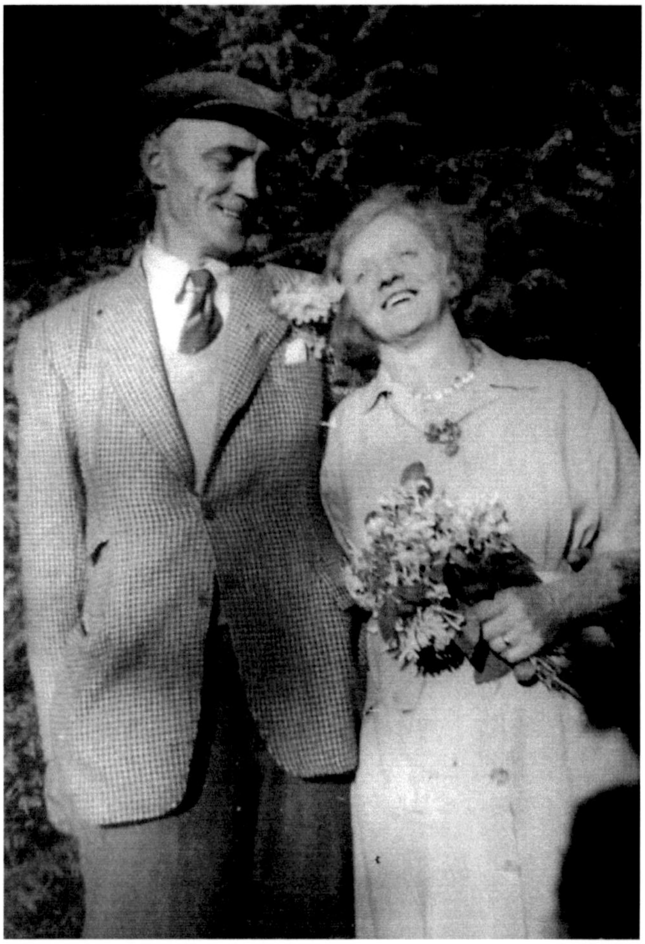

Margaret and William Raymond Egdell – were also long-term residents at Bilton Banks – and their children, Samuel, Gordon, Margery and Mildred were born there.

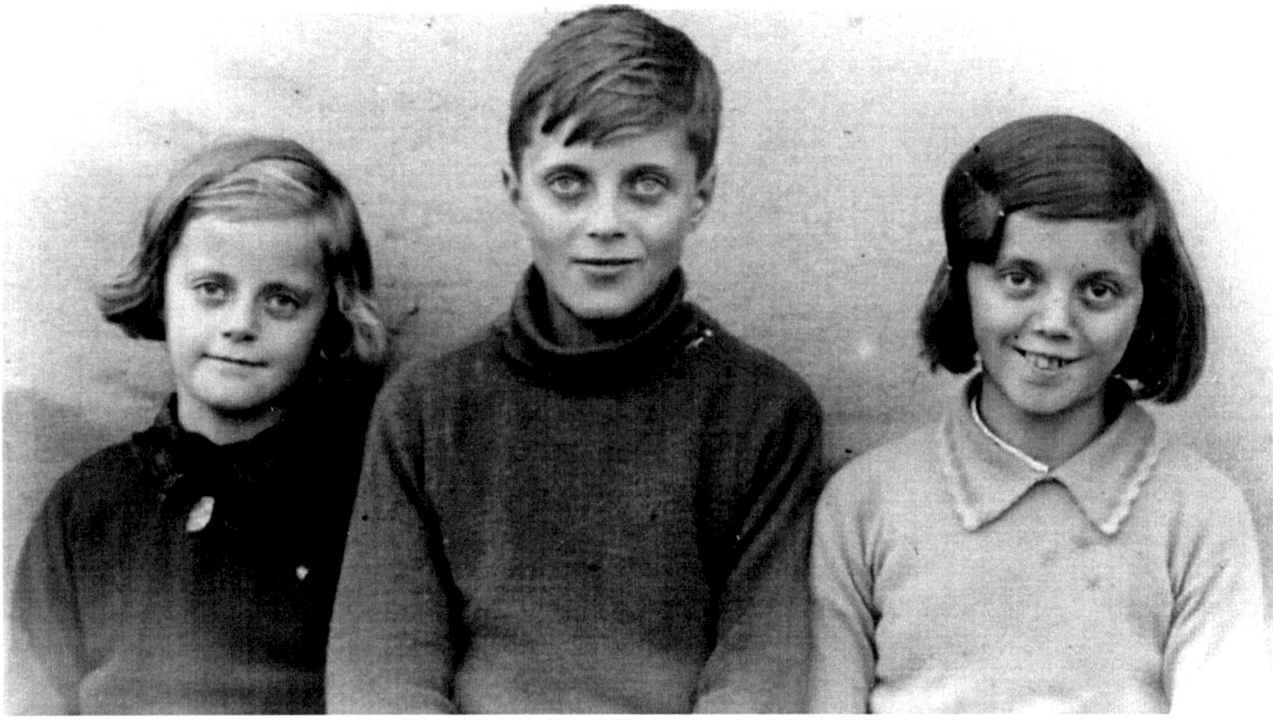

Margery, Samuel and Mildred Egdell *circa* 1942

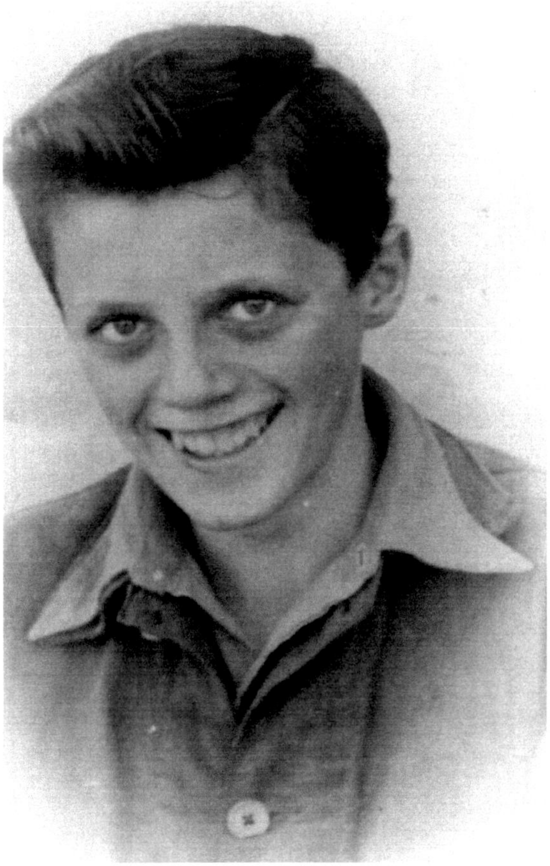

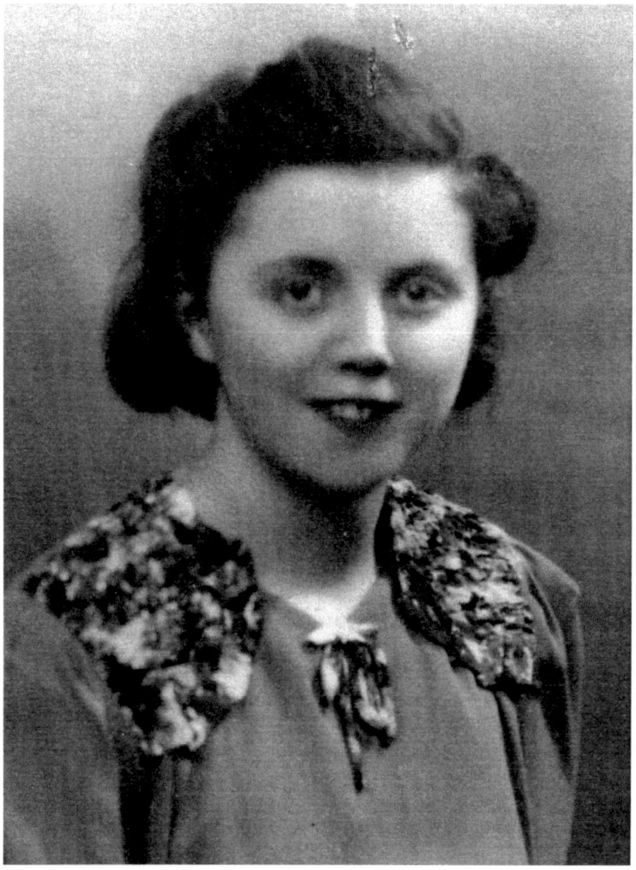

Gordon and Mildred Egdell

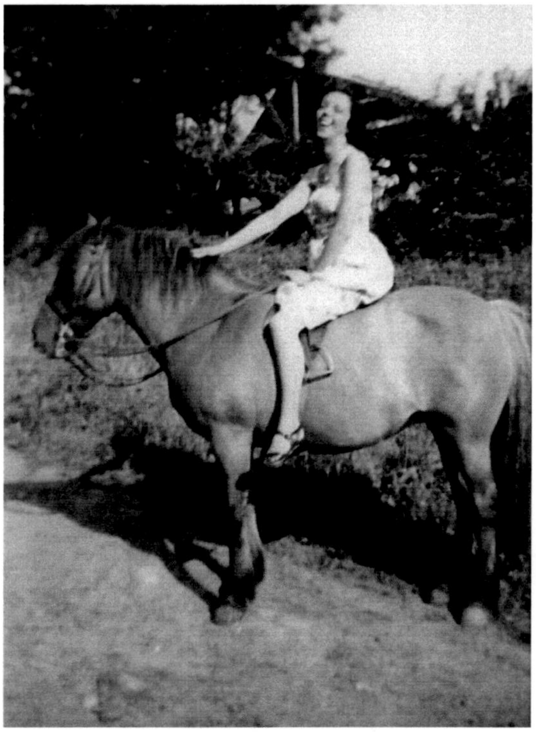

[159]

Mildred Egdell

[159] All six photographs from Gordon Egdell's collection.

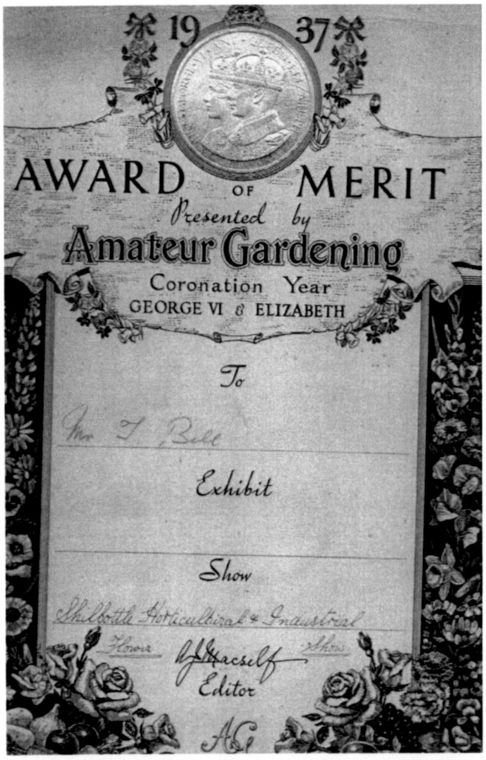

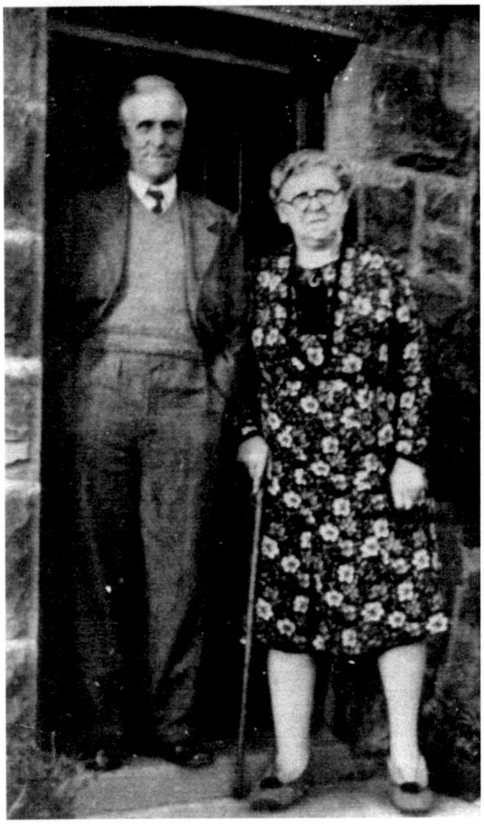

Above: Tommy Bell, with his wife Sarah (Sinna) at a later time.[161]

Gordon Egdell, when interviewed in November 2011, spoke of being quarantined as an infant when he was diagnosed with scarlet fever. He was moved out of the village and put in the isolation hospital which was then in the middle of a field midway between Alnwick and Deancroft. It was a primitive, corrugated-metal building. His parents couldn't visit; their only contact was through frantic waving at the hospital's windows. After six weeks in 'isolation' there he said that he was as much attached to his nurse – Bertha Knox, as he was to any of his relatives.[160] Notwithstanding surviving that experience, he contended that he was a lucky bloke to be alive. One afternoon, aged about nine or ten, when returning from the Council School in Shilbottle, he and Geordie Douglas were having *a bit of daft carry-on*. First they bought a bread bun off the baker in Collier's Close *because we were scranny* and then they pelted up the long field towards home. Their daftness carried on until they reached the pit yard. Geordie, out of breath, went straight for the stand-pipe outside Gordon's aunt Dora's house. *He had 'a canny' drink and then with his wet hands he took a dive for the pole we used as a sort of swing, something like a May-pole. The pole carried the electric cable to the manager's house. Geordie's fingers were dripping when he grabbed hold of the electric cable. Straight off, he shouted 'A'm dying', and that's what it looked like. His feet were off the ground and he was being threshed about like washing on a line in a gale. I didn't have time to think but if I'd grabbed him I would have been a gonner. I was lucky, I just shoulder charged him and knocked Geordie full length sprawling into the yard. His hands were all burnt and honest I thought Geordie was going to die. I ran up the Long Row shouting 'Geordie's dying'.*

Help arrived; Geordie's burnt hands were dressed and both boys survived for Gordon to tell the tale. Hopefully, the manager eliminated the danger for future young adventurers, but of that there is no record. At a later time, Gordon recalls that top-soil from his father's expertly tilled garden was removed after the family had moved to Shilbottle village. Gordon's dad was *a class gardener* and the colliery manager had the soil dug out for the garden at his house at the Grange Pit.

Raymond Egdell wasn't the only competent gardener. In the Coronation year of 1937, Tommy Bell was awarded 'Merit' in the Shilbottle Horticultural and Industrial Show.

---

[160] Bertha Knox was his aunt Dora's sister-in-law.

[161] Images provided by Audrey Bell (née Snaith) who features in the snow scene shown earlier.

Audrey Snaith and her parents lived at number 8 Long Row and their house was one of the last to be demolished in 1952.

[162]

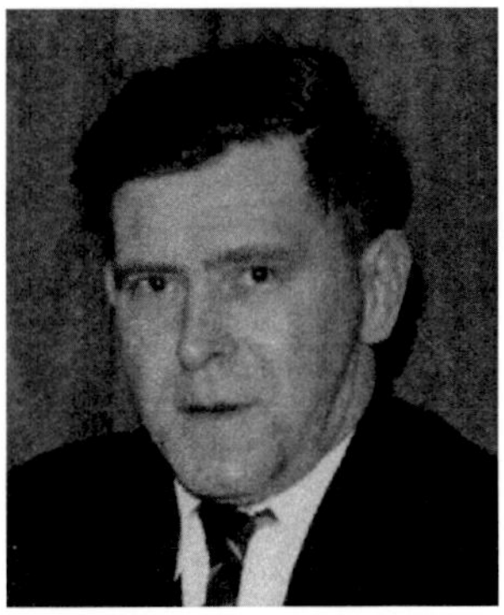

Lexie Bell

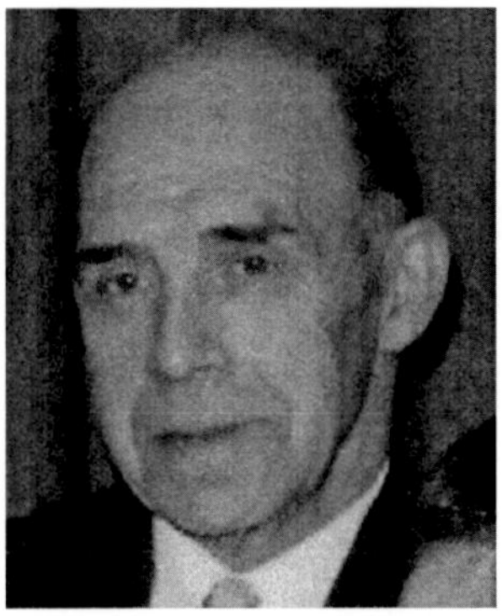

Jimmy Buglass

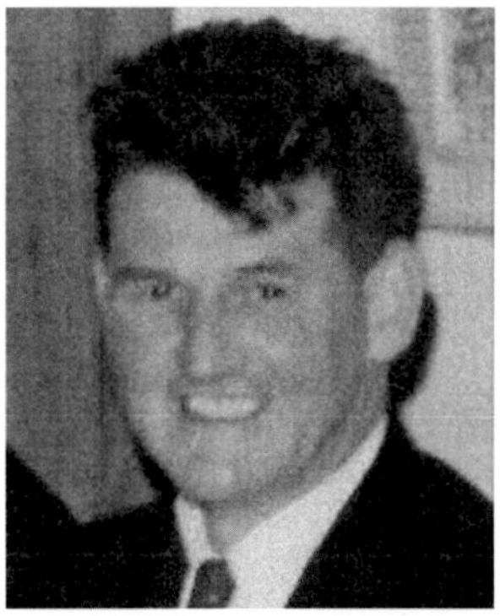

Jackie Ternent

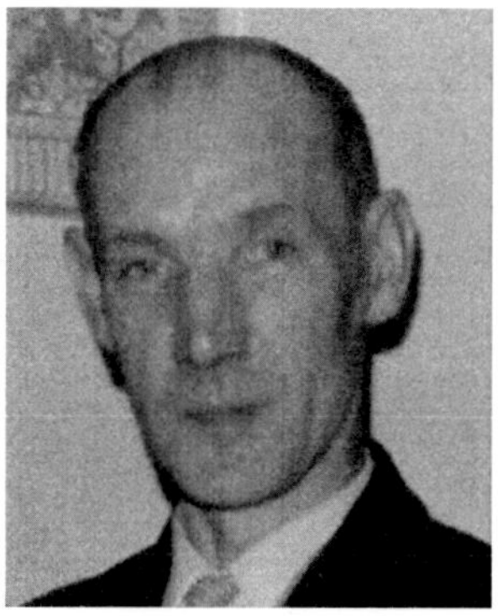

Alf Weightman

Further down the Long Row was Sadie Rennison (née Swordy)'s family

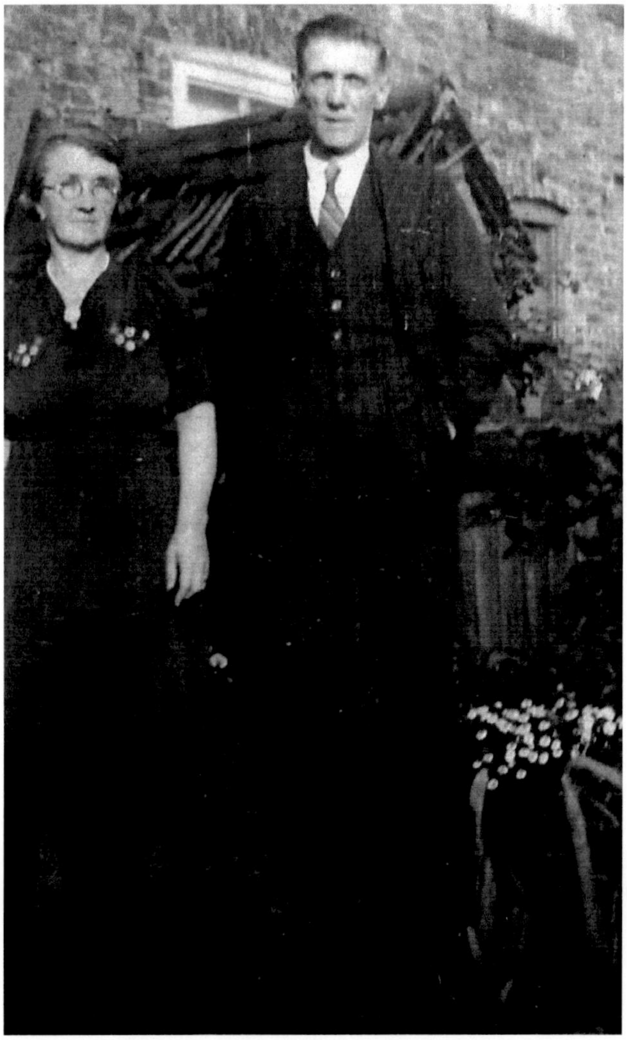

Jean Ann and John Swordy.

[162] Images cropped from a photograph of the Hussars dinner, provided by Audrey Bell – Lexie (George Alexander Bell) being Audrey's husband.

Next door to the Swordy family were the Rennisons and in due course Eric Rennison and Sadie Swordy were to be married. Before that happy event in 1947, there was a bit of growing to do.

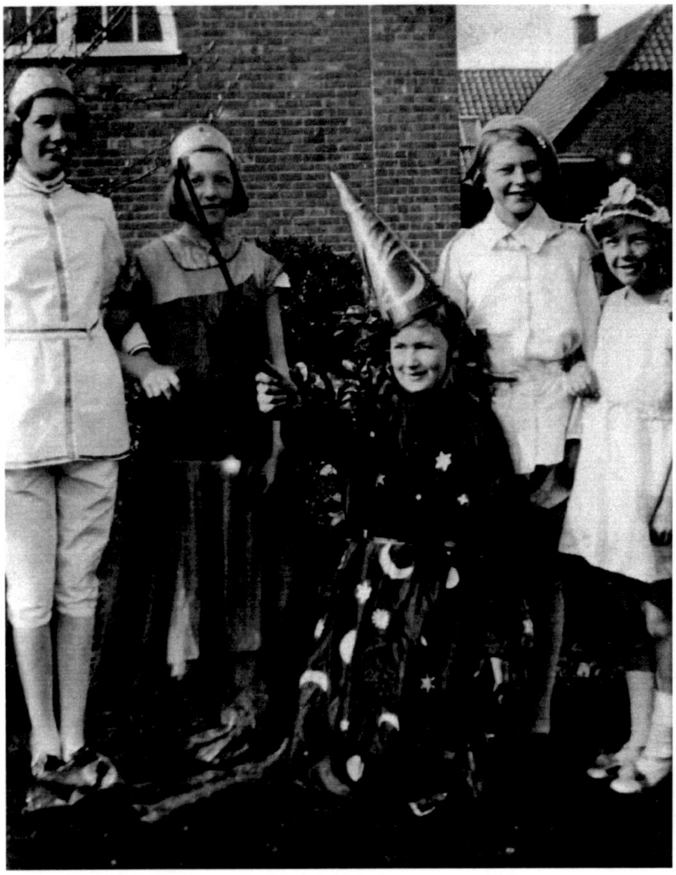

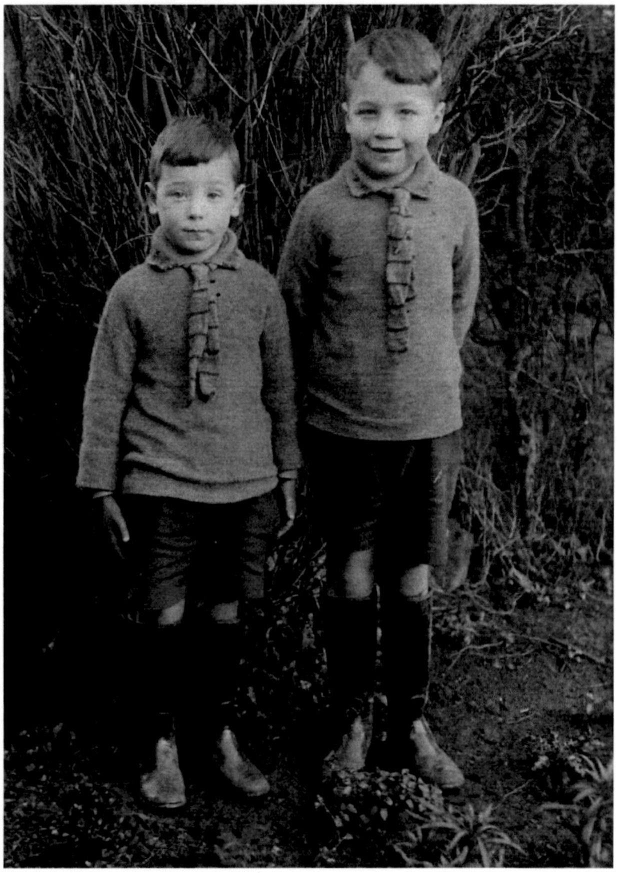

Above left: Elaine Weightman, Betty Swordy, Rene Inglis, Sylvia Punton and Sadie Swordy in a play at Shilbottle Council School, 1936.

Above right: Ron and Eric Rennison at Bilton Banks, 1932.

As happened in 1914, many men from Bilton Banks and Shilbottle joined up at the commencement of hostilities with Germany in 1939.

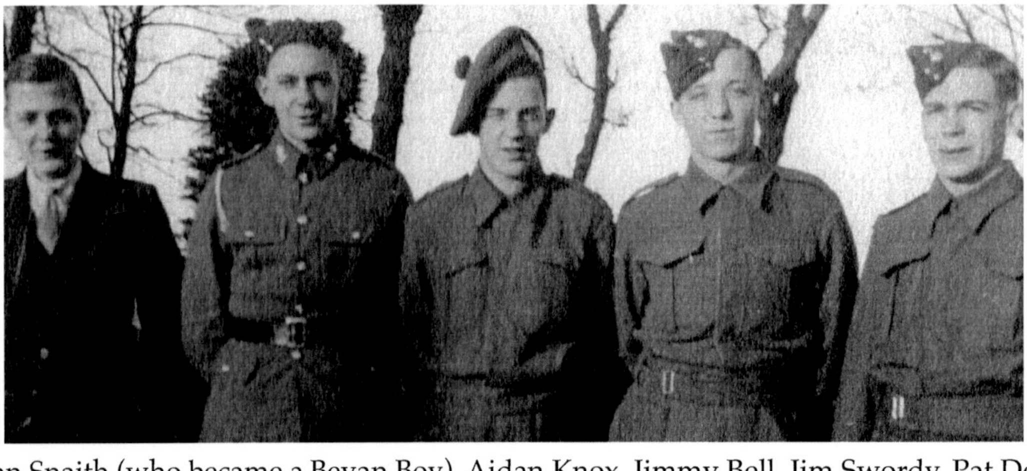
[163]

Norman Snaith (who became a Bevan Boy), Aidan Knox, Jimmy Bell, Jim Swordy, Pat Douglas.

[163] Above four photographs from Sadie Rennison's collection.

Roger Harrison's family were relatively late comers to Bilton Banks, but Roger (shown earlier) started work from there.

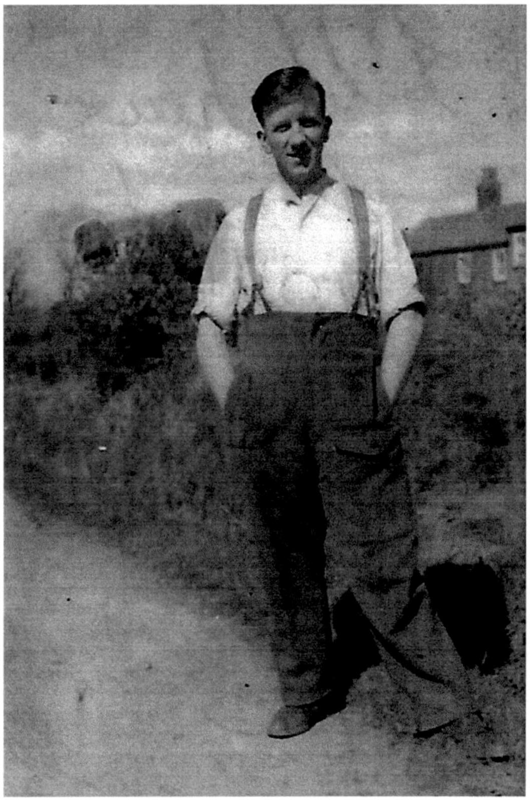

Henry William Harrison with the Long Row in the background.

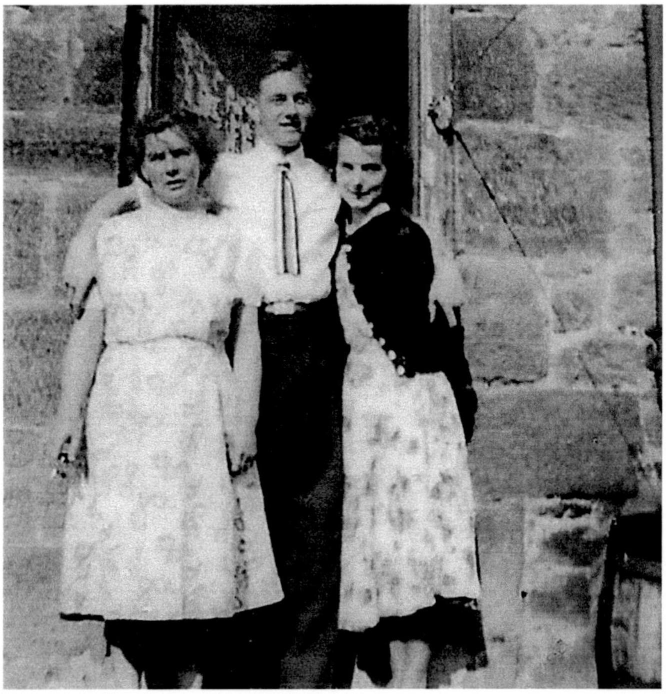

[164]

Roger Harrison with his mother Roberta (Robin) and Shirley Thompson. The Harrison's rain barrel is partially visible (as is their flaking back door).

[164] Above two images from Mr. Roger Harrison's collection.

The image (1951) below is not of Bilton Banks or Longdyke, but shows men who had worked there. They are placing cement plates around a dug-out for a settling pool to catch orange and black water which was seeping from the colliery's waste heaps and contaminating the water supply – including that of the single stand-pipe at Bilton Banks.

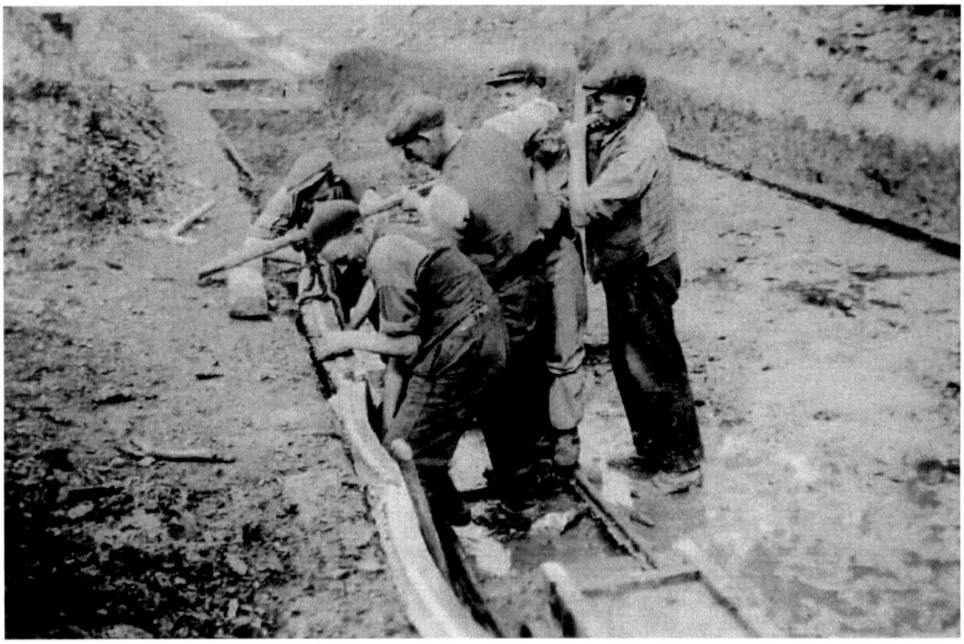

165

The men are – W. Lynn, Harry Lynn, Bill Shephed, C. Lillico and J. Ternent.

The Middlemist family may have been some of the people affected by poor water quality because they lived at Bilton Banks and later at Lesbury and Shilbottle. James Middlemist, on the left was blacksmith at Longdyke *circa* 1903 up until the outbreak of the war in 1914. In later life he was groundsman at Shilbottle Welfare.

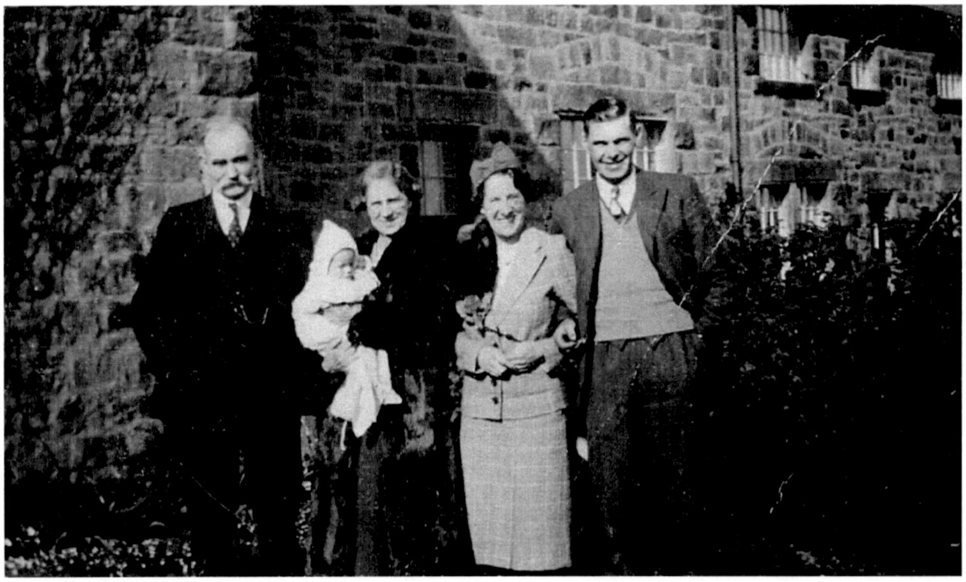

166

James Middlemist with his wife Ann (née Forrest of Shilbottle) and his son George and his wife Margaret (née Jobson).

[165] From Mr. Alan Gilholm's collection.
[166] From Mr. Ken Middlemist's collection.

James Middlemist was a skilled craftsman. In September 1918, an art exhibition of paintings, music and handicrafts was held in Baghdad. James was serving there during the First World War.

In the Exhibition class for metalwork, the 2nd and 3rd prizes were won by Private Middlemist, for his carved workbox and carved panel. The Committee of the Exhibition selected both exhibits for presentation to the Imperial War Museum in London.

The End of a Working Community

So, the 'Long and the Short' of this history is that, in due course, conditions underground made the winning of coal in Longdyke Pit too arduous, dangerous and unprofitable. The pit closed on 19th August 1925. When it did, most of the workforce moved to the Grange Pit.

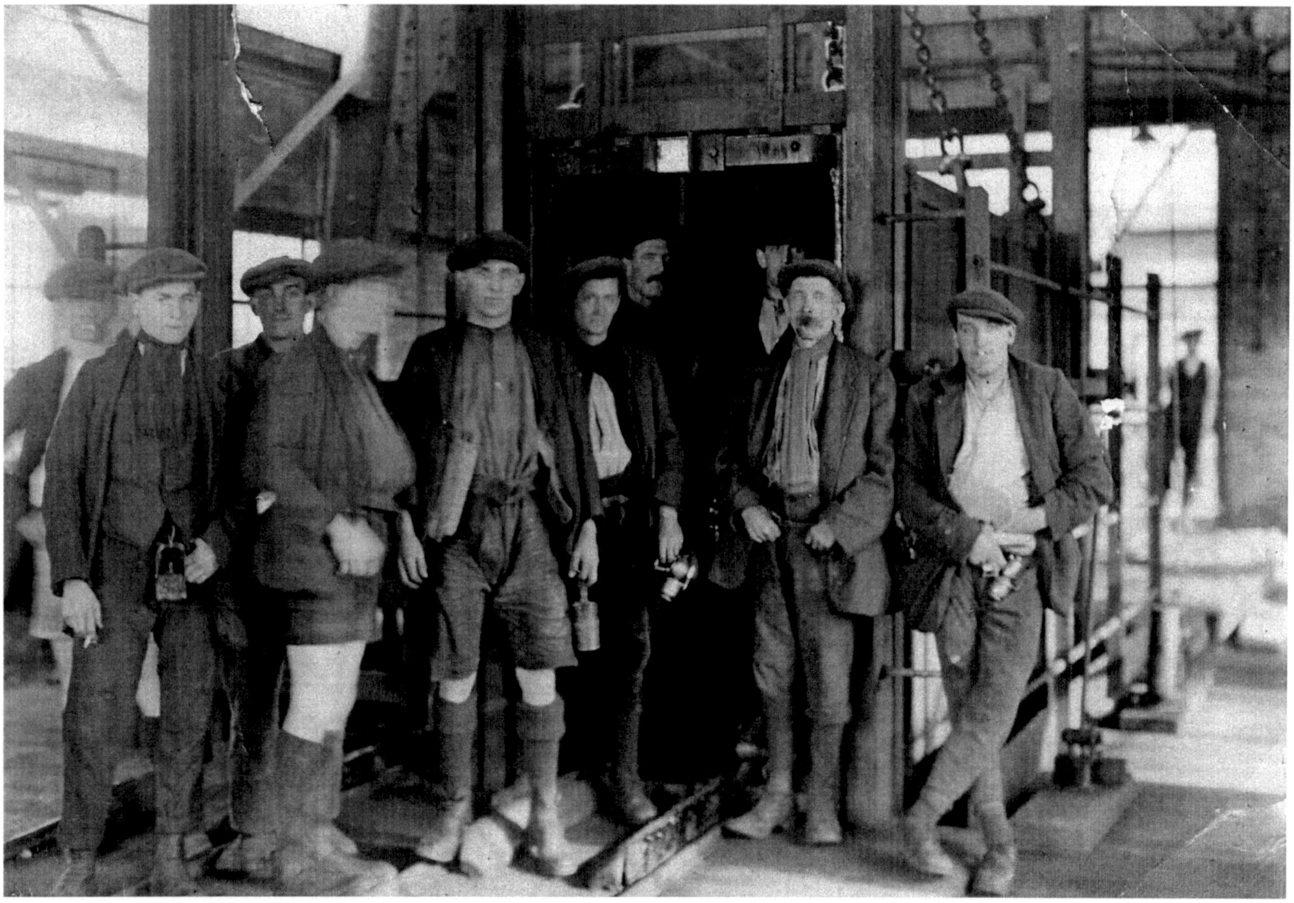

Above, some of the workforce (pre-1947) is ready to take the 'cage' from the North Shaft into the bowels of Grange Pit.[167] They and their colleagues would do this for another 35 years.

However, in 1982 the Grange Pit also closed and overleaf is the image of the North Shaft, in the process of being professionally capped.

Now, at that location, like Longdyke, there is little to remind passers by that once a colliery sustained a large workforce and a whole community.

[167] Photograph provided by Mrs Margery Slater.

168

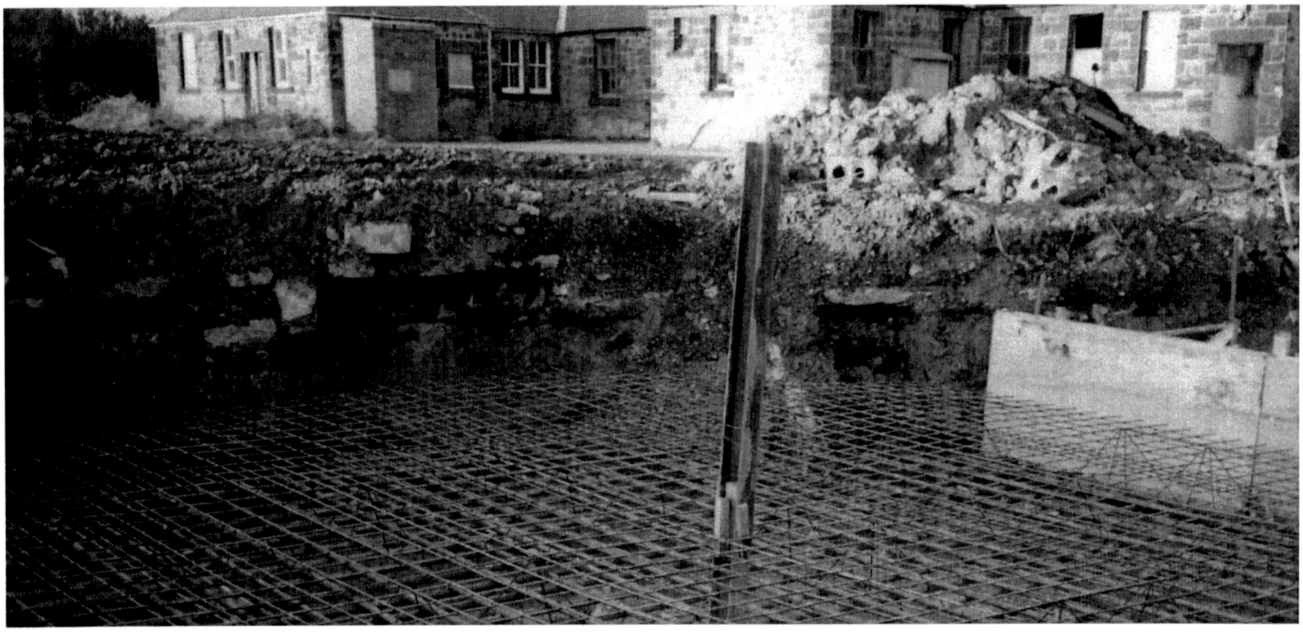

In the mid 1950s, after the workforce from Longdyke had relocated to Shilbottle Grange Pit, the houses at Bilton were demolished, but the foundations were still visible. Between 1973 and 1977 the site was finally cleared and the land restored to farmland.

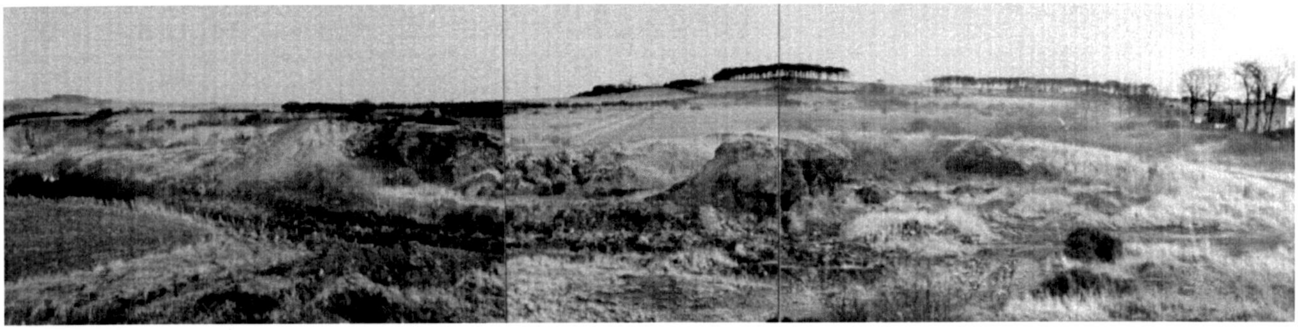

169

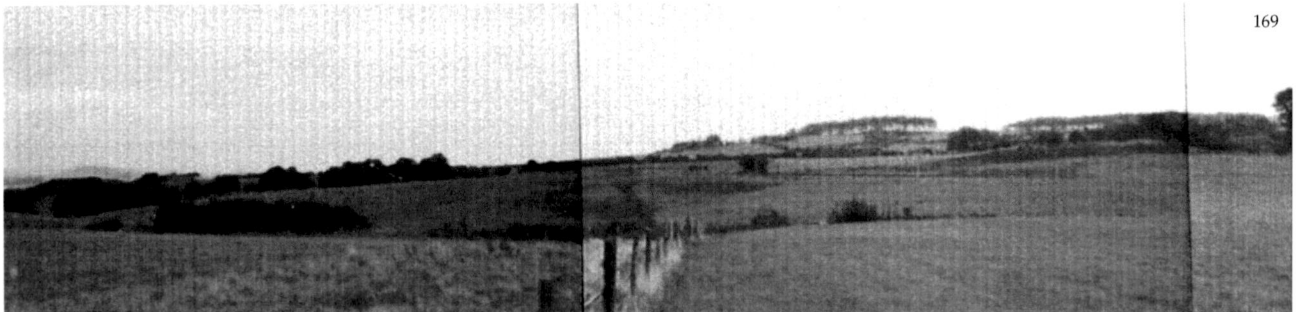

Beneath the reclaimed land, at Bilton Banks there are tunnels and waterways which have witnessed human endeavour over three quarters of a century. Present day visitors to the area may have no knowledge or comprehension of what went before, but I hope this small book will have helped remind people of times past. I hope also that my work has properly honoured, with respect and gratitude, those who lived at Bilton Banks and worked at Longdyke.

Barry Stewart

---

168 Photograph from Mr. Dave Young, Greenrigg, Bilton.
169 Northumberland Estates Archives reference AF: T 478.

Appendix 1

Census returns for Longdyke and Bilton Banks 1841–1901

Longdyke, Bilton Banks, 1841

Surname	Forename	Relationship	Age	Occupation	Born Northumberland
Jackson	George	Head	30	Ag Labourer	Yes
	Mary	Wife	25		Yes
	William	Son	6		Yes
Thompson	Mary	Head	50	Ag Labourer	Yes
	James	Son	20	Ag Labourer	Yes
	Mary	Daughter	15	Ag Labourer	Yes
Sanderson	Thomas	Head	40	Ag Labourer	Yes
	Ann	Wife	35		Yes
	Mary	Daughter	12		Yes
	Jane	Daughter	15		Yes
	Margaret	Daughter	8		Yes
	Elizabeth	Daughter	5		Yes
	Ellen	Daughter	2		Yes
Smith	Charlton	Head	55	Ag Labourer	Yes
	Mary	Wife	55	Ag Labourer	Yes

Longdyke Farm, 1851

Surname	Forename	Relationship	Age	Occupation	Place of Birth
Trobe	Thomas	Head	70	Labourer	Shilbottle
	Margery	Sister	72	Housekeeper	Shilbottle
Taylor	Ann	Boarder	22	Servant	Shilbottle
	Catherine	Boarder	18		Longdyke
White	Thomas	Boarder	35	Labourer	Chatton
Taylor	Henry	Boarder	50	Labourer	Shilbottle
Kinghorn	Robert	Head	32	Labourer	Chillingham
	Mary	Wife	29	Labourer	Chillingham
	James	Son	4		Hetton le Hole
Robinson	Thomas	Head	38	Labourer	Ancroft
	Jane	Wife	34	Labourer	Ancroft
	Joseph	Son	13		Ancroft
	Robert	Son	11		Ancroft
	Thomas	Son	9		Ancroft
	James	Son	7		Ancroft

Longdyke Farm, 1861

Surname	Forename	Relationship	Age	Occupation	Place of Birth
Hall	Thomas	Head	51	Coal Miner	Lucker
	Jane	Wife	38		Chillingham
Cruddas	Robert	Head	82	Ag Labourer	Whittingham
	Samuel	Son	42	Labourer	Rennington
	Mary	Daughter-in-law	34	Labourer	Scotland
	Jane	Granddaughter	1		Lesbury

Bilton Banks, 1871

Surname	Forename	Relationship	Age	Occupation	Place of Birth
Robson	Jane	Head	41	Ag Labourer	Alnwick
	Margaret	Daughter	12		Alnwick
	James	Son	6		Alnwick
	Elizabeth	Daughter	11 months		Whittle
Green	Francis	Head	55	Shepherd	Framlington
	Jane	Wife	53		Rothbury
	Francis	Son	28	Ag Labourer	Framlington
Green	Edward	Son	15	Ag Labourer	Rothbury
Cranston	John G	Boarder	26	Civil Engineer	Hexham

Census Data for Bilton Banks, 1881

Surname	Forename	Relationship	Age	Occupation	Place of Birth
Ray	James	Head	67	Horse keeper	?
	Ellenor	Wife	65		Chatton
	Thomas	Son	32	Miner	Kyloe
Wrigglesworth	Ellenor	Daughter	31		Lowick
Ray	Richard	Son	22	Miner	Lowick
	Ellen Jane	Granddaughter	4		Shilbottle
	Mary Ann	Granddaughter	5		Shilbottle
Retson	William	Head	29	Mining engineer	Merthyr
	Mary Ann	Wife	24		Newcastle
	William	Son	2		Bilton Banks
	George	Son	1		Bilton Banks
	Rettie	Daughter	2 months		Bilton Banks
Alexander	Mack	Cousin	29	Grocer	Hexham
Pegter	Alice	Servant	23	Nurse	Bath
Tone	Rachel A	Servant	19	Domestic	Gateshead
Cairns	Henry	Head	44	Engineman	?
	Rebecca	Wife	49		Chatton
	John	Son	21	Miner	Chatton
	Robert	Son	18	Miner	Embleton
	George H	Son	17	Miner	Embleton
	William	Son	15	Errand Boy	Bamburgh
	Jane	Daughter	13	Scholar	Bamburgh
	Thomas	Son	11	Scholar	Bamburgh
	Rebecca	Daughter	5		Lesbury
Bowey	Robert	Head	53	Winding Engineer	Amble
	Mary E	Daughter	14		Togston
	Catherine	Daughter	10		Togston
Wood	John	Head	55	Groom domestic	Rothbury
	Ellen	Wife	55		Chatton
	Thomas	Son	24	Miner	Shilbottle
	William	Son	22	Weighman	Shilbottle
	James	Son	20	Miner	Warkworth
	Ellen	Daughter	14	Scholar	Shilbottle
Thompson	Thomas	Head	37	Joiner	Alnwick
	Ellen	Wife	34		Shilbottle
	Mary	Daughter	11	Scholar	Shilbottle
	Ellen	Daughter	4		Lesbury
	Margaret	Daughter	2		Lesbury
	Jane	Daughter	1 month		Lesbury
Egdell	Edward	Head	41	Boiler Smith	Newton-by-Sea
	Mary Ann	Wife	35		Newcastle
	Mary Jane	Daughter	12	Scholar	Newcastle
	Edward Wm	Son	10	Scholar	Newcastle
	Samuel Jas	Son	8	Scholar	Howdon
	Agnes	Daughter	6	Scholar	Bilton Banks
Egdell	Thomas	Head	3	Engine Fitter	Acklington
	Mary Ann	Wife	30		Acklington
	Elizabeth	Daughter	12	Scholar	Shilbottle
	Samuel Ed	Son	10	Scholar	Shilbottle
Henderson	David	Head	28	Miner	Shilbottle

Surname	Forename	Relationship	Age	Occupation	Place of Birth
	Ann	Wife	22		Chatton
	Mary	Daughter	4		Cramlington
Robinson	Thomas	Head	29	Miner	Grindon
	Mary Ann	Wife	28		Berwick
	Robert	Son	8	Scholar	So Charlton
	Eliz Jane	Daughter	6	Scholar	Shilbottle
	Margt Ann	Daughter	5	Scholar	Shilbottle
	George W	Son	2		Shilbottle
Hall	John	Head	30	Miner	Beadnell
	Jane	Wife	28		Radcliffe
	Robert	Son	6	Scholar	Radcliffe
	Jane	Daughter	5	Scholar	Radcliffe
	Ann	Daughter	1		Shilbottle
Hutchinson	William	Head	39	Miner	Thropton
	Ann	Wife	40		Morpeth
	Robert	Son	14	Miner	Newcastle
	William	Son	13	Miner	No Shields
	Joseph	Son	7	Scholar	Spittal
	Thomas	Son	4	Scholar	Bebside
	Adam	Son	1		Hylton
Punton	James	Head	39	Miner	Ford Moss
	Alice	Wife	40		Alnwick
	Jas Rob	Son	7	Scholar	Amble
	Jos Ed	Son	5	Scholar	Alnwick
	Edward	Border	35	No occupation	Ford Moss
Weddle	William	Head	30	Miner	Biddleston
	Ann	Wife	32		Duns
	John	Son	6	Scholar	Shilbottle
	Christina	Daughter	5	Scholar	Shilbottle
	William	Son	1		Shilbottle
Weddle	John	Head	54	Miner	Lilburn
	Eleanor	Wife	55		Rabbit Hall
	Thomas	Son	26	Miner	Chathill
	Eleanor	Daughter	20	Domestic	Howback
	James	Son	18	Agric Lab	Howback
	John	Son	18	Agric Lab	Howback
	Adam	Son	14	Scholar	Shilbottle
Laidler	James	Head	26	Miner	Earsdon
	Jane	Wife	25		Lowick
	James	Son	3		Lesbury
	Joseph	Son	1		Lesbury
Dryden	Elandidle	Boarder	23	Coll Clerk	Blyth
Waddle	George	Head	28	Miner	Chathill
	Violet	Wife	25		Shilbottle
	Gibberson	Daughter	3		Shilbottle
Tweedy	John	Head	32	Miner	High Buston
	Mary	Wife	27		Wooden
Tweedy	Mary Ann	Daughter	4		Wooden
	Jane Isab	Daughter	1		Shilbottle
Forrest	William	Head	30	Miner	Brunton

Surname	Forename	Relationship	Age	Occupation	Place of Birth
Forrest	Esther	Wife	25		Shilbottle
	Mar Esther	Daughter	4 month		Bilton Banks
King	Robert	Head	23	Miner	Shilbottle
	Sarah	Wife	26		Newham
	Marg Ann	Daughter	4		Shilbottle
	James	Son	1		Shilbottle
Young	George	Head	50	Miner	Shilbottle
	Ellen	Wife	43		Shilbottle
	Emma	Daughter	14	Scholar	Shilbottle
	Isabella	Daughter	10	Scholar	Shilbottle
	Mary Jane	Daughter	7	Scholar	Shilbottle
	Ellen	Daughter	5		Shilbottle
Cowans	John	Head	48	Miner	Acklington
	Mary Ann	Wife	44		Hadstone
	William J	Son	19	Brakesman	Togston
Henderson	Edward	Head	26	Miner	Fleetham
	Maria	Wife	23		Shilbottle
	Mary	Daughter	1		Bilton Banks
Hall	Robert	Head	60	Engineman	Beadnell
	Isabella	Wife	62		Bowsdon
Johnson	Marg Ann	Granddaughter	19		Shilbottle
Buglas	Thomas	Head	46	Miner	Dorrington
	Margaret	Wife	44		Alnwick
	Thomas	Son	21	Miner	Shilbottle
	Charlotte	Daughter	13	Scholar	Shilbottle
	John	Son	12	Scholar	Shilbottle
	Elizabeth	Daughter	9	Scholar	Shilbottle
	James	Son	7	Scholar	Shilbottle
Smailes	William	Head	40	Miner	Shilbottle
	Alice	Wife	33		Lowick
	George	Son	15	Scholar	Alnwick
	William	Son	7	Scholar	Amble
	John	Son	4		Amble
	Joseph	Son	3		Shilbottle
Hutchinson	Robert	Boarder	23	Miner	Bamburgh
Green	W Ternent	Head	26	Miner	Shilbottle
	Mary	Wife	25		Embleton
	Elizabeth	Daughter	1		Shilbottle
Wilson	Thomas	Head	35	Miner	Shilbottle
	Elizabeth	Wife	34		Weldon Br.
	Ann Isab	Daughter	10	Scholar	Shilbottle
	Grace D	Daughter	7	Scholar	Shilbottle
	Thomas J	Son	5		Shilbottle
	Sarah	Daughter	5		Shilbottle
Telford	Albert E	Nephew	5 months		Shilbottle

Census Data, Bilton Banks, 1891

Surname	Forename	Relationship	Age	Occupation	Place of Birth
Thompson	Robert	Head	62	Miller	Ancroft
	Alice	Wife	51		Chillingham
	Mary	Daughter	30		Belford
	Dorothy	Daughter	25		Carham
	James	Son	20	Farm lab	Lowick
	Robert	Son	18	Miner	Lowick
	Thomas	Son	15	Miner	Lowick
	William	Son	13		Eglingham
	Alice Ann	Granddaughter	5		Rennington
Roschamp	John	Head	51	Mining Engineer	Wingate, Co Durham
	Ellen	Wife	47		Hetton le Hole
	Ellen	Daughter	23	Teacher	Acomb
	Mary	Daughter	17	Dressmaker	Acomb
	Harry	Son	7		Yorkshire
Young	George	Head	60	Miner	Shilbottle
	Ellen	Wife	52		Shilbottle
	Isabella	Daughter	20		Shilbottle
	Mary Jane	Daughter	17		Shilbottle
	Ellen	Daughter	15		Shilbottle
	Martin	Son	9		Lesbury
Clensy	William	Boarder	25	Miner	King William's Town, S.A.
Smith	Thomas	Boarder	21	Miner	
Straughan	John	Head	30	Coke Burner	Alnwick
	Joseph	Son	4		Shilbottle
	William	Son	2		Shilbottle
Wood	William	Head	32	Carter	Shilbottle
	James	Brother	31	Miner	Warkworth
	Ellen	Mother	62		Chatton
Reay	Richard	Head	33	Miner	Lowick
	Jane	Wife	28		Shilbottle
	James John	Son	2		Lesbury
	Adeline	Daughter	1 month		Lesbury
Thompson	Thomas	Head	42	Joiner	Alnwick
	Mary	Daughter	21		Shilbottle
	Ellen	Daughter	14		Lesbury
	Margaret	Daughter	12		Lesbury
	Jane	Daughter	10		Lesbury
	Thomas R	Son	2 months		Lesbury
Air	Robert	Head	55	Blacksmith	Kyloe
	Jane	Wife	62		Holy Island
	Robert	Son	26	Labourer	Kyloe
Egdell	Thomas	Head	45	Enginewright	Warkworth
	Samuel	Son	20	Blacksmith	Glamorgan
Cowens	John	Head	52	Blacksmith	Acklington
	Mary Ann	Wife	54		?
Robinson	Thomas	Head	38	Miner	Grindon
	Mary Ann	Wife	27		Berwick
	Robert	Son	18	Miner	Longlow Croft
	L Jane	Daughter	16	Servant	Shilbottle
	Mary Ann	Daughter	15		Shilbottle

Surname	Forename	Relationship	Age	Occupation	Place of Birth
Robinson	Mary	Daughter	8		Lesbury
	Thomas	Son	6		Lesbury
	Edith	Daughter	5		Lesbury
	Hannah	Daughter	3		Lesbury
Waddell	George	Head	38	Miner	Chathill
	Violet	Wife	33		Shilbottle
	Mary G	Daughter	13		Shilbottle
	John	Son	10		Lesbury
	Sarah	Daughter	4		Lesbury
	?	Son	1		Lesbury
Fenwick	Thomas	Head	42	Miner	Shilbottle
	Mary	Wife	36		Shilbottle
	Elizabeth	Daughter	11		Lesbury
	Annie	Daughter	9		Lesbury
	Jane	Daughter	6		Lesbury
	Francis Mary	Daughter	3 months		Lesbury
Punton	James	Head	49	Miner	Ford Common
	Alice	Wife	50		Shilbottle
	James Rob	Son	18	Miner	Amble
	Jos Edward	Son	15		Lesbury
	Andrew Bell	Son	8		Lesbury
	Joseph	Lodger	26	Miner	Scremerston
Smith	William	Head	59	Sinker	Cockermouth
	S ?	Wife	43		?
Weddell	John	Head	66	Miner	Wooler
	Thomas	Son	36	Miner	Ellingham
	Adam	Son	20	Miner	Shilbottle
Storey	Eleanor	Daughter	30		Whittingham
	John	Grandson	8		Lesbury
	Sarah E	Granddaughter	3		Lesbury
Tweedy	John	Head	42	Miner	High Buston
	Mary	Wife	35		Lesbury
	Mary Ann	Daughter	14		Shilbottle
	Catherine	Daughter	7		Lesbury
	Alexander	Son	6		Lesbury
Boyd	Thomas	Head	34	Engineman	Lesbury
	Mary Jane	Wife	30		Craster
	Geo Wm	Son	10		Alnwick
	Matth Jas	Son	6		Lesbury
	Stephen	Son	3		Alnwick
	Frances Mary	Daughter	1		Lesbury
Embleton	Thomas	Head	38	Miner	Embleton
	Elizabeth	Wife	39		Shilbottle
Fenwick	Geo Rob	Stepson	15	Miner	Shilbottle
	Mary Ann	Stepdaughter	9		Shilbottle
	John Wm	Son	11		Chevington
	Joseph Hill	Son	9		Pegswood
	Edward	Son	6		Acklington
	James	Son	2		Ohio, USA
Hutchinson	John	Head	46	Miner	Bamburgh

Surname	Forename	Relationship	Age	Occupation	Place of Birth
	Elizabeth	Wife	41		Warkworth
	Mary	Daughter	8		Warkworth
	Catherine	Daughter	6		Warkworth
	William	Son	4		Warkworth
Mather	Adam	Head	49	Labourer	Wooler
	Maria	Wife	51		Felton
	Robert	Son	25	Horse keeper	Yorkshire
	William	Son	19	Labourer	Alnwick
	George	Son	13		Shilbottle
Buglass	Thomas	Head	57	Dep. Foreman	Doddington
	Margaret	Wife	56		Alnwick
	Thomas	Son	21	Miner	Shilbottle
	John	Son	20		Shilbottle
	Elizabeth	Daughter	19		Shilbottle
	James	Son	17	Carpenter App	Shilbottle
	Jane	Granddaughter	7	Scholar	Shilbottle
Reay	Thomas	Head	43	Miner	Lowick
	Mary Ann	Daughter	15		Shilbottle
	Ella Jane	Daughter	14		Shilbottle
	James	Father	77	Road Labourer	Hazelrigg
Warwick	James	Head	63	Husbandman	Kirkoswald
	Hannah	Wife	48		N. Shields
Weightman	Isaac	Boarder	28	Miner	Bedlington
Brown	George	Son-in-law	16	Miner	Blyth
Warwick	Walter	Son	3		Shilbottle
Ferguson	Isabella	Niece	10		Backworth
Hall	Jos Robert	Head	35	Miner	Newcastle
	Margaret	Wife	31		Shipley Moor
	Matilda	Daughter	13		Shilbottle
	Annabella	Daughter	11		Broomhill
	Ethel	Daughter	3 months		Shilbottle
	Jas Rob	Son	3 months		Shilbottle
Jeffrey	William	Head	29	Blacksmith	Felton
	Ellen	Wife	24		Shilbottle
	Jane Ellen	Daughter	1		Shilbottle
Green	William Ternent	Head	36	Miner	Shilbottle
	Mary	Wife	35		Low Buston
	Elizabeth	Daughter	11		Shilbottle
	James Waddell	Son	8		Chevington
	John	Son	5		Lesbury
	Robert	Son	2		Lesbury
Taylor	William	Head	35	Miner	Bamburgh
	Ellen Pringle	Wife	41		Lowick
Haigh	Harry	Boarder	33	Contractor	Yorkshire
Frater	Robert	Head	33	Farmer	Alnwick
	Mary Eliz	Wife	28		Felton
	Jane	Daughter	5		Shilbottle
	John	Son	1		Lesbury
Bell	Marg Jane	Boarder	20	Servant	Shilbottle
Bradford	Thompson	Head	39	Farm Servant	Scotland

Surname	Forename	Relationship	Age	Occupation	Place of Birth
Bradford	Alice	Wife	41		Bamburgh
	Isabella	Daughter	11		Bamburgh
	Alexandra	Daughter	9		Bamburgh
	George	Son	6		Bamburgh
	Thomas	Son	3		Bamburgh
	Mary	Daughter	1		Lesbury
Bradford	Alexander	Head	65	Labourer	Berwickshire
	Mary	Wife	58		Berwickshire
	Rachel	Daughter	20	Servant	Bamburgh
	John	Son	17	Labourer	Bamburgh
	George	Son	14	Labourer	Bamburgh
Anderson	Jos Wm	Head	24	Stoker	Carlisle
	Marg Jane	Wife	24		Byker

Census Data, Bilton Banks, 1901

Surname	Forename	Relationship	Age	Occupation	Place of Birth
Smith	John	Head	34	Labourer	Lesbury
	Sarah	Wife	26		Morpeth
	Joseph	Son	2		Lesbury
	Mary		52		Lesbury
Bradford	John	Head	27	Shepherd	Northumberland
	Elizabeth	Wife	26		
	Mary	Daughter	4		
	Michael	Son	1		Shilbottle
Taylor	Catherine	Head	70	?	
	Michael	Son	37		Wooler
	Catherine	Daughter	42		Wooler
Hunter	Michael	Head	42	?	Alnwick
	Mary	Wife	37		Felton
	Jane	Daughter	18		Shilbottle
	Sarah	Daughter	13		Lesbury
	Matthew	Son	2		Lesbury
Jeffreys	William	Head	37	Col Engineer	Felling
	Ellen	Wife	22		Shilbottle
	Jane	Daughter	11		Lesbury
	John	Son	9		Lesbury
	Herbert	Son	4		Lesbury
May	Thomas	Head	29	Coal Miner	Lowick
	Mary A	Wife	24		Shilbottle
	Gloria	Mother	84		Beal
Temple	Thomas	Head	41	Col Deputy	Dipton
	Alice	Wife	38		Dipton
	Mary	Daughter	11		Dipton
	Maud	Daughter	5		Dipton
	Robert	Son	3		Annfield Plain
Egdell	Samuel	Head	32	Blacksmith	Shilbottle
	Elizabeth A	Wife	30		Bothal Barns
	Thomas E	Son	1		Lesbury
	Doora	Daughter	1		Lebury
	William	Son	3 months		Lesbury
Fordy	James	Head	32	Coal Miner	Newsham
	Caroline	Wife	23		Stakeford

Surname	Forename	Relationship	Age	Occupation	Place of Birth
Fordy	Samuel	Son	10		Newsham
	Margaret	Daughter	8		Newsham
	Frederick	Son	7		Newsham
	Mary J	Daughter	5		?
	Annie J	Visitor	5		Anfield Plain
Roschamp	John	Head	60	Manager	Hetton le Hole
	Ellen	Wife	57		Co Durham
	Jane	Daughter	25		Co Durham
	Jessie	Daughter	21		Co Durham
	Florence	Daughter	17		Co Durham
	Esther	Daughter	6		Co Durham
Roschamp	Thelma	Granddaughter	1 month		Co Durham
	Ralph	Grandson	1 month		Co Durham
Baxter	Robert	Head	49	Miner	Scotland
	Isabella	Wife	44		Norham
	James	Son	19	Miner	Ancroft
	Margaret	Daughter	19		Ancroft
	John	Son	15	Miner	Ancroft
	Robert	Son	16	Miner	Ancroft
	David	Son	7		Lesbury
	Georgina	Daughter	3		Lesbury
Nicholson	John	Head	45	Rope splicer	Bishop Auckland
	Jane	Wife	38		Earsdon
	Frederick	Son	14		Shildon
	Thomas	Son	12		Shildon
	Hannah	Daughter	10		Shildon
	Janis	Mother	64		Bishop Auckland
	James	Son	8		Shildon
	Arthur	Son	4		
	John	Son	2		
Wood	Michael	Head	41	Carter	?
	Margaret	Wife			
	Robert	Son	3		Lesbury
	Annie	Daughter	5		Lesbury
	Mary		3		Lesbury
	Isabella		1		
Brown	Alfred	Boarder	20	Miner	Ford
Elliot	John	Head	53	Miner	Newham
	Mary	Wife	40		
	John	Son	12		Newham
	Margaret	Daughter	12		Newham
Melville	David	Boarder	30	Stone Mason	Scotland
	Ann?	Wife	25		Scotland
Ayr	Robert	Head	65	Blacksmith	Fenwick
Punton	James R	Son-in-law	27	Miner	Amble
	Eleanor	Daughter	31		Fenwick
Ayr	Jane A	Granddaughter	5		Lesbury
Punton	James R	Grandson	2		Lesbury
	Richard L	Grandson	11 months		Lesbury
Causan	Sarah	Boarder	15		Yorkshire

Surname	Forename	Relationship	Age	Occupation	Place of Birth
Buglass	Thomas	Head	67	Miner	Alnwick
	Margaret	Wife	65		Shilbottle
	Thomas	Son	41	Miner	Shilbottle
	Elizabeth	Daughter	29	Servant	Shilbottle
Hudson	Edward	Head	55	Engineman	Alnwick
	Mary	Wife	44		Shilbottle
	Edward	Son	14		Shilbottle
Hindhaugh	John	Head	50	Miner	Edlington Hill
	Ann	Wife	50		Newcastle
	James	Son	17		Lesbury
	John	Son	14		Amble
	Elizabeth	Daughter	11		Choppington
	Richard	Son	8?		Lesbury
Sample	William	Head	48	Miner	Bamburgh
Ray	Margaret	Visitor	64		Lesbury
Ternent	Thomas	Head	53	Hewer	Shilbottle
	Mary	Wife	47		Shilbottle
	Jane	Daughter	16		Lesbury
	Margaret M	Daughter	13		Lesbury
Ternent	John	Son	7		Lesbury
Punton	James	Head	59	Hewer	Shilbottle
	Alice	Wife	62		Shilbottle
	Joseph	Son	25	Hewer	Shilbottle
Hogg	Ann	Aunt	79		Shilbottle
Green	William T	Head	46	Hewer	Shilbottle
	Mary	Wife	45		Shilbottle
	James H	Son	17	Hewer	Embleton
	John	Son	15	Hewer	Chevington
	Robert	Son	12		Lesbury
	Sarah	Daughter	7		Lesbury
	Mary	Daughter	6		Lesbury
	Henrietta	Daughter	3		Lesbury
Waddell	Thomas	Head	40	Hewer	Chathill
	Mary	Wife	46		Newcastle
	Annie ?	Daughter	14		Newcastle
	Sarah	Daughter	4		Lesbury
	John	Father	74	Drawer	Lillburn
Tweedy	John	Head	50	Hewer	High Buston
	Mary	Wife	47		Lesbury
	Catherine	Daughter	17		Lesbury
	John J	Son	12		Lesbury
	Jacob A	Son	10		Lesbury
	William P	Son	7		Lesbury
	Andrew	Uncle	84		Howick
Maddison	George	Visitor	12		Billingham
Boyd	Thomas	Head	46	Pump Engineer	Lesbury
	Mary	Wife	42		Craster
	George H	Son	21	Miner	Alnwick
	Thomas	Son	19	Filler	Lesbury
	Matthew	Son	16	Putter	Lesbury

Surname	Forename	Relationship	Age	Occupation	Place of Birth
Boyd	Charlie S	Son	13		Alnwick
	Andrew	Son	10		Lesbury
	Elizabeth	Daughter	8		Lesbury
	Arthur	Son	5		Lesbury
	Edith	Daughter	1		Lesbury
Hilton	John	Head	39	Dep. Manager	Shilbottle
	Mamry	Wife	36		?
	?	Daughter	6		Newburn
	Emma?	Daughter	2		Shilbottle
		Son	11 months		Shilbottle

Three other families, possibly Gray, Mather and Burton; decipherable forenames include – Jane, James, Ellen, Anthony, Rachael, Adam, William.

MEKIN IT SAFE

'Wi piece-work, good marras is key. If tha' not up fo it mind, wey ya stan'in bonny. Thu whole team's got t'work tigither one as hard as thu next – otherwise ya mekin nowt, A'm telling ya. Anyhow, wu waas in the wet. It waas just wor torn, A guess, dependin, strite up, on straas, n'wu draas thu short'n. Thu gaffer's mekin on it waas fair. Wey it might a' been, whey knaas? Anyhow, wu had t'mek thu most on it cos wu wo set there fo six months, foreshift n'back. It was off the edge of thu fyec, new cutting n'there waas maire stone than coal, wi wata drippin in aall thu time, hardly anywhere tu get ya bait in thu dry, if ya cud even sit up cos wu was bent double most u thu time. Eyghteen inches, that's aall it waas n'places.

Anyhow, Bill Dixon says, 'Check it oot.'

Wey fo' a Deputy he'd now't off cos he shud a'knaan. It was where wu torned the set. Course it waas wet. It had tu be; the whole effin place waas worse that a clarty midden. Mind he had a bett knee, kept swellin up that's why he waas med Deputy, and give'm his due, in fairness he wasn't aall bad.

So, A did like he says n'A meks mu way doon towards the fyec; hardly scraping in, n'by rights he shuda sent is in wey a marra but wu aall knaa'd that … 'so A just gans off, me heed bumpin where the fittas had stuck up thon daft bludy girda, far ower low. Well like, A was hardly through when A hears the timbas creekin.

If A'd been a youngin, me-be, A'd've got windy, might a'torned back but yu kna, A've got laddies doon here nuw n'Ad hord it aall afore. So A just bashes on, not far mind, n'afore A can say kiss me arse o out … A knaas what's comin, divn't A? Ya can sort-o sense it when the air whooshes n'gets bla'n oot ya, n'ya knaa what ya in for.

Anyhow, doon it cums, n'A was fast. Happed up: thowt A waas a gonna. N'A lies a bit waitin. Then A knaas like, realised like, tha not big stones like thu once waas, thu last time, but thu had is fast fo a bit – feet n'legs clamped doon, n'me arse gannin half-croon sixpence waitin fo' what's next, n'shootin pains like ya been kicked by a bullock. But there waas nowt was tha'? Nowt more anyhow. N'behind A can hear yellin n'carry on. Darkie Wilson's shootin like hell n'Billy Dixon clackin on like God kna's whaat.

Me lamp's on its side, pointing where the waatas gushin in nuw, fillin up; n'thu dust's settlin n'after a bit a'pullin n'pushin against the faal. A can craal, so A'm not that bad.

Thank God wu hadn't filled the tub otherwise A'd be buggered, wi hardly space tu torn roond o'nowt, but A managed. N'when A stops gaspin A still cannit hear me marra Tommy Ross.

Thu rest o'them are shootin on like nowt else.

'Jonty' tha shootin. 'Are ye aall reet, wuv had a faall.'

Wey A knaad that didn't A, cos A was in it as weell, wasn't A? And so was them lot; n'Billy Dixon was in thu shit. cud be anyhow, dependin.

He shud-a-seen wu hadn't propped thu wall right. Wu hardly ever dey mind; just mek it safe – not accordin tu thu manual like but gud enough fo pit-work as thu say. Anyhow, he shud-a-seen. He wuld-a-seen; must-a-dun, 'nd he shudn't a sent is up till it waas fixed.

Wey, thu dust settle like. That's thu only bludy gud thing ya can say aboot thu wet – it sharpens it up, meks it settle quick.

So A'm cogitatin aboot compensation like, when A'm on me way through thu duff, not serious like, but wund'rin as A'm craa'llin; anyhow, clearing the slate as A gan, n'there was muckle chunks on it, niver tuched in millions a'years A'm thinking n'just aboot fettled is, as if it's been hangin aboot waitin on is cumin.

Anyhow, A sees three lamps lang afore A sees any fyeces. That's cos thaa doon on that knees n'hunkas workin on wi Tommy.

Wey, as soon as A sees him A knaas like … it waas as plain as owt. It was pointless, waste a'time. Ha'f his fyec was missin. Now't ya cud dee, flattened he waas, poor bugger.

So, A just decided. Didn't ask or nowt, just did what ya have t'dee. A just gi' them a nudge oot thu way n'tecks me short off n'A lays it nice n'gentle ower Tommy's fyec. He might not a'minded but A did; them watchin n'that.

It waasn;t right was it? A wudn't a'liked it; A knaad that. Anyhow, it waas a lang trek in bye, n'why let every bugger's eyes see me marra like that. Let them wonda. They'd kna right enough what it's like getting felled. Some might a'seen it afore – but thu hadn't seen me marra.

N'then A did what wu shud a'done afore, strite off. A stuck a few extra props in, knaaing fine weel that thu Owerman n'then thu Manager wud hev to hev a look, n'thu Inspecta, n'thu whole works, mebe thu polis even. Might as weel mek it look aalreet.

'Cos if we didn't Billy Dixon's up shit creek – nare job, nare hoose, nare pension; A'm telling ya.

N'Tommy's Madge n'all; what thu hell waas she gan te get oot on it? Twice as much if the jobs dun reet, A knaa's that, so what's thu harm? Narebody said owt. A just bashed on. N'A let Billy Dixon pass tu mek his way doon, tu use the in-bye phone, keeping oot thu way n'aall as A'm finishin off. It was something tu dee; keep me mind off me legs, n'me marra. N'them lot cud see it, see it in me fyec, see it in how A waas knockin in thu props, n'thu just let is get on, mekin it safe … that's n'effin laugh … mekin it safe?[170]

[170] The author's winning 'Dialect Prose' entry in the Northumbrian Gathering at Morpeth in 2010.

Bibliography

Air, Harry, (handwritten), *Memories of Longdyke Colliery Working, (1988), 'Hand getting methods 1913 and developments.'*

Brewis, Henry, *A Stroll in the Country*, Newcastle, Powdene Publishing, 1999

Brown, Claire and Peter (et al), (Eds), *Memories of Shilbottle, Millennium Edition*, 2000

Cantrill, T.C., *Coal Mining*, Cambridge, CUP, 1914

Green, John, *Mining in Shilbottle,* (handwritten account), NRO 2205/1/2, Northumberland Archives

Hodgson, Crawford John, F.S.A., *History of Northumberland Vol. 5*, Newcastle, Andrew Reid, 1899

Jermy, Roger, *Northern Northumberland's Minor Railways, Vol.2 – Colliery & Associated Lines*, Usk, Mon. Oakwood Press, 2011

Mattusch, Carol, *'Metal Working and Tools'* in Oleson, John Peter (Ed.) *The Oxford Handbook of Engineering and Technology in the Classical World*, OUP, Oxford, 2008

Smith, Ken and Jean, *The Great Northern Miners,* Newcastle, Tyne Bridge Publishing, 2008

Stewart, Barry, *Mekin it Safe*, Morpeth, Northumbrian Gathering, 2010

Tuck, James T., *The Collieries of Northumberland Vol. 1,* Newcastle, Trade Union Printing Services, 1993

Wilson, Robert, *Transactions of Tyneside Naturalist Club, 1863-64 Vol. VI,* NEIMME, Neville Hall, Newcastle-upon-Tyne

www.ancestory.co.uk
www.britannica.com (Encyclopædia Britannica)
www.dmm.org.uk (Durham Mining Museum)
www.cmhrc.co.uk (The Coalmining History Resource Centre)